Remaking Chinese Urban Form: Modernity, Scarcity and Space, 1949–2005

Duanfang Lu

Routledge
Taylor & Francis Group

LONDON AND NEW YORK

First published 2006 by Routledge

This paperback edition first published 2011
by Routledge, 2 Park Square, Milton Park, Abingdon,
Oxfordshire OX14 4RN

Simultaneously published in the US and Canada
by Routledge
711 Third Avenue, New York, NY10017

Routledge is an imprint of the Taylor & Francis Group, an informa business

© 2006, 2011 Duanfang Lu

Typeset in Palatino and Humanist by PNR Design, Didcot
Printed and bound in Great Britain by CPI Antony Rowe, Chippenham, Wiltshire

This book was commissioned and edited by Alexandrine Press, Marcham, Oxfordshire

British Library Cataloguing in Publication Data
A catalogue record of this book is available from the British Library

Library of Congress Cataloging in Publication Data
Lu, Duanfang
Remaking Chinese urban form : modernity, scarcity and space, 1949–2005 / Duanfang
Lu.
      p. cm. — (Planning, history, and environment series)
   Includes bibliographical references and index.
   ISBN 0–415–35450–1 (hb : alk. paper)
      1. Sociology, Urban—China. 2. City planning—China—History. 3. Communism and
   architecture—China—History. 4. Danwei—History. I. Title. II. Planning, history, and
   the environment series.
   HT147.C6L8 2005
   307.76'0951—dc22

2005012255

ISBN13: 978–0–415–66569–8 (pbk)
ISBN13: 978–0–203–00119–6 (ebk)

Remaking Chinese Urban Form:
Modernity, Scarcity and Space, 1949–2005

7 DAY

Planning, History and Environment Series

Selection of published titles

Contents

Foreword

Chinese Urban Forms: A Surreal Affair

Here is a book that offers a rich collection of observations on China, postcolonialism, architecture, modernity and planning. For me, however, it had an uncanny ability, through the full registration of the import of planning, to open onto a different understanding of Chinese politics. It helped me to understand Chinese history and Mao in a new, novel and, I think, productive way. And here is how it did it…

I went to the Barbican the other day. I'd never been before. I was on my way to an exhibition called 'Surreal House', yet the surreal moment happened before I even got there. Walking through a forest of postmodernist skyscrapers interspersed with classical architectural heritage buildings, I took a 'high street' short cut that, quite literally, ramped me above the everyday of London and landed me squarely in the Barbican Estate. The Barbican Estate isn't just any housing estate, it's a vision of modernity's future. Ebenezer Howard's 'Garden City' meets the clean lines of Le Corbusier to produce a late 1960s George Jetson view of the year 2030 … talk about 'off-modern'![1]

There is a surrealism that now surrounds such late 1960s modernist attempts to project into the postmodern future. Oddly utopian, strangely uncanny, their promise of a more rationally ordered and scientific world where nature is tamed and every need catered for now stands, like this monumental estate itself, as a sign of the hubris of positivism.

Strange then, to have these thoughts while reading about China and the Maoist planning, for if one thinks of Mao Zedong, one invariably thinks of partisanship rather than positivism.[2] Yet flicking through the pages of Lu Duanfang's wonderful book, one could be forgiven for thinking otherwise. Page after page displays diagrams, designs and plans of Mao era urban planners and they, in turn, reveal a positivistic desire, not just to increase production, but to transform people's lives through the reorganization of the way they lived them. Here, in their plans for communities, urban clusters and micro-districts, the positivist urban planners of Mao's China tether their design plans to a revolutionary agenda demanding total social transformation. The politics of partisanship based in the production of enmity and kept alive through class struggle, yet strangely rational in the way it reorders the land and the body.

Entire urban communities would be re-organized into work unit housing estates redesigned in a manner similar to the small industrial villages of early capitalism. For the peasantry, from the late 1950s onwards, their life would be made revolutionary through the organization of the commune structure. Such changes were not just cosmetic administrative redesignations, but complete transformations of work and living space. Undertaken to improve industrial and agricultural output, this desire to reorganize life more efficiently is the revenge of Bogdanov's tecktological science of organization, a tendency alive within the early Bolshevik Party that had a strange echo and afterlife in the Stalinist era.[3] Even the name 'work unit' offered a hint of this sounding more like a unit of measurement rather than a place where people lived and worked.[4] This China, the China of the 'work unit' and of a positivist socialist imaginary, was one of total state calculation. The state becomes the sum total of all its unit parts and all that central planners seemed to need to do was to add them all up!

Yet it was precisely in getting those technologies that would enable this form of total calculation into place that the modernist obsession with rationally ordered space, functional forms and productive lives started to unravel. Faced with the Scylla of Party demands for rapid industrialization at any cost and the Charybdis of worker and peasant discontent at the quality of life produced, socialist modernity was forced to face up to the enduring problem of what Lu Duanfang has called Third World modernism. This form of modernism, more than any other, turns on the question of scarcity and, in Mao's China, Lu insists, scarcity becomes part of a new national imagination.

It was the desire of the Party to overcome scarcity quickly that led them to channel virtually all human and material resources into the industrialization effort and this, in turn, severely limited their ability to supply an adequate socialist provision to work units and communes. Scarcity led to cutbacks. It forced the ornamental 'big tops' off the roofs of ornate buildings and the abandonment of elaborate and expensive plans for urban redesign. It also, paradoxically, opened onto a more partisan, telluric, and vernacular politics of Mao Zedong.[5]

Mao Zedong had spoken of the virtue of a Chinese nation that was 'poor and blank'. Upon such a clean sheet, Mao insisted, beautiful characters could be written. The revolution would strive to write these characters and when they did they would spell out words like struggle, devotion and sacrifice and they would then attach these words to institutional forms such as the 'mass-line', the Party, and the government. Scarcity meant that the Party was forced increasingly to call upon people to use their own resources (self reliance) to use all available means (walking on two legs) and to sacrifice for the socialist cause (serve the people). Scarcity, Lu notes, introduces a 'not yet' quality to socialist utopianism. Perhaps more importantly for the Chinese communists, and the reason why scarcity could become part of the national imagination, was that it also reminded the Chinese communists of those moments in Party history when a form of utopian austerity practiced in their rural base camps in China eventually catapulted them to power.

From this experience in rural China, the communists not only learned how to rally people to their cause but, more importantly, rally them to a cause driven by a politicization of scarcity. Landlordism and capitalists were used to engender class hatred and that would then be channelled into an ethos of sacrifice through involvement in class struggle. Millions would join mass-line organizations and carry out endless austerity drives that were also, inevitably, campaigns against political backsliding. While working in tandem with the Party bureaucrats to promote the industrialization process, these mass-line organs, paradoxically, ended up introducing new complications that would eventually lead to their plans being undermined.

This process of conflict between planners and activists begins almost from the time they start building the work units. The work unit reorganization of everyday life resulted in those units being responsible, not just for production needs but also for the grass-root education, health, and housing needs of their members. The state, in allocating virtually all resources into factory and plant building, left the work unit leaders without the resources necessary to fulfil what could be called the socialist provision of their work. Yet the work unit leaders, fearful of being denounced by mass-line inspired political campaigns against Rightists, felt that they must, for local political reasons, provide this socialist provision.

The balancing act they had to achieve was to provide the state with enough products so as to fulfil their quota while, simultaneously, siphoning off enough material resources so as to provide the socialist provision of the work unit. To achieve this 'balance', work unit chiefs would often overstate the amount of land they would need for their unit and thereby ensure that they had the space to build hospitals, cinemas, schools and crèches (p. 91). They would also overstate their material needs and stockpile materials given to them by the state (p. 92). They even developed an elaborate barter system between stockpiling work units (p. 94). As Lu concludes (p. 98), with little by way of capitalist incentive to maximize profit, there was no reason why work unit leaders would not maximize their political capital within their units and provide low return facilities as part of the socialist provision. The result was a transformation of urban life. Work units, which had been essentially conceived of as production units, gradually began to develop into what Lu would call the 'basic unit of collective consumption'. The conclusions that one can draw from this are startling. It suggests that some of the crucial material aspects of socialism in Mao's China came not from Party planning but almost despite it. As Lu ruefully states, this was not part of the socialist plan (p. 98). If the consequences of the urban planner's action in the city were perverse, their actions when sent down to the countryside to reorganize the villages were utterly catastrophic.

The year was 1958. As part of a political drive, urban planners were sent down to the countryside to be rustified. If they were there to learn from the masses, they were also there to teach peasants something about scientific organization. As Lu notes, 'to raise the political consciousness of peasants and increase agricultural output, specialist planners believed that traditional rural settlements should be revolutionized through a fundamental reorganization of the physical environment' (p. 111). Planners, says Lu, held that the scattered and undersized villages system of China were wasteful and irrational. They deemed that villages should be amalgamated into large units, and that these units, known as communes, should build densely packed accommodation that would increase the arable land available for cultivation and contribute to the field, the factory and the home becoming more fully integrated. Architecturally, they designed buildings without toilets or kitchens to force people into a more communal lifestyle and, in terms of planning, worked out the optimum land use. This even went so far as to establish the appropriate distances between central residential zones and satellite clusters in order to maximize distributional efficiency. Here Lu's argument reminded me of William Skinners remarkable longitudinal study of marketing and social structures in China and his critique of the Great Leap Forward.[6]

Skinner's study begins by examining the traditional system of economic distribution in China. He notes the crucial role played by standard, intermediate and central market towns from the time of the Qing dynasty onwards. These, he argued, were crucial to the distribution of goods and services between urban and rural areas. These were the arteries of the entire rural distribution network and it was these that the communists destroyed as they introduced their own new more 'rational' and scientific system – the commune structure.

With far less detailed knowledge than Lu musters, Skinner persuasively argues that the infrastructure in rural China was inadequate and unable to support this more sophisticated and rational system. The failure of this new system and the total abandonment of the traditional one meant that the whole rural distribution network simply crashed when communists, for political reasons, tried to implement it with lightening speed. Here was one of the key factors for understanding the causes of the catastrophic Great Leap Forward famine. Lu's work allows us to see the causes of this problem differently. Far from the economy collapsing because of the forces unleashed by a pastoralist ultra-left politics, through Lu it now becomes clear that this is a problem of the hubris of the scientific management systems and the newly centralized distribution network system was unable to cope with the hugely complicated nature of distribution in rural China. The old system, denounced and destroyed, could not be resurrected and this left the countryside without any adequate means to respond when the starvation began. The famine inevitably follows.

There is much else in this work that could be spoken about and commented upon, but the key aspect that I have focused on is the way it opens onto a new understanding of the relationship between the revolution, politics and the various instantiations of modernity. One thing that shines through, however, is the way that this book has the capacity to enable one to envision an entirely new way of looking at the Chinese revolution and Chinese modernity. It's much more than a book on urban transformation, for it is one that allows us to see the effects of modernity as a style of thought. In this respect, at least, her book is no less surreal that the Barbican for it, too, offers an unusual take on modernism, and opens one's eyes to the role of the off-modernism in some of the great utopian failures of the twentieth century.

Michael Dutton
London

Notes

1. Svetlana Boym coins the term 'off modern' for 'architecture of adventure.' This, she insists includes architecture that goes beyond the Western European and American contexts, see Boym, Svetlana (2008) *Architecture of the Off-Modern*. New York: Princeton Architectural Press, New York, p. 7.
2. Note here the work of Carl Schmitt who, in 1963, wrote in his *Theory of the Partisan* that revolutionary China was 'an essentially new stage of partisanship, one at whose beginning we find the name Mao Tse-tung'. Quoted in Toscano, Alberto (2008) Carl Schmitt in Beijing: partisanship, geopolitics and the demolition of the Eurocentric world. *Postcolonial Studies*, **11**(4), pp. 417–433.
3. Bogdanov was a leading communist thinker who dueled with Lenin but who emerged as the leader of Prolecult in the Soviet Union in the 1920s. His major theoretical work was Bogdanov, A. (1984) *Essays on Tektology: The General Science of Organization* [translated by George Gorelik]. Seaside, CA: Intersystems Publications. For an argument suggesting he strongly influenced Stalin see Lecourt, Dominique (1977) *Proletarian Science? The Case of Lysenko*. London: New Left.
4. Yi Zhongtian (2006 [1996]) *Casually talking Chinese* [*xianhua zhongguoren*]. Bejiing: Beijing Hualing Publishing House.
5. It is Carl Schmitt who highlighted the uniquely political quality of Mao Zedong's work that is buried in telluric attachments, and opens onto a new stage of partisanship. Alberto Tuscano reads this as a new mode of understanding and operating in politics. See Carl Schmitt (2004 [1963]) *The Theory of the Partisan: A Commentary/Remark on the Concept of the Political*. Berlin: Duncker & Humblot. English translation © Michigan State University Press.
6. See Skinner, G. William (1965) Marketing and social structure in rural China, Part 3. *Journal of Asian Studies*, **24**(3), pp. 363–400.

献给我的祖父母卢郁蕴和曾瑾玲

For my grandparents Lu Yuyun and Zeng Jinling

Chapter One

Socialist Space, Postcolonial Time

Apart from their other characteristics, the outstanding thing about China's 600 million people is that they are 'poor and blank'. That may seem a bad thing, but in reality it is a good thing. Poverty gives rise to the desire for change, the desire for action and the desire for revolution. On a blank sheet of paper free from any mark, the freshest and most beautiful characters can be written, the freshest and most beautiful pictures can be painted.

Mao Zedong, 1958, 'Introducing a co-operative'

This book examines Chinese modernity as at once a socialist and a Third World one by tracing the profound spatial transformations against the backdrop of nation building practices in contemporary China. The ending of the Cold War has strengthened the dominant visions which perceive Western models of development as the universal paradigm for all human societies (Fukuyama, 1992). Meanwhile, there have been increasing challenges to the progress of economic liberalization and globalization at numerous local sites (Castells, 1996, 2004; AlSayyad, 2004). China's position in global space has shifted greatly amid the restructuring of the post-Cold War world order. It is time to re-imagine China. Will this nation gradually transform itself into a society with a set of social attributes similar to those of Western societies? Or will it retain its distinct identity and hold the potential for viable alternative rationalities?

From the perspective of urban transformation, the Chinese city is becoming capitalist in many respects: the emergence of central business districts (CBDs), the uneven growth of territorial units, and the rise of new urban spaces such as shopping malls, signature architecture buildings and luxury residential enclaves (Gaubatz, 1995, 2005; King and Kusno, 2000; Wu, 2005). At the same time, the socio-spatial template inherited from the previous era continues to shape post-reform urban development (Logan, 2002; Ma and Wu, 2005b; Friedmann, 2005). Among others, the influence of the work unit (danwei) still persists in many aspects. The city under Mao (1949–1976) was organized mainly through the work unit – the socialist enterprise or institute – which functioned not only as workplace but also as social institution (chapter 3). The work unit integrated work, housing and a variety of social facilities such as nurseries, canteens, clinics and shops in close proximity within its walled compound(s). The economic reforms since 1978 have gradually weakened the role of the work unit as the fundamental socio-spatial unit of the Chinese city. Deeply embedded in social expectations and practices, however, its many features are reproduced in new urban developments (Francis, 1996; Bray, 2005). With this and other factors (e.g., the mixed economy, urban-rural discrepancy, the informal sector), post-reform China displays a dazzling array of old and new, socialist and capitalist, Third World and First World elements (chapter 7).

This book represents an attempt to understand the perplexing present by re-examining past legacies through one particular field of knowledge, namely, that of the built environment. Specifically, the inquiry focuses on the development of the work unit as the dominant urban form under Chinese socialism. While most existing scholarship on the work unit has concentrated on its institutional aspect, this book investigates its physical dimension. The study is based on the premise that the built environment is not an autonomous arena but rather a social field with important political implications. Drawing on architectural and planning history, urban studies and cultural theory, I look at Chinese urban form in the broad social, ideological, economic and cultural context.

In the examination of socialist urban form, considerable debate on whether there is a socialist city has focused on the socio-spatial characteristics of cities in socialist society (French and Hamilton, 1979, pp. 1–22; Szelenyi, 1996, pp. 303–307). Today most agree that the distinctiveness of cities in socialist countries is questionable, as they are an amalgam of elements from diverse sources (French, 1995). This book shows that the characteristics of Chinese urban form did not necessarily match the creeds of socialism, nor were they always intended by socialist planners. By considering the production process of space, I argue that urban form and function under Mao were nonetheless 'socialist' in nature, as they were produced as part of socialist production and accumulation strategies. My study demonstrates that the integral spatial form of the work unit was the unique outcome generated by the conflicts between the needs of capital accumulation and the necessity of labour reproduction within a peculiar Socialist/Third World context. I show that work-unit-based urbanism was an alternative both to capitalist and to Soviet urbanism.

Much Chinese studies literature focuses on the socialist aspect of Chinese society, while its Third World facet is often largely ignored except in foreign policy research.[1] This book provides an alternative mapping of Chinese modernity by highlighting its Third Worldliness through the lens of scarcity. By doing so, I hope not only to offer a fresh angle to view contemporary China, but also to enrich current debates on postcolonialism.[2]

The rapid expansion of postcolonial studies in recent years has been accompanied by growing critical reflections on the subject. Among others, the literature has hitherto largely concentrated on modernity as a 'cultural' dilemma, examining the problems of the Third World by way of identity politics alone (Dirlik, 1997, 2000; Juan, 1988; Bartolovich, 2002). This book aims to tackle the lacunae by highlighting the fact that while the issue of identity politics is important, there remain, however, many social and spatial choices made in developing societies that cannot be explained well without including the dimension of scarcity. Much of urban transformation in contemporary China, as the book will demonstrate, can only be explained when scarcity, as a historically constituted condition, is taken into account. By using scarcity as an epistemic starting point for the understanding of Third World modernism, I hope to bring together political economy and the analysis of the postcolonial, the two spheres that have largely remained separated in current cultural debates (Hall, 1996, pp. 257–258).

The remainder of this introduction establishes historical and theoretical backgrounds referred to in the following chapters.

The Beginning of a New Time

Whereas the Chinese Republican state shifted the official year to Republic Year 1 when it was established in 1911, a subtle gesture was made by the socialist regime a few days before the announcement of the establishment of the People's Republic on 1 October 1949 – for the first time in history, China had adopted the Gregorian calendar as the nation's official calendar.[3]

This gesture not only represented a ruthless break with a self-referential national history, but also positioned socialist China in a relation of synchronic temporality with other nations of the world. I characterize the new temporality of post-1949 China as the 'postcolonial time'. By doing so, I am aware of the risk of applying the notion 'postcolonial' to a historical context that differs greatly from the one in which the notion was first formulated. The evocation of the term is, however, worth the risk, as it will not only help to comprehend some under-explored aspects of the Third Worldliness of Chinese socialism, but will also allow a reassessment of the claims of postcolonialism through Chinese experiences.

In traditional China, official time was referenced from the emperor's dynastic time. When an emperor ascended the throne, the year would be changed to Year One under the title of his reign. Through this, the emperor positioned himself at the centre of the specific celestial/temporal/spatial structure known as the Central Kingdom. According to Wu Hung (1997), this temporal concept was not challenged until the late nineteenth century, when foreign invasions brought not only changes to the country's political and economic life, but also changes to public time-telling. Wu identifies two shifts in temporal representation in 1900, in the city of Beijing (*Ibid.*, p. 345). First, the old Drum Tower, which used to announce the emperor's time by sending its thundering reverberations, was silenced, as its leather drumheads were destroyed by soldiers of the Eight-Power Allied Forces.[4] Second, time was instead told by the clocks of foreign banks, which linked Beijing to 'a huge colonial network marked by a chain of western "self-ringing clocks" in London, Singapore, Shanghai, and Hong Kong' (*Ibid.*, p. 345). In this process of weaving different places into a single system, countries 'were deterritorialized, stripped of their preceding significations, and then reterritorialized according to the convenience of colonial and imperial administration' (Harvey, 1989, p. 264; quoted from Wu, 1997, p. 345).

Changes in public time-telling during the early twentieth century were thus part of the process of subjugation. In contrast, the conjoining of the nation to a global temporality in 1949 was undertaken by the Chinese state itself. I consider this episode signifying that socialist China entered global history not as its object but as an independent subject. In his book *Postcolonial Developments*, Akhil Gupta (1998) observes that Western developmental discourses and institutions after the Second World War interpellated the newly independent nation-states of the Third World into particular temporal and spatial locations. Temporally, Third World nation-states were seen as lying in the 'dim recesses of the history' of the West. Spatially, they located in the periphery of a world system centred on the Euro-American axis. What constitutes 'the experience of modernity as "postcolonial" in a country such as India', Gupta argues, is the 'acute self-awareness of this temporal lag and spatial marginality' (*Ibid.*, p. 9).

Gupta's formulation of the postcolonial condition echoes Frantz Fanon's classic discussion of psychological violence (1968), and more recently, Homi Bhabha's theorization of the 'postcolonial time-lag' (1994, chapter 12). My polemic here is not to deny the continuity of the 'time-lag' complex, but to emphasize the rise of the newly institutionalized national subjectivity. In post-1949 China, this transition allowed the nation to conceptualize, according to its own interests and aspirations, a world not as a static one that was normatively bifurcated into a centre/periphery, but a dynamic one constantly being reconstructed. As Peter Van Ness (1993) points out, China has been through three lines of global mapping. First, the socialist-camp line (1950–1957) considered China as a 'junior member' of the Soviet-led alliance of communist countries. Second, the Third World line (1960–1970) assumed a South-versus-North global geometry, in which China attempted to lead a Third World challenge to superpower control.[5] Finally, the modernization/opening to the West line (1978–1988) adopted a policy that led to joining the capitalist world market system while still prescribing the South-North confrontation. Despite successive conceptual shifts, China has consistently identified itself with the Third World and considered 'strengthening unity and cooperation with other Third World nations' its basic foreign policy since the founding of the Third World coalition in 1955 (Harris and Worden, 1986, p. 1). Yet how 'Third World' is China?[6]

China is objectively a Third World country in some important aspects.[7] It is poor in terms of per capita gross national product, is culturally non-Western, and shares with other developing countries a common experience of humiliation and exploitation. Western Cold War research presented China as an essentially non-colonial national unit. As Tani Barlow (1997) points out, 'imperialism' and 'colonialism' were effectively banished from the lexicon of China scholarship as part of the process of making a Cold War ideological world order. Lucian Pye (1968, p. 73), for example, considers China 'not [colonized enough]' because colonialism failed to penetrate far enough into the Chinese political system. What is undeniable is that many Chinese found deep humiliation as their nation was subjected to partition by foreign powers (Dittmer and Kim, 1993; Unger, 1996). In his 1921 novel *Sinking,* for example, Yu Dafu (1989) created a portrait of a young Chinese student oppressed by feelings of shame and loneliness when he studied in Japan. While he yearned for a woman whose body and soul would belong to him, the hero suffered from an awareness that the Japanese despised and mocked at him because his country was weaker than Japan. Filled with frustration, he entered a brothel and spent the night there. The next morning, hating himself, the young man took his own life. In the closing words of the story he exhorted China to gain wealth and strength, for her weakness brought about his death.

Memories of national humiliation under foreign powers are continuously evoked in contemporary Chinese nationalistic discourse to construct and strengthen a Third World national identity (Van Ness, 1993; Gries, 2004). What is different is that, while in the previous era modernity was considered desirable, yet belonging to 'the Other', the post-1949 national space, to quote Dilip Gaonkar, was turned into a site 'where a people "make" themselves modern, as opposed to being "made" modern by alien and impersonal forces' (1999, p. 16).

I argue that it is within this context that modernity becomes something beyond its normal contours in Western discourse. The configuration of modernism in the West is complex, made up of a broad range of theories, experiences and tenets: from Marx's 'melting' version in which the explosive drives of capitalism liberated humanity from its own illusions, to Weber's 'iron cage' vision in which a purposive rationality ushered in a disenchanted world; from the Boudelairian appreciation of the aesthetic pleasure brought by the effervescence of modernity, to the Nietzschean claim of narcissistic self-absorption against an absurd modern world. More recently, Marshall Berman (1982) characterizes modernity as a historical experience that seeks ceaselessly to transform the very conditions that produce it. In the context of post-1949 China, I argue, *modernity is turned into the nation's new identity, something that directs a people's imagination about who they are, where they are now, and what they should collectively aspire to be.*

With this new identification, socialist sovereignty was inevitably mixed with developmentalism. Arturo Escobar (1995) points out that the development discourse since 1945 has to do with the exercise of Western power over the Third World through knowledge production and institutional structures. Desire for development, however, was motivated by a different set of conditions in China. Compared with other Third World countries, the traditional status of China was high, which made its experience of humiliation, since the 1830s, particularly unbearable. It was this mentality that motivated the nation's modernization programmes to achieve the goals of 'self-strengthening' (*ziqiang*) and pursuit of wealth (*qiufu*) during the late Qing and Republican periods (Tang, 1996; Gries, 2004, chapter 3). The mentality was carried on and institutionalized through post-revolutionary historiography after 1949, in which China was described as a semi-feudal, semi-colonial society (Gries, 2004). Meanwhile, socialist China was supremely confident that it could soon become the winner of the game because socialism was better able than capitalism to develop the forces of production. In turn, to prove the superiority of socialism, the state founded its legitimacy on its success in surpassing the advanced capitalist countries. Furthermore, within a Cold War context, the military threat from abroad was real. A sense of crisis strengthened the socialist state's conviction that the nation should quickly build its industry, especially heavy industry, which was considered the basis for national security (Zhongguo shehui kexue yuan and zhongyang dang'anguan, hereafter ZSKYZD, 1989, pp. 13–26).

Together these elements constituted the socialist Chinese variant of the catch-up complex – the urgent desire to take the fastest track to 'wealth and power' (*fuqiang*), keep up with the most developed countries, and establish international recognition. Under such a complex, the 'postcolonial time' was permeated by a combination of revolutionary drives, developmentalist aspirations and nationalistic concerns. This is evident in a famous paragraph from Mao's 1958 speech, 'Sixty points on working methods':

Our revolutions come one after another. Starting from the seizure of power in the whole country in 1949, there followed in quick succession the anti-feudal land reform, the agricultural cooperativization, and the socialist reconstruction of private industries, commerce, and handicrafts... Now we must start a technological revolution so that we may overtake Britain in fifteen or more years... After fifteen years, when our foodstuffs and iron and steel become plentiful, we shall take a much greater initiative. Our revolutions are like battles. After a victory, we must at once put forward a new task. (Chen, 1970, pp. 62–63)

What is particularly striking about this passage is its insistence on a perpetual search for an alternative future by constantly transcending the independent revolution, the socialist revolution, industrial modernity and more, 'one after another'. The vision shares with modernism as characterized by David Harvey (1989), an inner drive for creative destruction. In the course of this destruction, the very conditions that had produced revolutions continued to be transformed by new revolutions, and the point of fulfilment was immediately turned into the point of new departure. Berman's assertion that '[t]o be fully modern is to be antimodern' can be read with a different meaning in this context (Berman, 1982, p. 14). To be revolutionary, the revolution must endlessly transcend itself. I suggest that this forceful temporality to which the nation subscribed was the fundamental motor of Chinese socialism.

Scarcity and Third World Modernism

How to achieve modernization with limited resources is a problem faced by all Third World nations. Unlike the core countries in the world system of capitalism, the capital needed for industrialization in a peripheral country has to come from within rather than from other peripheral countries (Wallerstein, 1979, 1999).[8] Hence when the Chinese socialist state set out to build a modern industrial society, it found scarcity looming formidably along its road.

To be sure, scarcity, the condition of not having enough, is not a natural given; instead, it is a constructed notion whose meaning shifts across time and space (Xenos, 1989).[9] Whereas scarcity is the presupposition that underlies modern economic theory (Robbins, 1932), native Australians, for example, experience insufficiency as an episode rather than a general condition (Sahlins, 1972, p. 14). In Thomas Robert Malthus's (1798, 1960) dire warning of overpopulation, scarcity is a permanent feature of human society as subsistence increases only in an arithmetical ratio while population increases in a geometrical ratio. Neo-Malthusian discourse since the mid-1980s stresses the scarcity of resources as an important conditioning and motivating factor for environmental deterioration, ethnic violence and civil unrest (Homer-Dixon, 1991, 1999; Ophuls and Boyan, 1992; Kaplan, 1994, 2000; Reynolds, 2002; Simpson, Toman and Ayres, 2005).

Marxist thinkers tend to focus their attention on the unjust distribution of surplus goods while under-estimating the degree of scarcity as a variable in their analysis of social practices. Nancy Lee Peluso and Michael Watts (2001, p. 5), for example, argue that violence in the context of environmental conflict should be viewed in the light of 'the political economy of access to and control over resources' rather than being attributed to scarcity. While I agree with Peluso and Watts that power relations and the workings of capital are important, I contend that scarcity makes a difference within the same structures of political economy. Among others, scarcity has profound effects on human agency. This is especially true when even a subsistence level of existence cannot be maintained (Wu, 2003). With a strong desire for survival, scarcity becomes a powerful magic wand, transforming individuals into collective human movements, with the virtues required to bring about revolutions – sacrifice, self-discipline, and fearlessness in the face of death, to name just a few. I believe this can partially explain why movements against capitalist domination, contrary to what Marx had predicted, were de-radicalized in the 'overripe' core, but succeeded in the underdeveloped periphery. In fact, it was widely held in post-World War II Western political discourses that poverty was the main factor that helped the spread of communism and increased the appeal of the socialist development model (Packenham, 1973, p. 52).

Scarcity matters. Following Marx and others, I consider scarcity a historical condition, as material needs are socially constituted within the structure of meanings: 'so-called necessary wants, as also the mode of satisfying them, are themselves the product of historical development and depend therefore to a great extent on the degree of civilization of a country' (Marx, 1976, p. 275).[10] For post-1949 China, scarcity was the result of multiple historical forces. First, scarcity was an inherited condition from the previous era. The spread of Western imperialism greatly changed the flows of resources at a global scale (Frank, 1998). While China's per capita income was the highest in the world in 1500, it became half that of Western Europe by 1820, and less than one-tenth of the latter by 1950 (A. Lu, 2000, p. 57; Maddison, 1991, p. 10). The Sino-Japanese War and the ensuing Civil War left many cities in ruins.

Second, scarcity was exacerbated by a comprehensive blockade and embargo against China taken by the West from the end of 1950 (A. Lu, 2000, chapter 5; Zheng, 2000). In contrast to some commentators' assumptions, 'delinking' was not initiated as a voluntary choice but instead as an imposed condition in the Cold War context (A. Lu, 2000, pp. 78–81). With the US-led embargo and other punitive economic policies, China's trade with Western industrial countries dropped from 36 per cent of its total trade to less than 8 per cent between 1950 and 1955 (*Ibid.*, p. 78). The share of trade with Southeast Asian nations also fell from 6.5 to 1.4 per cent during the same period. China, for the first time in history, was almost entirely excluded from the normal world trade system of which it had been a major regional centre (Arrighi, 2002). The embargo caused a great shortage in the country of some key materials for industrialization and construction (Zheng, 2000; ZSKYZD, 1989, pp. 545–559).

Third, scarcity was structurally created by the new socialist economic system. Facing enormous difficulties in achieving industrialization in a poor country, the Chinese state adopted two basic strategies to obtain maximum accumulation of capital and surplus value: privileging production over consumption, and extracting surplus value from agriculture (Liu and Wu, 1986). China's accumulation rates were even higher than the Soviet Union in comparable phases. While in the Soviet Union the rate averaged about 25 per cent for the first ten 5-year plans, in China it was above 25 per cent for most of the years between 1949 and 1978 (Chan, 1994, p. 60). The level of accumulation was pushed to extremes in 1958 and 1959 (the period of the Great Leap Forward) when the rate reached 33.9 per cent and 43.8 per cent respectively, while a rate between 31 and 34 per cent was maintained throughout the 1970s (*Ibid.*). High levels of accumulation led to severe scarcity in social provision (chapter 4).

Fourth, social scarcity was created with major changes taking place in human needs as an integral part of China's modernization. New desires were systematically directed towards machinery, technology and other things related to industrial modernity. The images of material well-being and national progress frequently appeared in newspapers and magazines, illustrating what a new way of life should look like. A new desiring population was produced: workers came to expect that every aspect of their lives would be taken care of by the state, while peasants, living amid scarcity, envisioned a life of abundance (chapters 4 and 5). The disparity between expectation and reality only intensified the feeling of scarcity. During the 1950s, much political strife and conflict was generated among workers by the shortage of housing and social facilities in the city (*Renmin ribao*, 1956*b*, 1957*b*, 1957*c*, 1957*h*).

In fact, the sense of being lacking was so powerful that the Chinese state quickly conceptualized the nation as one of scarcity. An 'anti-waste' (*fan langfei*) discourse arose soon after 1949 (ZSKYZD, 1989, pp. 564–577). The rhetoric received a new impetus in 1955 when a resolution was made in the Soviet Union which denounced the tendency of impractical extravagances in construction (ZSKYZD, 1998, pp. 1082–1135). The national austerity policy was reinforced, and everything, including quality of life, had to be sacrificed to achieve industrialization.

The Soviet Union's housing design standard, per capita living floor space of 9 square metres, for example, was initially adopted as the model for Chinese residential planning. Under the austerity policy, however, planners continued to question whether the imported Soviet 'socialist standards' were proper practices in China, as the latter was perceived as a much poorer country than the former. The housing standard was adjusted to 4.5 square metres per capita in the mid-1950s (*Ibid.*, p. 811).

In architectural practice, nationalistic structures with big roofs and traditional ornamentation were condemned as wasteful in 1955 (Rowe and Kuan, 2002, pp. 87–106). Liang Sicheng, the Vice-Chairman of the Beijing Urban Planning Committee, became the object of severe political attack for being the main proponent of the national style (*Jianzhu xuebao*, 1955, nos 1 and 2). Structures were built according to an ultra-economical standard thereafter. In the early 1960s, Chinese architects started to take their inspirations from other Third World countries to design modernist architecture based on local conditions instead of Western paradigms (Lu, 2004). New indigenous know-how was produced, and the architectural practices of other developing nations were conceptually linked with those of China, creating a new vision of Chinese architecture (Lu, 2005; chapter 5).

China's quest for modernity, therefore, created a perpetual scarcity not only as a social reality but also as a national imagination. This prominent element of Third World modernism, however, is curiously left out of the discussion of the postcolonial. My focus here is on Homi Bhabha's theory of postcoloniality. Through sophisticated poststructuralist procedures, Bhabha (1994) weaves a fine analysis of the failures of colonialist and nationalist discourse (Young, 1995; Fludernik, 1998). His thesis is centred on discursive failures caused by miscommunication and misinterpretation (Radhakrishnan, 2000, p. 55). To Bhabha, it is enough to conceive of (post)colonial subjectivity as both doubling and partial prescence (AlSayyad, 2001, pp. 6–7). The key problem I have with such concepts as hybridity and mimicry is that, by grounding his analysis in the state of being 'less than one and double', Bhabha (1994, p. 116) never goes beyond the subtle tactics of manipulation in reaction to the dominator. As such, the failure of both the dominated and the dominator is absolute; there is no way out of it.

I have argued elsewhere the need to historicize hybridity in attempts to understand opposition and domination in specific times and places (Lu, 2000). I propose here that scarcity must be added as a key dimension in the examination of the complexity of the postcolonial dilemma. This new orientation allows me to pose the question: What happens after a transposition of national identity from the state of 'being less' to the state of 'being lacking'? I suggest that, in the context of post-1949 China, a number of important conceptual shifts are made possible through this transposition. These can be briefly summarized as follows. First, the failure of desire is externalized by considering that the failure is due to scarcity – being lacking in means to achieve the goals – instead of due to its being 'less than one and double' or 'less civilized'. Second, as the failure becomes an exterior condition, the distance between the nation's current state and its projected identity is justified as a relational term that exists only during a certain period and can be shortened via specific strategies.[11] Third, in the battles against failure, as the possibility to learn from the failure is opened up, there arises a new need for self-knowledge and other knowledges besides Western knowledge.

The recognition that the failure is historical and can be reversed helps to resolve the crisis of agency that often confronts people after the revolution. Thus, in the epigraph to this chapter, Mao indeed celebrated the fact that the Chinese were 'poor and blank' (1971, p. 500). He proclaimed that it was precisely because of such conditions that the desire for 'change', 'action' and 'revolution' would be incited (*Ibid.*). In his modernist vision of Chinese society, Mao was a real life Faust who aspired to 'build a brave new world out of the ashes of the old' by eliminating anything that stood in the way of modernization (Harvey, 1989, p. 16). With characteristically Maoist thinking, scarcity was ironically turned into a favoured condition – 'a blank sheet of paper free from any mark' – in the push for modernization, so that scarcity and modernity were conceptually reconciled. Yet this synthesis, as we shall see, was a fragile one, constantly in danger of disintegrating into new contradictions.

Spatial Practices under Chinese Socialism

In *The Production of Space*, Henri Lefèbvre (1991*a*) reminds us that space is not an innocent backdrop or neutral material substratum. Instead, space is a fundamental component of the capitalist mode of production and social domination; the production of space can be likened to the production of any other sort of commodity. Along this line, urban studies literature has worked out an impressive research agenda on the development and maintenance of urban space under the capitalist mode of production (e.g., Castells, 1978; Harvey, 1985; Gottdiener, 1985; Ball, 1986; Smith, 1996; Crysler, 2003, chapter 5). This study is informed by such writings but focuses instead on the production of the built environment under state socialism. While accepting a broad framework of political economy, I argue that spatial production in Maoist China was not only due to the socialist mode of production, but also due to the historical condition of scarcity and weak planning power within a peculiar socialist/Third World national context. Before outlining the mechanisms behind the production of space under Chinese socialism between 1949 and 1978 , I shall start with a brief history of Chinese urban form.

China has a long and distinguished history of urban planning. Classical texts on the appropriate form of the royal city became available as early as the Zhou dynasty (eleventh century BC to 256 BC) (Wheatley, 1971). Imperial capitals and regional administrative centres in successive dynasties were more or less constructed according to the classical model. Cities were surrounded by high walls, with a north–south, east–west grid of streets setting the framework for the walled ward system where enceintes, market quarters and residential districts were housed in separate wards (Yang, 1993). This model reached its maturity by the Sui (581–618 AD) and early Tang dynasties (618–907 AD) but was gradually replaced by an open street system during the late Tang and early Southern Song periods (1127–1279 AD) (Heng, 1999). By the late imperial period, with the intensification of a market economy and urbanization, Chinese cities developed a dense morphology with mixed commercial and living spaces (Skinner, 1977a).

The Opium War (1839–1842) opened up a series of encroachments by Western powers, under whose influence new urban forms, such as treaty ports and railway cities, appeared (Esherick, 2000a). Both native and Western urban reformers considered Chinese cities disorderly, unhealthy and inefficient. Hence the Republican era (1911–1949) saw a major effort to redevelop Chinese cities through urban reform (Cody, 1996; Tsin, 1999; Esherick, 2000b; Staleton, 2000). Modern infrastructure, new regulations promoting hygiene and safety, and Western planning concepts were introduced to some Chinese cities, creating urban patterns similar to those found in other modern cities (MacPherson, 1990; Dong, 1999; Wang, 2004). A new commercialism transformed cities such as Shanghai into glittering pleasure domes, alive with a variety of modern functions (Lee, 2001). Despite changes in a number of major cities, however, traditional spatial patterns persisted in the vast majority of China: walled, intensive and compact in morphology.

With the founding of the People's Republic in 1949, fundamental societal transitions brought a new wave of spatial transformation. While most urban reforms were carried out at the municipal level during the Republican period,

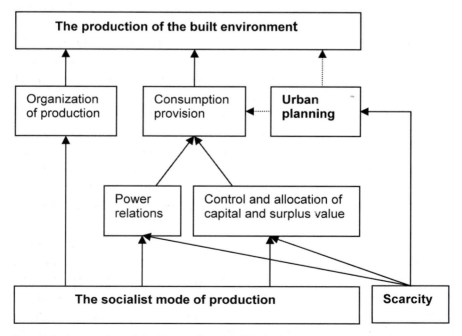

Figure 1.1. A research model of the production of the built environment under Chinese socialism, 1949–1978.

the new socialist state acquired unprecedented responsibility for urban planning on a nationwide scale. Urban development was controlled by a series of national 5-year plans and largely driven by industrialization (Ma and Hanten, 1981). New urban construction was accomplished mainly through the accretion of work units in near suburban areas. While initially designed as a unit of production, the work unit gradually developed into the basic unit of collective consumption which integrated workplace, residence and social services (chapters 3 and 4). The Maoist city achieved a morphology made up in large part of a jigsaw puzzle of self-contained and spatially demarcated work units surrounding the old city core. This morphology contrasts sharply with that of modern capitalist cities, where urban space is characterized by the separation of land use into commercial, industrial and residential districts.

Figure 1.1 is presented as an organizing framework for this and other research to come to grips with the dynamics behind the production of the built environment under Chinese socialism.[12] Beginning at the bottom left of the framework is the socialist mode of production, which provides the foundation for two main categories of influence upon the production of the built environment: the organization of production and consumption provision.

As industrialization was the key engine that drove urban growth in Maoist China, the organization of production played a major role in shaping the skeleton of the built environment. Efficient organization required a balance between a number of antagonistic elements, including the specialization of production vs. the scale of the production unit, the separation of polluting industry vs. the minimization of transport costs, production near raw materials vs. production near consumers, etc. The calculation of these relations was mirrored in the rational organization of the built environment (ZSKYZD, 1989, pp. 538–550).

Following Ball (1986), consumption provision here refers to the design, production, distribution and management of crucial means of consumption such as housing, nurseries, schools and health facilities. I propose seeing consumption provision in pre-reform China as influenced by two major factors: control and allocation of capital and surplus value, and power relations. Each factor featured specific characteristics and had important implications for spatial production:

1. Capital and surplus value were controlled and allocated through vertical linkages in the centrally planned socialist system. The central state distributed resources through ministries to work units according to national plans, while work units turned over most of surplus value to the state. As such, economic plans and state policies were implemented through individual work units without too much interference from the local government (Shue, 1994; Cartier, 2005, p. 26). The municipality received only a small share of capital and thus had little

control over urban development (Gong and Chen, 1994; Wu, 1999, p. 207). In spite of official state ownership, the users and occupants of state property had *de facto* control upon the property. Therefore, actual property rights were scattered among different levels of jurisdictions, sectoral departments and work units; transactions and negotiations often took place in *ad hoc* manner (Walder, 1986, 1992; Wu, 1997). The vertical distribution system and the dispersed property structure led to the uncoordinated pattern of urban growth (chapter 4).

2.   Although the Chinese state was depicted as a totalitarian regime in Cold War-era research, recent studies have shown that its power structure was fragmented, leaving much room for individual jurisdictions and social agents to assert their respective agency, at times ignoring or distorting the initial plans (Shue, 1988, 1994; Wu, 1997; Cartier, 2005). The weak control of the socialist state over enterprises and labour was structurally produced. Under socialism, enterprises operate within soft budget constraints – that is, if a production unit suffers financial losses, the state will cover it sooner or later (Kornai, 1980). Hence a socialist economic system does not possess the kind of disciplinary mechanisms over enterprises characteristic of capitalism.[13] Due to the lack of labour markets, layoffs, bankruptcies and so on, the means for disciplining labour under socialism are less efficient than those under capitalism (Verdery, 1991, p. 427; Bray, 2005, p. 166). The strong bargaining power of the work unit over the local government and the planning department, and workers over their work unit, played a key role in redirecting capital from production to consumption construction (chapter 4).

Although the structures of political economy were vital, I consider scarcity an important category of influence in the context of Third World socialism. Whereas the structures of political economy provided the basic rules for agents to operate in a social field, scarcity distorted the rules, changed social and spatial imaginations, modified the interrelations between social agents, and incited human agency and action.

As mentioned earlier, under the condition of scarcity, the Chinese state adopted the policy of privileging production over consumption to accumulate maximum capital for industrialization. This policy was quickly translated into new conceptualizations of urban space and construction. There were major efforts to convert the 'cities of consumption' into the 'cities of production' during the 1950s (ZSKYZD, 1989, pp. 581–583). Urban functions in commerce, finance and services were suppressed; most of the city's manpower and resources were transferred to industrial development. State investment in urban development was tilted heavily towards productive construction – the erection of structures that were directly related to production – and biased against non-productive construction – the erection of structures which rendered services for people (Zhang, Zheng and Dai, 1982).

As Chapter 4 will show, the resulting huge scarcity of consumption facilities at the municipal level caused severe political tension and strife during the 1950s. The state responded by imposing the responsibility of urban provision upon the work unit. Related institutional rules were established step by step to strengthen the social function of the work unit.[14] Faced with political pressure from employees below and administrators above, unit leaders strived to meet the needs of their workers. One of the important findings of this book is that as state resources for non-productive construction were scarce, the building of living facilities within work units were often accomplished through construction outside the state plan and by resource hoarding. The study demonstrates that some insights about the mechanisms of state socialism noted by the scholars of East European socialist countries, such as 'second economy' and 'shortage economy', are valid in the context of Maoist China, and that these mechanisms had important impacts upon the built environment (Knorád and Szelényi, 1979; Kornai, 1980, 1992).[15]

This book reveals that Chinese urban form, as it exists today, bears little resemblance to what Chinese socialist planners had in mind. China's residential planning pedigree was derived from Western and Soviet repertoire. Specifically, the microdistrict (*xiaoqu* in Chinese and *mikrorayon* in Russian) schema was introduced to China in 1956 and established as the dominant residential planning model in the early 1960s (chapter 2). However, due to limited resources and weak planning powers, planners failed to realize the model to any great extent before 1978. In theory, public ownership and the centrally planned system should provide favourable conditions for the realization of planning ideas. In practice, construction investment was channelled through all-powerful vertical sectoral lines, over which the planning department had little control. In theory, all construction projects should be put under the supervision of planners. In practice, planners operated in the lower echelon of the power system and did not possess adequate means for regulation. Consequently, although planners worked hard to reverse the self-contained development model of the work unit by consistently stressing the microdistrict schema and coordinated urban growth, their actual influence was feeble (chapter 4). Urban planning turned out to be a weak intermediate element in the socialist production of space, unable to correct biases created by the system according to the profession's own criteria.

The Structure of the Book

This book is organized thematically, focusing on selected episodes that epitomize critical moments in the development of the contemporary Chinese built environment. Each chapter takes up a relatively independent topic, so the book can be best read as a kind of collage in which the parts interact in a complementary pattern, instead of being synthesized into an overarching general history.

Chapters 2 and 3, which comprise Part I of the book, set the stage for the analysis that follows by introducing China's residential planning ideals and urban reality. Chapter 2 represents the first attempt to investigate the diachronic development of two important residential planning schemas in China: the neighbourhood unit and its Soviet variant the microdistrict. The study traces their multiple involvements in China's nation building practices, ranging from urban reforms in the Republican era, socialist building under Mao, and housing commodification and community building in the reform era. Chapter 3 provides an account of the physical features and spatial experiences of the work unit, and a comprehensive evaluation of its socio-spatial implications for the Chinese city.

In Chapters 4 and 5, which comprise Part II of the book, I address the distortion of planning ideals under Chinese socialism. While much of existing literature on the formation of the work unit concentrates on its institutional origins, Chapter 4 provides an inquiry into the development of its physical form. It does so by using archival study to examine the conflicting relationships between the state, work units and planners in the construction of living facilities in Beijing between 1949 and 1965. Chapter 5 looks into the planning experiments during the people's commune movement launched in 1958. Concurrent with sweeping institutional changes, architects and planners boldly experimented with modernist design. Yet despite the energy and enthusiasm instilled in commune proposals, they rarely progressed from paper. The study reveals an intriguing aspect of Third World modernism – the utopianization of modernity.

Chapters 6 and 7, Part III of the book, examine the ways in which the Chinese built environment was transformed, adapted and contested over time. In Chapter 6, I identify the persistence of the wall-building tradition during successive political changes as a medium through which to understand the relationship between modernity and tradition in contemporary China. Upon the consolidation of socialist control in 1949, the utility of city walls was called into question. As the era of the city wall in Chinese culture ended, a new one began. By the 1960s work units were building walls not only as a security measure, but also as a means of defining territories and hoarding land. The importance of walls has not decreased in the reform era; instead, the need for walls has been strengthened in private developments. Chapter 7 examines the transition of the work unit from an enclosed entity to a more fluid space and the conflicts generated by this process through a case study of a research institute located in Beijing. I show post-reform Chinese urban space as a site where urban and rural residents both run parallel to each other in close proximity and disrupt each other's life in unpredictable ways.

The book closes with a brief epilogue.

Notes

1. Coined by French economist Alfred Sauvy during the early 1950s, the term 'Third World' was the ideological by-product of the dramatic changes in the world order after World War II. The Asia-Africa Conference in Bandung, Indonesia, in 1955, symbolized the appearance of developing nations that had gained independence from colonial rule as newly emergent forces in the world system. The term was used during the Cold War to distinguish nations that aligned neither with the West nor with the East (Hermassi, 1980). More recently, the 'Third World' has been used as the general term to describe poor countries whose populations had a per capita income below US$3,000 in 1978 or a life expectancy of less than 70 years (The World Bank, 1980). China has consistently identified itself with the Third World since the founding of the Third World coalition in 1955 (Harris and Worden, 1986, p. 1). Mao's theory of the three worlds was one of the primary objects of research during the Cold War period (see note 5). Since 1978, China's position in global space has changed greatly, but the official statements of the Chinese government continue to claim a Third World identity for the nation (Van Ness, 1993, pp. 213–214). More recently, Arif Dirlik (1994, 2000) provides seminal theoretical explorations on the Third World aspect of Chinese socialism.
2. Postcolonialism has arisen as part of the critical toolbox in cultural studies since the 1970s, with Edward Said's *Orientalism* (1978) as one of its founding theses. The theory deals broadly with the cultural, social and political issues in response and resistance to colonialism and the continuing dominance of Western hegemony. Prasenjit Duara in his book *Rescuing History from the Nation*, for example, stresses postcolonialism as 'the critique of the ways in which modern, independent nation-states continue to operate within the old (colonial/Enlightenment) problematic of History and its hierarchy of different modes of living and time' (1995, p. 9). The field of postcolonial studies has produced some of the most exciting theoretical imaginations of the Third World in recent years. For the discussion on postcoloniality and the built environment, see King, 1990, 2004; AlSayyad, 1992, 2001; Nalbantoglu and Thai, 1997; Kusno, 2000; Lu, 2000; Cairns, 2004.
3. On 28 September 1949, *Renmin ribao* (People's Daily) changed the year from the Republic Year 38 (*minguo 38 nian*) to 1949.
4. The Eight-Power Allied Forces were sent by Britain, France, the United States, Japan, Germany, Italy, Austria and Russia.
5. Mao's famous theory of the three worlds saw global space differently from the normal division of the three worlds. It considered the First World consisting of the two superpowers, the United States and the USSR, the Second World including the developed countries of Europe and Japan, and the Third World made of both socialist and underdeveloped capitalist countries (Harris and Worden, 1986, pp. 12–13). As the Second World War was 'controlled and bullied by the superpowers', the contradiction between the two could be exploited by the Third World to unite the Second 'in the common struggle for self-determination' (*Ibid.*).
6. China's Third World identity is controversial in Western discourses. Lillian Harris and Robert Worden, for example, list a number of anomalies regarding this self-positioning: better than other developing nations in per capita GNP, GNP growth rate, life expectancy and so on; not having the direct colonial occupation experience of many Third World states; and large in size compared with most developing countries (1986, p. 1).
7. Peter Van Ness (1993, p. 196) summarizes the commonalities shared by Third World nations in five categories: 'economic (underdeveloped), cultural (non-Western), racial (non-white), political (non-aligned), and geographic (situated in Asia, Africa, or Latin America)'.
8. Immanuel Wallerstein's world-systems analysis (1979, 1999) argues that based on a

transnational social division of labour and global commodity chains, capitalism as a historical system involves an interstate system comprised of national states. These states have been brought into the world capitalist system with differing positions in its structure. Certain nation-states occupying core positions absorb much of the surplus value produced within countries at peripheral positions via unequal exchange. Peripheral countries are dependent on the export of lower value-added products or raw materials to core countries; workers in the former are paid much less than those in the latter for the same amount of labour time. There are semi-peripheral countries featuring a combination of core and peripheral production processes. The work of Wallerstein, Samir Amin, Andre G. Frank and others on the world capitalist system forms an important area of contemporary Marxist research.

9. Nicholas Xenos (1989) argues that the concept of scarcity as a universal human condition is indeed a modern invention. For the ancient Greeks, *spanis*, the idea of insufficiency, was accompanied by a concept of needs as naturally limited. The English word 'scarcity' retained this limited sense until modern times. From the eighteenth century on, the concept of scarcity was transformed from a limited notion to a universal condition (*Ibid.*, p. 3). Xenos considers this conceptual transition a result of the creation of an environment of boundless desire, as an endless pursuit of luxury is necessitated by a world of affluence (*Ibid.*, p. 5).

10. From a different perspective, Jean-Paul Sartre considers scarcity a constructed human condition under capitalist modernity. In his *Critique of Dialectical Reason*, Sartre sees history as 'born and developed within the permanent framework of a field of tension produced by scarcity' (1960, 1976, p. 125). As human beings construct a social field in which there is not enough for everyone, Sartre argues, they cannot recognize their mutual humanity (*Ibid.*, p. 127).

11. I owe the point to R. Radhakrishnan's discussion on Bhabha's reading of the narration of nation (2004, pp. 54–55).

12. My design of the framework was informed by the findings of this study and existing scholarship, especially Castells, 1977; Ball, 1986; Kornai, 1980, 1992; Verdery, 1991; Wu, 1997; Ma and Wu, 2005a.

13. Although János Kornai's insights were derived from Hungarian experience, they are equally valid in the context of Maoist socialism. See chapter 4 in this book.

14. For a discussion of the institutional origins of the work unit, see Lü, 1997; Perry, 1997; Yeh, 1997; Yang and Zhou, 1999; Bray, 2005, chapters 3, 4 and 5.

15. I choose to use the term 'scarcity' instead of 'shortage' in this book. The term 'shortage economy' is used by János Kornai (1980, 1992) and others to describe the chronic shortages as a systemic flaw of the centrally planned economy in Eastern European socialist countries. My use of the term 'scarcity' stresses the experience of being lacking shared by poor countries in general.

Chapter Two

Travelling Urban Form: The Neighbourhood Unit in China[1]

The term 'origin' does not mean the process by which the existent came into being, but rather what emerges from the process of becoming and disappearing. Origin is an eddy in the stream of becoming.

Walter Benjamin, 1928, *The Origin of German Tragic Drama*

In his book *The World, the Text, and the Critic*, Edward Said (1983) introduces the notion of travelling theory to address the movement of ideas across space. According to Said, the travel of theories and ideas occurs in four major stages. First, there is 'the point of origin': the location at which the idea first entered discourse. Second, there is 'a passage through the pressure of various contexts' as the idea moves. Third, there is a set of conditions which allows the introduction or toleration of the transplanted idea. Fourth, the now fully or partly accommodated idea occupies 'a new position in a new time and place' (*Ibid.*, pp. 226–227). Said's 'travelling theory' opens up a crucial research agenda, which establishes the displacements of ideas in different cultural or national sites as an important aspect of the production of knowledge.[2]

This potentially rich approach, however, remains relatively underutilized in planning history. Conventional studies on the international diffusion of planning ideas often imply a linear path and tend to reduce the complexities surrounding local appropriations, (mis)interpretations, reinventions and resistances. In light of the fact that the development of many modern planning ideas occurred at intersecting regional, national and transnational levels, the neglect of their travel aspect has clouded some important connections that otherwise could be pursued. This chapter looks into the travel trajectories of the neighbourhood unit concept in China. First articulated by the American social reformer Clarence Perry in the

1920s, the neighbourhood unit schema provides a model layout for a residential district, with specific prescriptions for the spatial arrangement of residences, streets and services. Over the past eight decades, the neighbourhood unit plan has traversed national boundaries and spread widely throughout the world. It has served as an important template for contemporary Chinese residential planning.

The idea of the neighbourhood unit was employed by Japanese colonial planners in the planning of cities such as Changchun and Datong in the 1930s. During the late 1940s, Chinese planners initiated planning proposals for several major cities based on the neighbourhood unit and other modern planning concepts. Due to civil unrest and war, however, the actual realization of the neighbourhood unit idea did not take place until the founding of the People's Republic in 1949. Socialist planners experimented with several competing residential planning ideas during the 1950s. The microdistrict (*xiaoqu* in Chinese and *mikrorayon* in Russian), an idea transmitted from the Soviet Union and essentially similar to the neighbourhood unit schema, gradually gained favour. Except a few built examples of the microdistrict, however, planners failed to actualize the model to any great extent under Mao (1949–1976). Economic reforms since 1978 have created new opportunities for the implementation of the microdistrict planning principles. At the turn of millennium, the microdistrict schema gained new vitality as a national 'community building' (*shequ jianshe*) campaign was launched to establish the residential community as the new basic unit of urban governance.

Drawing on Said's 'travelling theory' and recent scholarship on knowledge and representation (Foucault, 1972; Bhabha, 1994; Fairclough, 1995; Marianne and Phillips, 2002), this study is focused on the diffuseness with which the neighbourhood unit idea was apprehended and applied by reference to the shifting social exigencies in the Chinese nation-building process. As such, the questions discussed have not been concerned with a description of the application of the neighbourhood unit schema in a particular city. Rather, the study stresses how ideas and forms were interpreted, negotiated and contested in a constant flux of historical practices. It asks the following questions: in what context did the neighbourhood unit concept enter the Chinese social discourse?[3] How did the connotations of the idea shift in the process of translation and adaptation? At which moment were certain streams of thought preferred and legitimized over others? And how has the idea been repeatedly evocated and reconstructed under new social conditions? The chapter shows that the travel of the neighbourhood unit concept in China involved multiple associations, successive discursive conversions and *ad hoc* pragmatic decisions. Its domestication was a continual process of translating, taking, selecting, combining and reinventing, instead of direct borrowing of foreign ideas; or, to use Walter Benjamin's poetic language, it is 'an eddy in the stream of becoming' (1977, p. 45).

The chapter is divided into four sections. The first is a brief introduction to the neighbourhood unit concept as a specific constellation of modern thought, vision and action. The second section then discusses the various routes through which the concept travelled to China in the Republican era. The third examines some early socialist experiments with neighbourhood planning during the 1950s, emphasizing the transformations and resistances the transplanted ideas provoked in China. The final section seeks to understand the emergence of the microdistrict as a norm for residential planning and its new roles in the reform era.

The Neighbourhood Unit: A Brief History

The neighbourhood has long been the basic spatial unit to organize cities and towns. In ancient China, a normative principle of urban planning which organized the city into separate wards had been established since Zhou times (c. the eleventh century BC to 256 BC) (Wheatley, 1971; Yang, 1993; Heng, 1999). The medieval European town consisted of autonomous quarters, each with its own centre and market (Mumford, 1961). The new scale of industrial production, however, severed intimate human associations of the pre-industrial era. Based on an impersonal spatial system, the modern city supported a new way of life hostile to neighbourliness. By the late nineteenth century, the Western social elite had identified the rehumanization of the modern city as an urgent obligation (Boyer, 1983).

The turn of the twentieth century was arguably one of the most imaginative periods for new conceptualizations of society and space. Ebenezer Howard's book *To-Morrow: A Peaceful Path to Real Reform* (1898) established a novel spatial linkage between society, nature and economy through a new type of urbanism in a planned town. The idea became the basis for the garden city movement in various parts of the world (Hall, 2002). The settlement house movement was launched in Britain in the late nineteenth century as part of a broad attempt to preserve human values in poorer urban districts and soon spread to the United States (Weiner, 1994; Carson, 1990). Meanwhile, developments in social sciences provided new theoretical linkages between social interaction and the physical environment. Charles H. Cooley, an Ann-Arbor based sociologist, in his book *Social Organization* (1909) argued that face-to-face human relationship had a geographical basis. Chicago School sociologists, including Robert Park and Ernest Burgess, also produced a rich body of literature on community development. Burgess (1925), for instance, held that an ecological community of geographic location would have an effect on the building of a local culture.

Starting his career in teaching service, Clarence Perry was attached to the Playground and Recreation Association of America in 1909 as its second field officer, whose main responsibility was to investigate the prospects for promoting an extended use of public schools for after-hours social and civic uses (Birtles, 1994, pp. 1–3). His book *Wider Use of the School Plant* received acclaim from the settlement house movement which Perry considered a major influence on his earlier thinking (1911, pp. 2–3). He was later involved in the community centre movement, which advocated that 'Every schoolhouse a community capital and every community a little democracy' (Seligman, 1934, p. 250). Although the movement failed to develop coherent community life, the experiments provided a basis for Perry and others to explore further the idea of the 'socially planned neighbourhood'. The first public presentation of the idea occurred at a joint meeting of the National Community Centre Association and the American Sociological Society in Washington on 26 December 1923, when Perry gave an illustrated lecture entitled 'A community unit in city planning and development' (Dahir, 1947, p. 24). In his 1924 presentation at the National Conference of Social Work in Toronto, Perry further elaborated a number of key points for the model planned neighbourhood, in which he made reference to his own residential suburb Forest Hills Gardens as an example of the planned neighbourhood (Perry, 1924).[4] Much of his ideas were later incorporated in Perry's book *The Urban Community* (1926). The concept found its most complete description in Perry's treatise 'The neighbourhood unit, a scheme of arrangement for the family-life community' (1929) and gained wide acceptance shortly thereafter.

Some, including Lewis Mumford, point out that Clarence Stein and Henry Wright had already included many similar neighbourhood planning principles in their design of Sunnyside Gardens in New York before Perry's neighbourhood unit schema was fully crystallized (Mumford, 1951; Patricios, 2002).[5] Regardless of who deserves the laurels for originality, a new and readily usable planning schema was emerging. The neighbourhood unit fused a range of early twentieth-century visions and actions into a few tangible design principles. First, clear boundaries determined by wide, arterial streets to control the movement of through traffic past the neighbourhood; second, a primary school within easy walking distance; third, grouped local shops located at the periphery of the neighbourhood; and fourth, neighbourhood parks and playgrounds to comprise about 10 per cent of the whole area (Perry, 1929). The neighbourhood unit represents a design solution that brings together urban functions and social interactions. With schools, shops, parks and community facilities connected with but not bisected by main traffic arteries, residents can find convenience and safety. The provision of community facilities on a manageable scale creates an environment which strengthens neighbourliness and moral bonds.

The neighbourhood unit concept quickly won acclaim from architects, planners, government agencies and private developers. Tracy Augur, in an address delivered at the 1935 national housing conference, regarded Ebenezer Howard's garden city idea and Perry's neighbourhood unit schema as twin pillars to rear a stable urban order (Augur, 1935). Quite a few garden suburbs were built according to the neighbourhood unit plan in the United States. Famous examples include the three greenbelt towns of the Resettlement Administration, suburbs of Cincinnati (Greenhills), Milwaukee (Greendale) and Washington (Greenbelt, Maryland). A number of planners envisioned organizing the entire city according to the neighbourhood and community planning principles. The 1946 *Preliminary Comprehensive City Plan of Chicago*, for instance, was based on the concept of the city being comprised of 514 self-contained neighbourhoods and 59 communities (Chicago Plan Commission, 1946). Agencies of the federal government gave unequivocal support to the neighbourhood unit plan. The 1941 Federal Housing Administration (FHA) bulletin, *Successful Subdivisions*, adopted the idea as the basis for planning the residential environment (Federal Housing Administration, 1941).

The neighbourhood unit concept has been the subject of worldwide interest since its inception (Dahir, 1947, p. 70). The 1930 Third Congress meeting of the CIAM (Congrès Internationaux d'Architecture Moderne), whose speakers included Le Corbusier and Walter Gropius, discussed the question of 'how to organize whole groups of dwellings into neighbourhood units in such a way that human needs could be satisfied' (*Ibid.*, p. 71). British academic discussion of the neighbourhood unit concept in the 1930s led to wide acceptance of the idea as a way to correct past planning mistakes. The semi-official British adoption of the neighbourhood unit took place with the publication of *The Dudley Report* and *The Housing Manual* in 1944 (Ministry of Health, 1944; Ministry of Housing, 1944). Following Perry's notion of a hierarchy of service centres, British planners developed a three-tier retailing system of neighbourhood, district and town centre (Birtles, 1994, pp. 32–33). Certainly, in a number of aspects British interpretations of the neighbourhood unit differed from Perry's 1929 formulation (*Ibid.*): shopping facilities at the centre rather than at the periphery of each neighbourhood; public open space at the perimeter rather than at the centre to act as a buffer between neighbourhoods; and the size of the neighbourhood unit set at about 10,000 residents, a major departure from Perry's 1929 formulation.

The neighbourhood unit concept provided the basis for the development of British new towns after World War II, which in turn offered important lessons for other countries around the world (Goss, 1961; Burke, 1971). To name just a few, plans for new towns in Israel during the 1950s, including Beersheba, Ashqelon and Migdal, were modelled on the British Mark II new town plans (Shaked, 1970). A wide application of neighbourhood planning in Australia was found in Canberra since the formation of the National Capital Development Commission in 1958

(National Capital Development Commission, 1965; Moseley, 1974; Linge, 1975). The basic components of the Soviet neighbourhood plan, which had developed since 1931, were similar to those of the neighbourhood unit schema (Kaufmann, 1936). In Brazil, the residential planning of the new capital Brasilia was based on the *superquadra*, which followed organizational rules similar to those of the neighbourhood plan (Holston, 1989, chapter 5). The neighbourhood unit was also the fundamental spatial unit in Le Corbusier's plan for Chandigarh in India in the 1950s (Kalia, 1999).

With the wide international recognition it has received, the neighbourhood unit is arguably a 'global urban form' of the twentieth century. Its spread has been characterized by an internationalization of modern planning knowledge, large-scale residential developments, and the rise of welfare society. It serves as a major landmark in shaping human settlements in various parts of the world. Yet the neighbourhood unit, as this chapter will demonstrate, is far more than another instance of Western expansionist aspirations and uniform technologies of homogenization. Instead, it has been variously localized into nation-building programmes and social welfare projects. The sections that follow will provide an account of the Chinese variant of the planning experimentation with the schema.

Routes in Republican China

One of the earliest residential developments in China, which was based on the neighbourhood unit concept, was developed by Japanese colonial planners in Changchun in 1934. Following Japan's military occupation of Manchuria in 1931 and the establishment of the puppet state Manzhoukuo in the following year, Changchun was renamed Xinjing ('New Capital', or Shinkyo to the Japanese) and set up as the capital (Buck, 2000; Tucher, 1999; Li, 1997; Guo, 2004). The first five-year plan of Xinjing (1932–1937) was carried out by Sano Toshikata and his associates, who produced a comprehensive design for the entire new city (Buck, 2000, pp. 79–84). The plan aimed to remould Xinjing according to modern planning ideas (Tucher, 1999, chapter 8).[6]

The neighbourhood unit concept was adopted in the residential planning of Xinjing, and its application was inevitably shaped by the specific colonial circumstances. Planner Hideshima Kan classified urban neighbourhoods into different types according to life style, profession, city scale and the distance to urban centre (Li, 1997, p. 228). The neighbourhood unit schema was employed to plan modern 'new Manchurian' residential districts, serving the elite class – the Japanese. Each unit consisted of 6,000 residents and 1,500 households in an area of 1.7 square kilometres (*Ibid.*, p. 226). Public facilities were divided into two levels: the first consisted of schools, community centres, clinics, shops, parks, sports fields, police stations and so on, located on the periphery of the central square; the second consisted of kindergartens, sports fields and offices, placed at four different locations according to their optimum service radii. The Shuntian residential district (1934–1941) located near the palace area was the first project built according to these principles. By 1942, it had a population of 16,760 (mostly Japanese) and 3,504 households (*Ibid.*, pp. 231–32).

Following Japan's occupation of Datong in 1937, in June 1938 the North Shanxi Autonomous Government began to consult Tokyo University professor Uchida Yoshikazu (also written as Yoshizo) about the expansion of the city as a mining, transport and political centre (Tucher, 1999, p. 153). Uchida and his team arrived in Datong on 23 September 1938 and stayed there for three weeks. The Datong plan they produced incorporated some of the most advanced standards and up-to-date planning concepts, including the satellite city, the neighbourhood unit and the greenbelt (*Ibid.*, 153–159). Each neighbourhood unit in the plan was about 0.8 square kilometres and consisted of 1,000 households (Li, 1997, p. 256). The unit was centred on the primary school and the park adjacent to it; public space was in a four to six ratio to private space. Residence was divided into three classes, all with extensive walls (Tucher, 1999, p. 163). Uchida published the Datong plan in the journal *Kenchiku zasshi* in 1939, which was hailed by some Japanese planners as one of the most sophisticated master plans at the time (1939*a*; 1939*b*). Despite the fact that the military occupation provided cheap land and financial investment, most projects in the Datong plan were never realized.

The early twentieth century saw wide ranging efforts to reform Chinese cities. Many modern planning concepts were introduced by Western planners and Western-trained Chinese specialists (Esherick, 2000*b*). For example, during the 1920s and 1930s, Nanjing, Guangzhou and Shanghai were at the forefront of establishing the US planning connections through various channels (MacPherson, 1990; Cody, 1996; Tsin, 1999). Jeffrey Cody (2001, p. 189) notes that Nanjing's 1929 residential development plan, designed by American architect Henry Murphy and others, showed some influence of Perry's neighbourhood idea (although he also points out that the connection cannot be completely substantiated). Most urban experiments, however, were suspended during the Sino-Japanese war (1937–1945), and it is unclear how far the Japanese planning experiments influenced the spread of the neighbourhood unit concept in China. After the war, Chinese planners embraced the latest planning techniques to rebuild the nation. Among others, the neighbourhood unit was widely adopted by Chinese planners in the organization of several major cities. A 'Ten-Year Plan' was produced in 1946 for the wartime capital Chongqing, which was made the 'permanent second capital' (*yongjiu peidu*) after the Kuomintang government moved back to Nanjing (figure 2.1) (Dong, 1999, pp. 257–259). American consultants were invited by the Chinese Ministry

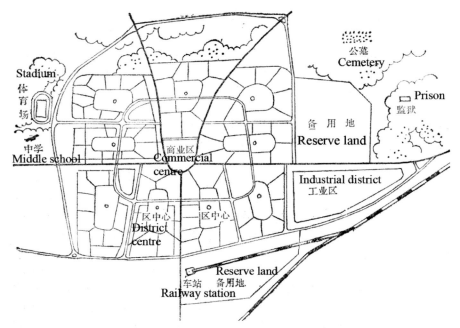

Figure 2.1. Master plan for the satellite city of Chongqing, 1946 (translation added).

of Interior to participate in planning decision-making. Under their influence, the neighbourhood unit concept was adopted to structure the city's satellite settlements, and there were attempts to integrate it with the *baojia* neighbourhood system (Gordon, 1946).

Baojia was a household registration and surveillance system adopted in late-imperial China to strengthen the state's control over urban residents. The system organized ten *jia* of about one hundred households into a *bao*, each with a headman who was responsible for registering everyone and maintaining order (Dutton, 1992, pp. 85–88). American planner Norman Gordon, who advised the Chinese Ministry of Interior on city planning and housing, suggested that this social institution could be combined with the neighbourhood unit schema. In his 1946 article 'China and the neighbourhood unit' published in the journal *The American City*, Gordon (1946, p. 113) stated that while the Americans were given credit for having contributed the neighbourhood unit concept, the idea of consciously building up a community with neighbourhoods had its origin in ancient China. With Chinese planners, he attempted to integrate the traditional *baojia* system with 'the neighbourhood planning standards of 20th Century United States' (*Ibid*.). Each *bao*, consisting of 19 *jia* with 19 families per *jia*, would make one neighbourhood unit, served by an elementary school with 200 to 400 pupils. Recognizing that families in China were usually larger than in the US, Gordon proposed that each

Chinese neighbourhood unit could have 2,000 residents, slightly larger than the American standard (*Ibid.*).

The adaptation of the neighbourhood unit schema to the *baojia* system in the Chongqing plan represented an attempt to use history and culture as sources of legitimacy for modern urbanism. In contrast, in the post-war Greater Shanghai Plan, planners attempted to bypass previous socio-cultural constraints and articulate a purely functional urban form in the name of science and welfare. The first plan for greater Shanghai was made during the late 1920s aiming to strengthen nation building and foster urban growth and municipal pride, but its implementation was interrupted by the Sino-Japanese war (MacPherson, 1998; Wang, 1999; Wang, 2004, pp. 38–41). Right after the war ended in 1945, Zhao Zukang, head of the Shanghai Public Affairs Bureau, vigorously advocated making a new Greater Shanghai Plan (Wang, 2004, pp. 51–52). In October 1945, the municipal government convened local specialists to collaborate with the Public Affairs Bureau to plan for Shanghai. A municipal planning commission was established in March 1946, and the first draft of the new Greater Shanghai Plan was made in December of the same year (MacPherson, 1998, pp. 325–326). Planners, mostly Western-trained Chinese designers and engineers, experimented boldly with modern planning ideas including zoning, the self-contained satellite city and the neighbourhood unit. While the 1929 plan emphasized the Beaux-Arts concern for formal grandeur, the new plan stressed universalistic standards of functionality and efficiency. The plan divided the municipal area of Shanghai into a hierarchical stratification; on the lowest level of the division was a neighbourhood unit with 4,000 residents (Dong, 1999, pp. 209–212). Heavily influenced by Euro-American planning standards, the 1946 proposal was criticized for being too idealistic. Adjustments were made in the second and third drafts, produced in February 1948 and May 1949 respectively, to create a more feasible general plan (Wang, 2004, pp. 51–52).

The neighbourhood unit idea entered the Chinese social discourse in the late 1940s when the Sino-Japanese War left many destroyed cities in urgent need of large-scale housing development (Lin, 1948). It is worth noting that, while the concept was originally designed in its American context to strengthen social democracy and community bonds, such connotation was largely lost in Chinese planning discourse. Chinese urbanists and social reformers saw the neighbourhood unit schema mainly as a straightforward technical means to organize planned residential areas and distribute urban services effectively. In his article 'New urban neighbourhood planning' published in *Construction Review* (*Jianshe pinglun*), for example, Peng Yumo (1948) held that a well-planned neighbourhood could prevent the devaluation of real estate and the rise of slums in newly developed areas. Citing *Successful Subdivision*, published by the Federal Housing Administration of the US, Peng listed various ways to plan land use and street systems to achieve optimum benefits. In his discussion, imported planning norms and forms were considered transparent scientific criteria that were universally applicable, while variables of society, culture and geography were completely ignored.

A number of planners questioned the actual effects of the neighbourhood unit schema. In another article appearing in the same journal, Yi Zhi (1948) called for innovative approaches to collective housing design according to changing social conditions. With a tone of annoyance, he pointed out that modern Shanghai *lilong* housing exerted a bad moral influence upon the younger generation and a new housing form would help to breed a decent life style. Like Western reformists of the time, Yi preached that housing forms must serve to regulate modern society. Yet Yi held a critical view of the dominant Western planning ideas including the garden city and the neighbourhood unit. He argued that the two planning models put too much emphasis on the separation of different land uses, hence preventing the creation of an aesthetically and functionally harmonized urban environment.

Due to civil unrest and war, neither the Chongqing plan nor the Greater Shanghai Plan was realized. Yet through the proliferating discourses of the neighbourhood unit and other modern planning ideas, a new spatial conceptualization for society was gradually established: one in which planners claimed legitimacy in the name of the welfare of the population. Despite the fact that Republican urbanists consistently expressed frustration with social and economic constraints, their practices provided elements and techniques for later experimentation.

Early Socialist Experiments

The founding of the People's Republic in 1949 marked a major turning point in urban development. The Chinese Communist Party (CCP) vowed to create an egalitarian society based on a socialist economic system. Urban development was controlled by a series of national five-year plans (Yeh and Wu, 1999). Planners found themselves facing massive tasks: allocating functions to cities, deciding on developmental priorities, and controlling the rate of urban growth, to name just a few.

A new chapter for planning had begun, yet there were far more continuities with what had gone before than what one would envisage. In the field of residential planning, socialist experiments during the transition period (1949–1952) were heavily influenced by developments that had already taken place in the Republican era. As a massive construction programme was launched to ease housing shortages, the neighbourhood unit schema was adopted to plan large-scale residential development (Kwok, 1981). The planning of Caoyang New

Village in Shanghai is exemplary. Its chief designer, Wang Dingzeng, a graduate of the University of Illinois at Urbana-Champaign, learned the neighbourhood unit idea from a booklet published by the Shanghai Public Affairs Bureau in the mid-1940s.[7] In a 1947 *Construction Review* article, Wang proposed that housing scarcity (*fanghuang*) in post-war Shanghai could be solved by large-scale redevelopment projects (Wang, 1947). He suggested that the adoption of the neighbourhood unit schema could improve housing conditions and the welfare of urban residents. While Wang's proposal was never implemented in the Republican era, the

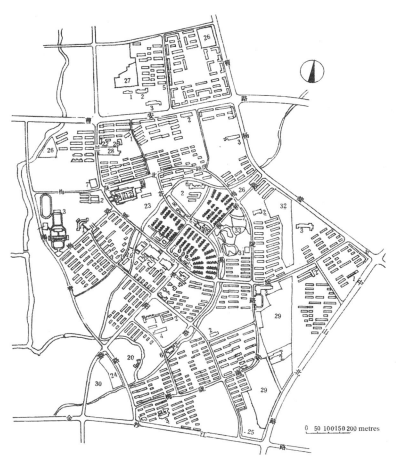

Figure 2.2. Caoyang New Village, designed by Wang Dingzeng *et al.*, Shanghai, 1951–1953.
Key: 1 Nursery; 2 Primary school; 3 Middle school; 4 School of Commerce; 5 Service station; 6 Shops; 7 Food market; 8 Comprehensive service station; 9 Shops; 10 Public bathhouse; 11 Restaurant; 12 Hospital; 13 Neighbourhood hospital; 14 Cultural centre; 15 Cinema theatre; 16 Police substation; 17 Neighbourhood office; 18 Housing management department; 19 Housing management office; 20 Park management office; 21 Parking area; 22 Fire department; 23 Nursery of young plants; 24–28 Factories; 29 Storage; 30 Reserve land; 31 Swimming pool; 32 Prefabrication plant; 33 Park

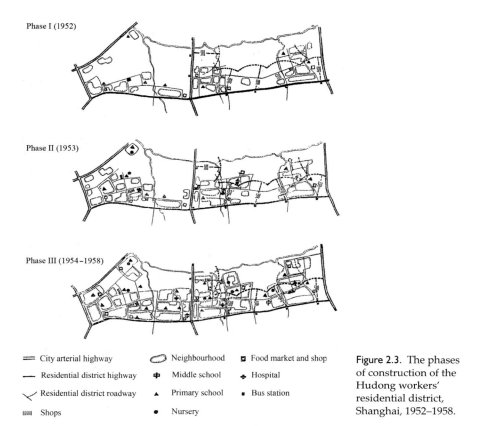

Phase I (1952)

Phase II (1953)

Phase III (1954–1958)

═ City arterial highway	◯ Neighbourhood	▣ Food market and shop
── Residential district highway	╬ Middle school	✚ Hospital
⤸ Residential district roadway	▲ Primary school	■ Bus station
⸺ Shops	● Nursery	

Figure 2.3. The phases of construction of the Hudong workers' residential district, Shanghai, 1952–1958.

socialist ways of distributing material, financial and human resources provided an optimum environment for the realization of his ideas.

Built between 1951 and 1953, Caoyang New Village occupied a total area of 94.63 hectares and provided an integrated residential area (figure 2.2) (D. Wang, 1956). While accommodating a larger population than a neighbourhood unit normally would allow, Wang admitted that the village plan followed the basic principles of the neighbourhood unit with some minor adjustments. The plan was divided into three hierarchical levels: neighbourhood, cluster, and village. Each cluster had its own nurseries, kindergartens and primary schools, which were located at independent blocks within easy walking distance (less than ten minutes). The village had community facilities such as co-op shops, post offices, cinema theatres, and cultural clubs at the centre, while commercial establishments at the periphery. Bounded by city thoroughfares, the village street system was laid out in a flexible pattern to accommodate the unevenness of the site. Shortly after the completion of Caoyang, four Hudong villages were constructed based on similar principles. Together they provided housing for 20,000 residents (figure 2.3). This scale of operation was unthinkable in the previous era: the acquisition

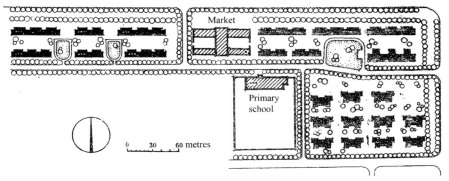

Figure 2.4. Fuxingmenwai neighbourhood unit, Beijing, Phase 1 (1951).

of large plots of land, the full provision of social services, and the coordination between adjacent projects were all unprecedented.

The neighbourhood unit idea was adopted in Beijing's master plans (Zhang, 2001, pp. 126–127), and several residential districts were built according to the schema (figure 2.4). Yet the triumph of the neighbourhood unit was only provisional. Very soon, Soviet influence began to permeate every aspect of Chinese urban reconstruction. During the 1950s, more than 10,000 Russian advisors were invited to assist various modernization programmes in China, and their opinions often outweighed local objections to key decisions (Spence, 1969, p. 282). In the sphere of residential design, Soviet advisors sought to transplant to China the superblock (*dajiefang*) schema (figure 2.5). This consisted of a grouping of four- to six-storey blocks of flats arranged around a quadrangle with public facilities in the centre. The schema stressed symmetrical axes and aesthetically coordinated street façades, which was more directly influenced by the Beaux-Arts concern for formal grandeur than by Marxist theory. During the Stalin era, Soviet planners set their superblock schema against its Western counterpart – the neighbourhood unit – by arguing that unlike the latter, which was isolated in the suburb, the superblock remained 'the organic component' of the city and was a most economical approach to urban construction (D. Wang, 1956, p. 2).

As links with the Euro-American world were cut off, theory and practice from the Soviet Union and Eastern European socialist countries were promoted in every way. A large volume of books and articles translated from Russian strongly influenced Chinese professionals. Half of the articles in the 1954 *Architectural Journal* (*Jianzhu xuebao*), the nation's most influential journal in the field, were about architecture and urban planning in Russia and Eastern Europe. As the superblock schema was established as the new 'orthodoxy', there was a major shift in the connotations of the neighbourhood unit, which was now considered bourgeois in nature and fell into disrepute. In his 1956 article on Caoyang New Village, Wang

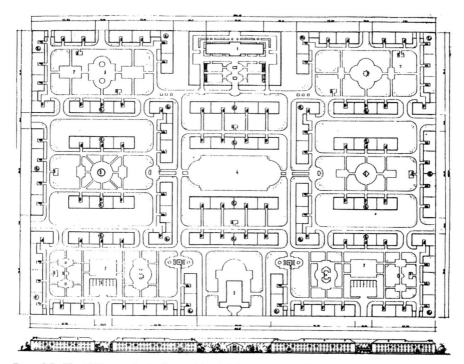

Figure 2.5. The 1955 award-winning residential design proposal based on the Soviet superblock schema.

provoked self-criticism for not including the latest Soviet techniques in planning but adopting the wasteful bourgeois neighbourhood unit idea (*Ibid.*, p. 2). During the early 1950s, quite a few residential districts and factory living quarters were designed according to the superblock schema. Famous examples of this included Baiwanzhuang Residential District in Beijing (figure 2.6) and the living quarter of the No. 1 Automobile Plant in Changchun (Li, 1956; *Huadong gongye jianzhu shejiyuan*, 1955).

Yet Chinese planners soon found that the superblock model was problematic in several aspects: the perimeter layout caused a large number of westward windows, street-facing units suffered from noise and pollution, and it was difficult to achieve cross-ventilation. In a 1956 article on residential planning, architect Wang Ye pointed out that it was unfair to make people live in westward-facing dwellings for no other reason than formalistic concern (Y. Wang, 1956). Meanwhile, the Soviet leader Joseph Stalin died on 5 March 1953; references to him gradually disappeared in various realms (Åman, 1992). Internally, since 1955 the Chinese Communist Party had increasingly put economic emphasis on industrial development. As the state conceptualized the nation as one of scarcity, economy and utility became new priorities in housing construction. The stern layout of the

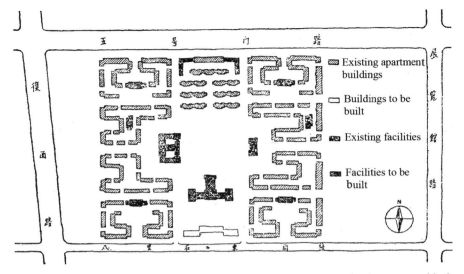

Figure 2.6. Baiwanzhuang Residential District planned according to the Soviet superblock schema, Beijing, 1956.

superblock was abandoned and more flexible plans were favoured (Lü, Rowe and Zhang, 2001, pp. 128–130).

Another major spatial experiment during this period, which is rarely mentioned but worthy of note, is the Soviet-style company town. A company town is defined as a settlement built and operated by a single business enterprise (Garner, 1992). A large number of company towns in capitalist society, such as mining camps and mill towns, appeared between 1830 and 1930. Dependent on resource sites, they were often situated in remote, isolated locations, where the companies had little alternative but to build housing for workers (Crawford, 1995; Allen, 1966). The earliest company towns were sites characterized by human suffering and environmental deterioration. From the late nineteenth century on, some industrialists attempted to make the company town a testing ground for utopian city planning. A model company town was one in which the paternalism of the owner extended beyond the basic requirements of factories and mines. Well-designed houses, parks, schools, libraries, and social halls, were all set within an attractive landscape, representing the developer's unusually high degree of interest in the well-being of workers (Crawford, 1995, pp. 137–40). The model company town required, however, high maintenance costs while producing low returns on investment. Therefore, in the US, the last construction boom in the model company town ended with the Great Depression.

The model company town idea was introduced to the Soviet Union through a number of inspection tours Russian industry representatives made in the

1920s (Castillo, 2003). Taylorism was introduced to Russian mills as a new model of socialist labour during the same period. Albert Kahn Associates, which was contracted for work in the USSR in 1929, played an important role in the development of Soviet factory design (Castillo, 2003; Bucci, 1993, pp. 90–96; Cody, 2003, pp. 100–108). During its operation in Moscow the firm designed more than 500 factories, including many key projects in the Soviet First Five-Year Plan such as steelworks at Magnitogorsk and aeronautic facilities at Kramotorsk (Castillo, 2003). Kahn office staff also coached thousands of Soviet apprentices on factory planning. Yet the Kahn practice largely focused on the production section of industrial works; the planning of the service sector lay on the shoulders of Russian designers. A remarkable consensus existed among professionals at the time, that is, ideally, industry and residence should be physically separated by green belts, yet located in sufficient proximity to each other to minimize the journey to work (French and Hamilton, 1979). These objectives were codified by Russian planner Nikolai A. Miliutin into the 'linear city' concept in the late 1920s (Bater, 1980, p. 24; Miliutin, 1974). The schema comprised parallel strips of residences and factories separated by an amenity greenbelt, with parks and water bodies to windward and industrial zones to leeward of housing. Although the schema was altered in actual application, its basic principles remained accepted in the planning of many Soviet company towns. Ivanovo-Voznesensk, one of the Soviet's pioneering company towns, for instance, consisted of working and living quarters segregated by greenbelts (Castillo, 2003, pp. 140–141).

With the First Five-Year Plan (1953–1957) launched in China, more than one hundred key industrial projects were designed directly by Russian experts, and many others were built based on standard Soviet blueprints. Among others, the Soviet-style company town was introduced. Following the model, living quarters (*shenghuoqu*) and workshops were planned simultaneously for projects located in rural and suburban areas. The master plan for the No. 1 Automobile Plant in Changchun, for instance, included both working and living quarters (Wang, 1955). The design of the living quarters was based on the then dominant superblock model. After the superblock layout was abandoned, the planning of factory living quarters followed the basic principles of the neighbourhood unit schema. The 1956 standardized schema for a state farm, for example, offered offices, housing, the primary school and other facilities, based on the statistic projection of the population served (*Nongyebu changbu guihuazu*, 1956). Yet these were no longer designed according to the superblock paradigm but arranged in a rather more flexible layout (figure 2.7).

The integral pattern of the Soviet-style company town sometimes extended to the design of institutions located in urban areas, but in much more compact formulas. In a 1956 *Architectural Journal* article on hospital design, Zhao Dongri

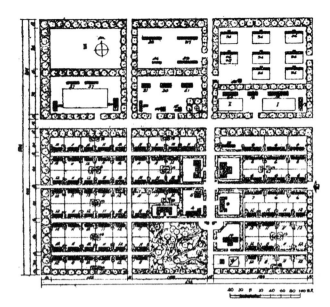

Figure 2.7. The standard
site plan for the state
cotton farm, 1956.

introduced the four hospitals constructed in Beijing during the early and mid 1950s
(Zhao, 1956). In all these cases except Tongren Hospital, employees' canteens,
dormitories, and apartments were developed in conjunction with hospital facilities
(figure 2.8). In contrast to the Soviet company town paradigm, however, there was
no attempt to separate the hospital and the living quarters. Instead, the various
facilities were economically integrated to form a functionally organized whole.
There was little theoretical discussion available on this type of urban form, but
subsequent developments demonstrated that this under-analysed form gradually
became the dominant form to organize Chinese cities. I shall come back to this in
the next section.

The Microdistrict: From Plan to Market

The Chinese planners' experimentation with the superblock was short lived,
and was soon suspended due to both international and internal changes. After
an interim period, some basic principles of the neighbourhood unit concept
reappeared, but in a new guise. First used in the 1935 Moscow Plan, the
'microdistrict' (*mikrorayon*) was defined as a self-contained residential district with
an area of 75–125 acres and a population ranging between 5,000 and 15,000 (Sawers,
1978; Bater, 1980, pp. 109–111). Four to five microdistricts, each with a service
radius of 300–400 metres, made a residential complex. Although the microdistrict
schema articulated a more sophisticated hierarchy and allowed a larger scale,

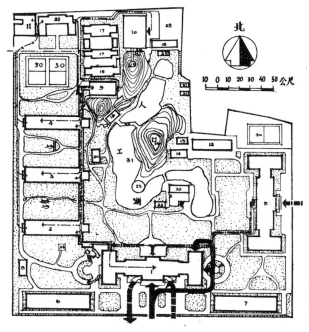

Figure 2.8. Site plan for Jishuitan Hospital, Beijing, 1956.

Key: 1 Outpatient section; 2–4 Inpatient section; 5 Classrooms; 6 Dormitory for doctors; 7 Dormitory for students and staff; 8 Transformer substation; 9 Nutrition section; 10 Boiler room; 11 Mortuary and garage; 12 Student canteen; 13 Kitchen for Hui people; 14 Canteen for Hui people; 15 Staff canteen; 16 Chimney; 17 Dormitory; 18 Dormitory for attendants; 19 Trade union office; 20 Lounge and reading room; 21 Laundry and general affairs section; 22 Nursery; 23 Outdoor dance floor; 24 Crematorium; 25. Hanxu pavilion; 26. Kiosk; 27. Greenhouse; 28 Coal store; 29 Flower rack; 30 Playing field; 31 Artificial lake; 32 Bridge

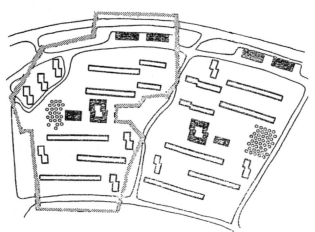

Figure 2.9. Planning proposal for a microdistrict consisting of two residential groups, Moscow, 1963.

its basic principles of spatial organization (i.e., the integration of housing and facilities, optimum service distances and the hierarchical spatial structure) were essentially similar to those of the neighbourhood unit (figure 2.9). During the Stalin era, the use of the microdistrict was supplanted by the superblock schema. After Stalin's death, as the new Party leader Nikita Khrushchev was determined to set the Soviet Union on a modified path, the microdistrict idea re-emerged and received wide acceptance almost immediately.

The microdistrict concept was introduced to China in a 1956 article translated from Russian (Tewei'ersikeyi, 1956). It was soon employed as the basic unit for residential planning in the 1957 preliminary master plan proposal for Beijing (Sit, 1995, pp. 96–97). Yet the concept did not receive any systematic treatment until the following year. The first issue of the 1958 *Architectural Journal* featured four articles related to the microdistrict. A detailed introduction of the concept was offered in the article titled 'Planning and construction of an urban residential district' by Luben Taneff (1958), a Bulgarian professor and architect. Luben explained the rationale and application of the microdistrict as a socialist planning device. He argued that well-organized, self-contained microdistricts could strengthen local-level political participation. Examples from Sofia and other Bulgarian cities were cited to illustrate the microdistrict planning principles. The other three articles were case studies of residential planning in Shanghai and Beijing, in which the term 'microdistrict' received frequent usage without further explanation of the sudden shift in planning discourse (Xu and Fang, 1958; Fu, et al., 1958; Zhao, *et al.,* 1958). In the concluding section of the article on Hudong development in Shanghai by Xu Qingqiu and Fang Renqiu (1958, p. 9), a brief discussion of the neighbourhood unit and the Soviet microdistrict was provided. The authors divided the Soviet model into the superblock type and the neighbourhood group type. The authors acknowledged that the planning principles of the latter, the scheme adopted in their design, were similar to those of the neighbourhood unit. The discussion indicated that the adoption of the microdistrict did not involve essential changes in basic residential planning principles. The transition from the neighbourhood unit to the microdistrict, therefore, was largely a strategic manoeuvre to revive the old practices under a new name.

The microdistrict received frequent discursive usage in the rural planning practices during the people's commune movement launched in August 1958. Concurrent with sweeping institutional changes, designers boldly experimented with commune planning between 1958 and 1960 (chapter 5). Planners believed that peasants could be rehabilitated fundamentally by revolutionizing rural settlements. They proposed a complete reorganization of scattered, small villages into concentrated, large residential clusters (*jumin dian*) according to modern urban and regional planning principles (Pei, Liu and Shen, 1958; Wang and Cheng, 1959; Wu, 1959). The microdistrict planning principles were adapted to plan the commune as a combination of economic activities, civic administration and residence (figure 2.10).

Although the experimentation with rural planning was soon stifled, the microdistrict gradually became a well-established fixture through the discussion of commune plans. The notion was systematically explicated in 1962. Wang Shuoke (1962) summarized Shanghai's residential planning experiences in his article and proposed a three-tier system consisting of the basic living unit, the

Figure 2.10. Site plan for Zaojiatun Residential Cluster, Hongqing People's Commune, Changping, Beijing, 1958.
Key: 1 Commercial facilities; 2 Printing house; 3 Shoe plant; 4 Clothing plant; 5 Storage; 6 Bus station; 7 Hospital; 8 Office; 9 Middle school; 10 Garden of Happiness; 11 Cultural palace; 12 Theatre; 13 Children's palace; 14 Hongzhuan University; 15 Children's facilities; 16 Canteen and boiler room; 17 Club; 18 Primary school

neighbourhood and the residential microdistrict (figure 2.11). A later article by Wang Dingzeng and Xu Rongchun (1962) divided the residential system into four levels: the residential group, the neighbourhood cluster, the microdistrict, and the satellite town or larger residential district (figure 2.12). Each level correspond to a respective organization in the urban administrative system and was provided with proper commercial and community facilities (*Ibid.*, pp. 6–7). This new classification laid the basis for later discussion of the microdistrict.

Establishing a new foundation for the microdistrict in Chinese planning discourse necessarily involved an articulation of its relationship with the neighbourhood unit idea. In an article published in November 1962, Shui Yayou

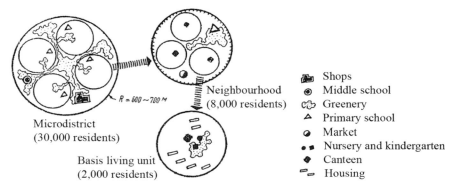

Figure 2.11. The three-tier residential system, Shanghai, 1959–1960.

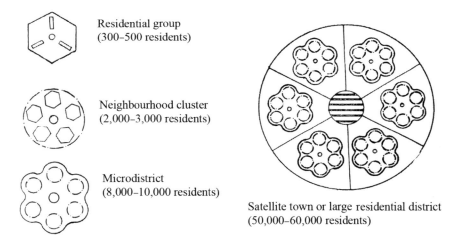

Figure 2.12. Residential system by Wang Dingzeng and Xu Rongchun, 1962.

provided a comparison between the two concepts (Shui, 1962). The analysis was primarily focused on differences in their respective objectives. The microdistrict aimed to organize residents' lives efficiently, distribute facilities economically, and create an aesthetic living space. The neighbourhood unit, in contrast, disguised class conflicts in capitalist society by creating a social and geographical unity. Despite his initial attempt to sustain a tension between the two concepts, Shui suggested in the subsequent discussion that the two were equivalent in terms of their nature, spatial structure and organizational rationales. Notably, Czechoslovakia, the Soviet Union, Poland, the German Democratic Republic, Britain, France and Sweden were juxtaposed in the same table to compare the standards adopted for the scale of residential units in these countries (Shui, 1962, p. 22). In this way, the microdistrict and the neighbourhood unit were reunited,

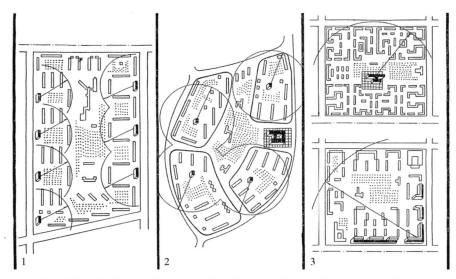

Figure 2.13. The distribution of commercial and social facilities within the microdistrict, 1963. *Key*: 1 Scattered; 2 Mixed; 3 Centralized

and a swirl of social, historical and natural variables were synthesized into a universal urbanism.

The microdistrict has since been established as a planning norm in China. A few design principles for residential districts were firmly established (Wang and Xu, 1962). First, housing and facilities should be integrated. Second, through traffic should be discouraged. Third, residential grouping should be determined by the 'service radii', the optimum distances between housing and services (figure 2.13). Fourth, the levels of hierarchy and the optimum numbers of community facilities should be based on the number of residents they served. Planners envisioned that all urban residential districts could be designed and constructed based on the microdistrict schema. Some microdistricts were built in major cities between the 1950s and 1970s (Min, 1993; *'Juzhuqu xiangxi guihua' keti yanjiu zu*, 1985) (figures 2.14, 2.15, 2.16, 2.17, 2.18). Yet when planners attempted to expand the implementation of the schema to a larger scope, they encountered tremendous difficulties (chapter 4). Piece-meal development of the compact variant of the company town model prevailed under Mao. A characteristic work-unit based urbanism which integrated production and residence was widely adopted throughout China (Chapter 3, Committee of Concerned Asian Scholars, 1972).

The shift from planned to market economy since 1978 has created new opportunities for the implementation of the microdistrict schema (Yeh and Wu, 1999). With a series of reforms targeting housing commodification, the task of residential development was gradually transferred from the government to

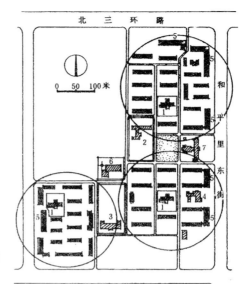

Figure 2.14. Site plan of the 7th district of Hepingli, Beijing, constructed in 1959–1961.

Key: 1 Nursery and kindergarten; 2 Primary school; 3 Middle school; 4 Canteen; 5 Shops (on the ground floor of apartment buildings); 6 Boiler room; 7 Office building

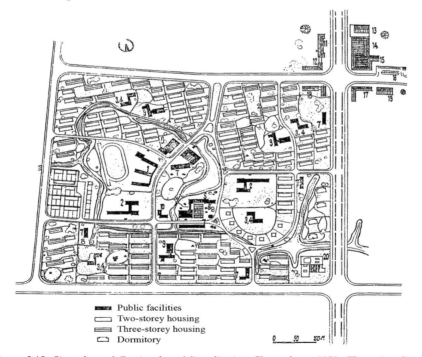

Figure 2.15. Site plan of Puqianzhen Microdistrict, Changzhou, 1959. The microdistrict was laid out on 40 hectares of land, with a total floor space of 106,905 square metres and a population of 10,452 (according to the short-term plan).
Key: 1 Middle school; 2 Primary school; 3 Nursery; 4 Kindergarten; 5 Cultural centre; 6 Office building; 7 Shops; 8 Food market; 9 Canteen; 10 Clinic and toilets; 11 Office building; 12 Post Office and bank; 13 Cinema theatre; 14 Club; 15 Stores; 16 Parking area; 17 Shops; 18 Services; 19 Book store; 20 Exhibition hall

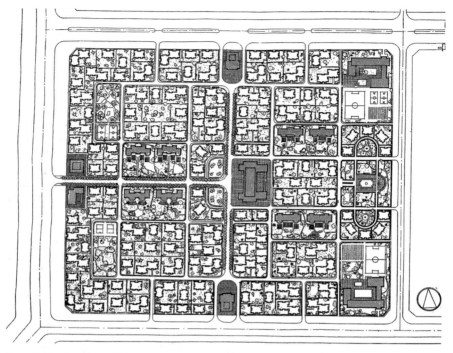

Figure 2.16. Site plan of Beiyangcun Experimental Microdistrict, Beijing, 1963. The microdistrict was planned for a population of 12,000, with 193,400 square metres of residential floor space and 37,800 square metres of service floor space.

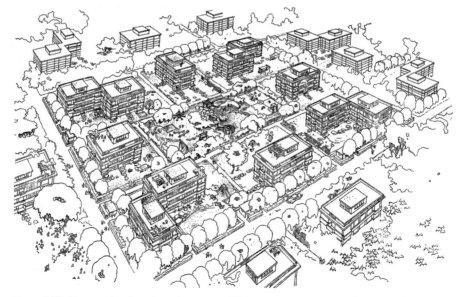

Figure 2.17. Perspective drawing of a corner of Beiyangcun Experimental Microdistrict.

Table 2.1. Urban residential district hierarchy.

Level of residential grouping		Cluster	Microdistrict	Residential District
Number of households		300–1,000	3,000–5,000	10,000–16,000
Number of residents		1,000–3,000	10,000–15,000	30,000–50,000
Land use	Residential	70–80	55–65	50–60
composition	Public facilities	6–12	12–22	15–25
(percentage	Transport	7–15	9–17	10–18
of total)	Parks and open spaces	3–6	5–15	7.5–18

Source: Zhonghua renmin gongheguo jianshebu, 2002.

private developers (Chen, 1993; Wang, 1995; Wu, 1996). Meanwhile, the central and local planning departments created an arsenal of codes in line with the inherited microdistrict schema to ensure an adequate provision of social facilities in commercial residential developments (table 2.1). Thanks to the unprecedented rate of construction and the planning department's increased power to regulate construction through planning codes, the design principles of the microdistrict schema were for the first time widely implemented. Most commercial residential tracts were planned in conjunction with nurseries, parks, stores and recreational facilities (figures 2.18 and 2.19).

Driven by commercial interests and new consumption needs, a number of features were introduced by developers. First, the community clubhouse (huiguan), comprising various recreational and dining facilities, was gradually established as a normative component in new residential developments and well received by consumers (figure 2.20). Second, many services are now undertaken

Figure 2.18. Site plan of Rover Palace (Luofushigong) Microdistrict designed by GZ Architects, Chengdu, 2000–2002. The microdistrict consists of 18 high-rise buildings, with a total floor space of 308,920 square metres and 1,499 apartment units.

Figure 2.19. A corner of Rover Palace Microdistrict (photo taken in 2003).

Figure 2.20. The community club of Boyaxiyuan, a middle-class residential district with 1,187 appartment units in Beijing, designed by Lu Duanmin *et al.*, and completed in 2004 (photo taken in 2005).

by professional property management companies, which collect service fees from residents. Third, despite the fact that most urban housing in China (including all work-unit owned housing) is enclosed within walled compounds, new commercial housing developments are equipped with more elaborate round-the-clock security systems than older residential areas. The wide implementation of the microdistrict schema, therefore, does not lead to a more open and even urban service system. Instead, enclosed commercial residential tracts reproduced the exclusive feature of the Chinese work units and the 'gated communities' found in other parts of the world (Wu, 2005; Huang, 2005; Blakely and Snyder, 1999; Caldeira, 2000).

Economic reforms led to the decline of the work unit system and the increased mobility of the population, which created new challenges for urban governance (Wu, 2002b; Howell, 2004; Bray, 2005, chapter 7). An official discourse on 'community building' arose in the mid-1990s in response to the changed urban conditions. Under the new initiative, the 'community' is conceptualized as a form of grassroots organization with a defined territory (Bray, 2005, p. 182). As there are more and more urban residents who move from urban-block-type and work-unit-type to microdistrict-type communities, the microdistrict has emerged as the dominant basic unit of urban governance (Ibid.). Each microdistrict has a Residents' Committee (jumin weiyuanhui), which operates as a mass organization under the Street Office (jiedao banshichu), the sub-district urban government. The main function of the Residents' Committee is to organize a corps of volunteers to perform daily maintenance and security work for the community; each apartment building has a volunteer 'building leader', and each building in turn has 'floor leaders' or 'section leaders'. The volunteers help to collect maintenance fees, organize group leisure activities, disseminate official and community notifications and so on.[8] Together these volunteers form a seamless network to link residents in individual microdistricts to the local government.

Concluding Remarks

This chapter has traced the diachronic changes that the neighbourhood unit schema and its variants underwent in China. It shows that some seemingly long-established Chinese norms for residential planning are results of transnational appropriations and successive discursive conversions. In particular, the chapter shows that the development of Chinese residential planning was informed by events, sources and inspirations from various parts of the world. It reveals the history of modern planning as a narration of intertwined global and local experiences.

By emphasizing crossover practices, I do not mean to suggest that such processes exist outside the hegemony of nationality. Instead, the study shows that it is necessary to grasp the implications of travelling planning ideas against the backdrop of Chinese nation building practices since the Republican era. The chapter reveals that the interpretations and revisions of the neighbourhood unit schema are often conjunctural and cannot be deducted purely from theoretical principles. Various disruptions – the wars, the socialist revolution and the reforms – were continuously brought into the itinerary of the concept. The neighbourhood unit idea hence travelled with 'inevitable displacements, revisions, and challenges' within the specific historical context of Chinese modernity (Clifford, 1989, p.

179). The neighbourhood unit schema, in the end, is far more than another sign of globalized repetition; instead, it has been constantly tamed into different programmes of modernization in new times and places.

Notes

1. An edited version of this chapter will appear in *Planning Perspectives*, Volume 24, no. 4.
2. The journal *Inscriptions* published a special issue on 'Traveling theories and traveling theorists' in 1989. For attempts to extend Said's formulation, see, for example, Clifford, 1989, 1997; Liu, 1995.
3. Following Michel Foucault (1972), the word 'discourse' here refers to a system of representation that has developed socially and has been naturalized over time. In the approach of critical discourse analysis, language is considered connecting with 'the social through being the primary domain of ideology, and through being both a site of, and a stake in, struggles for power' (Fairclough, 1989, p. 15). This approach has been widely used to unmask obscured structures of power, political control and dominance in the study of texts.
4. Located on Long Island, Forest Hills Gardens was an estate planned by Frederick Law Olmsted Jr, and developed by the Sage Foundation Homes Company. Its design featured clear boundaries on two sides, a differentiated local street system, the public school at a central location and variations in house size and cost, among others. It was built on 175 acres of open land and had a population of nearly 4,000 by 1923. Perry was one of the earliest residents when the first homes were occupied in 1912. He played an active role in the development of various community facilities. See Birtles, 1994, pp. 17–19.
5. Donald L. Johnson (2002) maintains that the idea of the neighbourhood unit was formulated by the Chicago-based architect William E. Drummond during 1913–1922.
6. Although Japan imported many Western planning ideas at the time, there were few opportunities to apply them in Japanese cities due to the land ownership system and weak planning powers. Japanese colonies offered new laboratories for the realization of modern urban plans. See Hein, 2003; Tucher, 1999, chapter 3.
7. Interview with Wang Dingzeng by author, 30 October 2004.
8. Interview with a Beijing resident by author, 2 February 2005.

Chapter Three

Work Unit Urbanism

It's like being in a womb. You can't escape.

Fox Butterfield, the *New York Times* journalist, ended his article entitled 'Getting a hotel room in China: you're nothing without a unit' with the above quote regarding the Chinese work unit (Butterfield, 1979). In this article, Butterfield recounts his frustrating experience of trying to get a room at the Beijing Hotel. 'What is your work unit?' the clerk repeatedly asked the baffled Butterfield. The latter soon realized the crucial role the work unit played in contemporary Chinese society: 'Every Chinese has a unit. It provides him with the necessities of life – housing and ration cards – gets his children into school and offers welfare in his old age' (*Ibid.*). Urban China was organized for work units, not individuals; being an individual '[w]ithout a unit, you are lost' (*Ibid.*). In the end, Butterfield's hotel room dilemma was solved only when the Chinese Ministry of Foreign Affairs agreed to allow him to use the Ministry as his temporary unit.

This story is a vivid illustration of an outsider's first shocking exposure to the peculiar Chinese urbanism centred on the work unit when China first relaxed its control upon foreign visitors in the late 1970s. After the founding of the People's Republic in 1949, most factories, schools and government offices were organized into a state production unit administrative system; the work unit was the basic unit of this system (Schurmann, 1968; Lü and Perry, 1997*b*). Since then, the work unit has functioned not only as workplace but also the principal social institution in which the lives of most urban residents are organized. By 1978, around 95 per cent of urban workers belonged to a work unit of one kind or another (*Guojia tongjiju shehui tongjisi*, 1994).

The fundamental importance of the work unit in Chinese society lies in its unique combination of economic, political and social functions (Parish and Parish,

1986, p. 25). The work unit offers its employees lifetime employment and attendant welfare such as public housing and medical care.[1] Each work unit has its own Communist Party branch in charge of transmitting party policy, implementing social campaigns, providing political education, awarding moral merit and making notes on employees' performance in personnel dossiers (dang'an). The work unit runs a variety of social services including shops, canteens, clinics, nurseries and libraries. It administrates many facets of everyday life: orchestrating group leisure activities, organizing local sanitation and mediating civic disputes, to name just a few (Lü and Perry, 1997b; Dutton, 1998). The work unit is a territorial unit that possesses a distinctive spatial form (Bjorklund, 1986; Chai, 1996). A typical work unit integrates workplace, residence and social facilities in close proximity within one or several walled compound(s). Residents may conduct most daily affairs without leaving their unit. The characteristic form of the work unit had a profound effect on urbanism under Mao. Economic reforms since 1978 have brought enormous change to the work unit, especially with the acceleration in urban restructuring since 1992 (Ma and Wu, 2005b, pp. 4–8). Despite the changes, the influence of the work unit still persists in many aspects (Bray, 2005, chapter 7).

As the basic building block of urban China, the work unit has been studied by scholars in disciplines ranging from sociology to political science. Important monographs include Andrew Walder's analysis of 'organized dependence' that flourished in the work unit (1986), David Bray's study of work-unit-based urban governance (2005), Yang Xiaoming and Zhou Yuhu's Zhongguo danwei zhidu on the institutional features of the Chinese work unit system (1999), Gail Henderson and Myron Cohen's account of daily life in a Chinese hospital (1984), and Marc Blecher and Gordon White's investigation into power and politics within the work unit during and after the Cultural Revolution (1979), among others. A volume examining the work unit as a social institution from historical and comparative perspectives was put together by Xiaopo Lü and Elizabeth Perry (1997a). The number of journal articles is also growing rapidly (e.g., Yang, 1989; Dittmer and Lü, 1996; Lu, 1989; Yi, 1991; and Li et al., 1996).

Apart from a handful of studies (Bjorklund, 1986; Rofel, 1992; Gaubatz, 1995; Chai, 1996; Bray, 2005), most existing literature focuses on socio-political aspects of the work unit. Although the characteristic spatiality of the danwei has profound effects on contemporary Chinese society, disciplinary limitations have made many social researchers reluctant to include the spatial dimension in their interpretations of Chinese society. This chapter provides an examination of the work unit as an urban form and its spatial implications for the Chinese city. Following an introduction to the position of the work unit within the Maoist urban system to establish the context, it moves to a study of the physical form of the work unit, followed by a discussion of its socio-spatial effects and the resulting urbanism.

The chapter closes with a discussion of change and continuity in the work unit during the reform era.

The City under Mao: A Brief Introduction

The Maoist city featured a geography made up in large part of a jigsaw puzzle of spatially demarcated work units surrounding the old city core. During the Republican period (1911–1949), despite urban reforms in a number of cities, traditional dense and compact urban patterns persisted in most parts of China. After 1949, new construction was concentrated in the areas outside the inner city, where urban growth was accomplished mainly through the accretion of work units (Committee of Asian Concerned Scholars, 1972; Gaubatz, 1996). This development pattern had resulted in an urban structure with a series of concentric zones of land use (Pannell, 1977, 1990; Ma, 1981; Wu, 1993). The old city core continued to accommodate commercial establishments and residential neighbourhoods inherited from the pre-revolutionary era. Municipal administration offices were often housed in this area. In some major cities, following the Soviet model, part of the central district was redeveloped into a monumental centre with ceremonial squares, which served as the stage for public spectacles during major holidays. Surrounding the core areas was a belt of relatively new urban development, where work units including institutions, universities and clean factories were arranged in a less intensive way compared with the old city centre. As in traditional China, the city's administrative territory incorporated large adjacent areas, including an agricultural belt as producer of provisions for the city (Pannell, 1977). Hence outside the urban area was a belt of suburban districts, where industrial enterprises, satellite communities and villages existed in juxtaposition with agricultural land. Beyond this area lay a number of counties, each of which had its own administrative centre.

As individual work units integrated many essential urban functions within their own territories, the functional roles of business districts were greatly reduced. The newly built areas of the Maoist city consisted of similar functionally mixed districts, rather than interdependent differentiated districts such as 'central business districts' (CBDs), 'industrial districts' and 'residential suburbs'. Meanwhile, as work units were not required to pay for the land they occupied and low-rise buildings were cheaper to build, low-density development became the dominant choice (Gaubatz, 1995). Many Chinese cities expanded well beyond the earlier limits of built-up areas and became vast metropolitan regions yet without a high-density CBD as normally found in capitalist cities.

The city under Mao was structured through a dual administrative system consisting of the urban neighbourhood and work unit system (Parish and Parish,

1986, chapter 2). The urban area was divided into urban districts (*qu*) on a territorial basis, under which were Street Offices (*jiedao banshichu*) encompassing 2,000–10,000 households. The Street Office, the sub-district government, was the lowest level of formal urban government administration, which consisted of dozens of Residents' Committees (*jumin weiyuanhui*), each encompassing up to 800 households. Similar to the work unit, the Residents' Committee was multifunctional: it transmitted state policy to the local level, managed social services and administered many facets of everyday life (Whyte and Parish, 1984). The Residents' Committee was sometimes further divided into smaller residents' groups with dozens of households (Pannell and Ma, 1983, pp. 84–86).

The relationship between the work unit and neighbourhood system was supplementary and overlapping. The work unit supervised those who were formally employed, while the neighbourhood system mainly served to integrate those who were not employed (for example, housewives, students and the retired) and those employed in small neighbourhood workshops and services (Chan, 1993). Those employed by the work unit while living outside the unit might turn to their work unit for some needs, and to their Residents' Committees for others. The neighbourhood system extended into the work unit compound. A larger work unit's residential district might be divided into several Residents' Committees. When someone retired from the work unit, he or she fell under the supervision of the Residents' Committee. As the majority of urban residents belonged to work units, the role of Residents' Committees was comparatively weak (Bray, 2005, p. 183).

The work units were classified according to their status in the national administrative hierarchy. 'Central units' (*zhongyang danwei*) received the initial investment from the central government, 'local units' (*difang danwei*) were work units established by the local government, while below both of these were basic units (*jiceng danwei*) (Lü and Perry, 1997a, pp. 7–8). In principle, each work unit was subject to dual subordination: it was placed under the jurisdiction of both the local government and its appropriate occupational bureaucracy (e.g., a factory under the Ministry of Industry, a university under the Ministry of Education and a hospital under the Ministry of Health). Yet within the centrally-planned socialist system, the vertical rule through ministries was dominant (Cartier, 2005, p. 26). National plans and state policies were implemented through individual work units without too much interference from the municipality (Shue, 1994). Because of a lack of a society-wide welfare system, the city relied heavily on individual work units to provide welfare for urban residents (Dixon, 1981). Hence the city under Mao was a relatively weak entity characterized by the dominance of work units (Cartier, 2005).

The Work Unit as an Urban Form[2]

The site planning of a new work unit was carried out by professionals, but the subsequent development was often planned by the work unit's own Department of Basic Construction. Beginning with essential production structures and dormitories for single workers, the work unit grew naturally, expanding as the enterprise matured (table 3.1). During the early years, a few basic living facilities were built: apartment buildings, canteens, boiler rooms, public bathhouses and nurseries.[3] Depending on the availability of construction funds and land, the work unit gradually built more apartments and other supporting structures such as social halls, guesthouses and primary schools.[4] Rather than being built in a separate area, housing and facilities often occupied space adjacent to the workplace.

Table 3.1. Construction completion at the General Institute of Iron and Steel Research, Beijing, 1950–1999.

Construction time period	Floor space (in square metres)			% of total floor space
	Total	Working quarter	Living quarter	
1950–1959	67,028	49,261	17,767	21.4
1960–1969	51,275	27,120	24,155	16.4
1970–1979	19,041	7,741	11,300	6.1
1980–1989	85,874	21,846	64,027	27.5
1990-1999	89,470	25,562	63,908	28.6
Total	312,687	131,530	181,157	100

Source: The Basic Construction and Planning Department, the General Institute of Iron and Steel Research, Beijing.

There is wide variation in spatial layout, resources and size of individual work units. Units in Shanghai, for instance, are more likely to have their employees living in separate residential areas than those in Beijing. Work units in far suburban and rural areas are generally well equipped, while units near downtown areas and in small towns are less so. Depending on their rank in the bureaucratic system, the resources available to the work units vary considerably. Central units generally fare better than local units, and those in privileged fields, such as universities and major factories, are likely to receive more funding and land for construction than others. Work units also differ greatly from one another in area and population size, from those with a few hundred square metres and dozens of members, to those with thousands of square metres and hundreds or thousands of residents.

Despite the seemingly haphazard construction of individual units, some spatial characteristics are widely shared (except very small work units), be they administrative units, educational institutes or industrial works. The common physical features can be summarized as: (1) a walled and gated enclosure; (2) a well-integrated internal circulation system; (3) close association of work and residence; (4) a high level of provision of social facilities; and (5) rationalist architectural layout and style. As mentioned earlier, economic restructuring since 1978 has brought fundamental changes to the work unit; some of the above features are no longer universal. In this and the next section, however, I treat the work unit as an archetype, leaving discussion of changes in the reform era until the last section.

Every work unit is a walled enclosure, or, if large enough, a cluster of several walled enclosures. The wall, in most cases made of brick, sets the work unit physically apart from its surroundings. There are usually several entrances through the wall from city boulevards. The main entrances are staffed by security personnel and fortified with heavy wrought-iron gates (figure 3.1). A small janitor's room is set on one side of the main gate, which provides working and living space for the gatekeeper, on duty around the clock. There is sometimes a mailroom beside the janitor's room; unit residents come to collect mail on a daily basis.

The level of security at entrances varies from unit to unit. Some institutions, such as major administrative offices and military-related units, may subject all persons to identification procedures. Others are relatively easy to enter; only those obviously not belonging to the work unit would be stopped for an identity check by the gatekeeper. The gate is closed at midnight and opened in the early morning. Once closed, coming and going for both residents and outsiders becomes difficult. Passage can only be obtained by waking the understandably displeased gatekeeper, who would only open the door for unit members he (rarely she) recognized. The working and living quarters are usually circled by separate walls. The gates between them may remain closed during work hours to prevent

Figure 3.1. Gate with the janitor's room on one side, Beijing (photo taken in 2005).

employees from slipping back home.

From the entrance there are roadways that form the means of circulation for pedestrians and vehicles. Far from being part of a larger urban highway system, the roadways of the work unit form a system of their own. Bounded by long boulevards for the rapid movement of city traffic, the work unit's internal circulation system is broken into short streets which give easy circulation within the unit but do not allow outside vehicles to run uninterruptedly through the unit compound. Rather than following the regular gridiron street system, the streets are laid out in a flexible pattern to fit the geography and particular needs of the unit (figure 3.2). Most streets remain straight to facilitate the movement of modern modes of transport. Yet without stop signs or traffic lights, the motorist must proceed cautiously, watching for vehicles, pedestrians and bicycles. Street widths vary to fit different traffic loads based on types of use: main streets are usually 7 to 9 metres wide, secondary streets 4 to 6 metres, and the roads leading to individual apartment buildings are 1.5 to 2 metres. Main streets are well-paved and flanked with sidewalks, gutters and drains, streetlights, curbs, trees and other planting. Streets are under close maintenance through regular tending of gardens, street sweeping and rubbish removal (Bjorklund, 1986).

The work unit provides public housing for its employees and their families. Usually, the living quarters (*shenghuo qu*) are close to the workplace. The only exceptions are factories that pollute the environment and work units located in highly-developed urban areas where land is scarce and housing space is limited. In these cases, employees may live in separate housing areas, or spill over into downtown neighbourhoods or residential tracts managed by the municipal government. Small work units may have workplace and residence within a compact area (figure 3.2), while larger ones tend to separate them into distinct areas with walls or roadways (figure 3.3).

Both the working and living quarters of the work unit are provided with a modern infrastructure, including electricity, running water and a sewage system. This is connected to that of the city, forming an integrated urban infrastructure system. In the case of work units in rural areas, the infrastructure is constructed from scratch at a new site and thus often forms a system of its own rather than joining with neighbouring villages. Local residents wishing to take advantage of the facilities are not allowed to do so, sometimes resulting in violent conflicts between peasants and the work unit.

The work unit provides various community facilities. Small work units have canteens, social halls, clinics and public bathhouses. Medium-sized units may add nurseries, kindergartens, parks, libraries, sports fields, guesthouses and shops (figure 3.4). Large work units, especially universities and work units in remote suburban or rural areas, have such elaborate social service systems that they

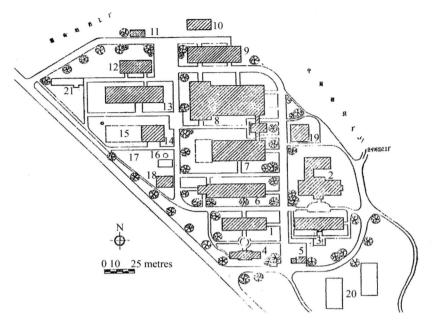

Figure 3.2. Site plan of a small chemical plant, Hunan, 1958.
Key: 1 Office building; 2 Canteen; 3 Dormitory; 4–15 Workshops; 16 Backwater tower; 17 Coal storage; 18 Repair shop; 19 Wooden-trunk room

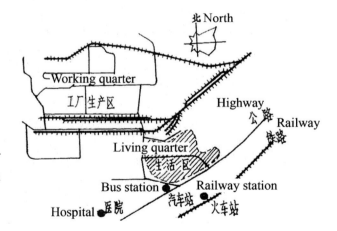

Figure 3.3. Master plan of Meishan Ironworks, Nanjing, built 1969–1971. The living quarter was located on the windward side and separated from the working quarter (translation added).

resemble a miniature city (figures 3.5). In addition to the facilities listed above, they have food markets, hospitals, post offices, banks, movie theatres, workers' clubs, barbershops and primary and high schools. While facilities in small work units are scattered in buildings throughout the unit compound, large units may have a district set aside for social services, which forms an area similar to a city's downtown (figure 3.6). Children's playgrounds, parking for bicycles, sports

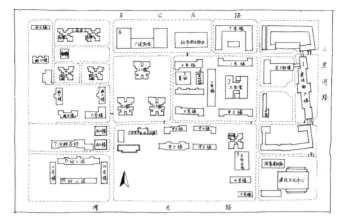

Figure 3.4. Map of the Ministry of Construction, Beijing (drawn by Gai Shijie in 2000).
Key: 1 Main building; 2 Canteen; 3 Food market; 4 Community centre; 5 Parking structure; 6 Kindergarten; 7 Xiangqun School; 8 Guangjian Hotel. The rest of the buildings are either office buildings or apartment buildings

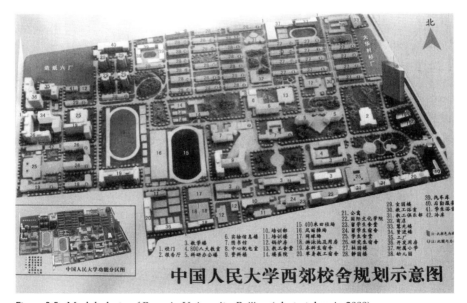

Figure 3.5. Model photo of Renmin University, Beijing (photo taken in 2000).
Key: 1 Main entrance; 2 Conference hall; 3 Classrooms; 4 400-student classroom; 5 Office and research building; 6 Information centre; 7 Library; 8 Central power distribution room; 9 Archive; 10 Training centre; 11 Training building; 12 Boiler room; 13 Faculty canteen; 14 Hospital; 15 400-metre track and field; 16 Playing field; 17 Tennis court; 18 Swimming pool; 19 Undergraduate dormitory; 20 Staff dormitory; 21 Apartment building; 22 International Cultural College; 23 International student canteen; 24 International student dormitory; 25 Student canteen; 26 Graduate student dormitory; 27 Lin-Yuan Building; 28 Jin-Yuan Building; 29 Yi-Yuan Building; 30 Faculty bathhouse; 31 Faculty club; 32 Shop; 33 Hui-Guan Building; 34 Xian-Jin Building; 35 Factory; 36 Development building; 37 Primary school; 38 Kindergarten; 39 Garage; 40 Services; 41 Public bathhouse; 42 Storage

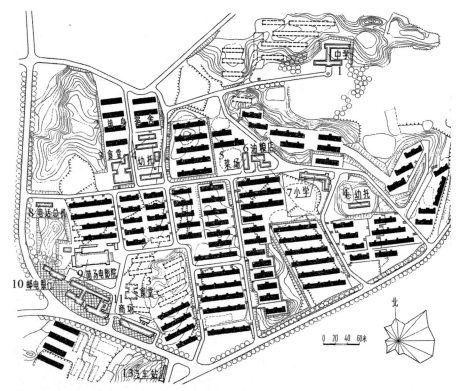

Figure 3.6. Site plan of the living quarter of Meishan Ironworks (1969–1971). Twenty kilometres from the city of Nanjing, the factory was developed as a company town complete with housing and essential social facilities. The floor space of the living quarter constructed in Phase 1 was 160,000 square metres.

Key: 1 Middle school; 2 Dormitory for single workers; 3 Canteen; 4 Nursery and kindergarten; 5 Market; 6 Grocery shops; 7 Primary school; 8 Headquarters of telephone; 9 Simply-built cinema theatre; 10 Post office and bank; 11 Shops. The rest of the buildings were apartment buildings

fields, parks and other recreation spaces are provided in the open areas between buildings (figures 3.7 and 3.8). All these facilities are designed for the exclusive use of unit members, but enforcing such exclusivity depends on the strength of individual work units. In some cases, neighbouring units cooperate to support the joint use of such facilities as schools and hospitals (figure 3.9).

The close proximity of work, housing and social facilities results in a peculiar pattern of local comings and goings. Many unit residents can carry out their daily business within the unit compound, although some do daily travel beyond the unit walls. Children of small work units go to schools outside the compound. Adults living with their spouses or parents in work units other than their own have to commute by bus or bicycle. Weekends are a time when many make trips of

Figure 3.7. Playground at a research institute, Beijing (photo taken in 2003).

Figure 3.8. Bicycle shed, Beijing (photo taken in 2005).

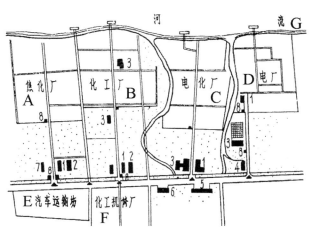

Figure 3.9. Four factories cooperated to support the joint use of both living (e.g., shops and the fire station) and production facilities (e.g., the transportation centre and the repair shop).

Key: A Coking plant; B Chemical plant; C Electrochemical plant; D Power plant; E Transportation centre; F Chemical machinery repair shop; G River. 1 Office building; 2 Laboratory; 3 Canteen; 4 Technical school; 5 Shop, post office and bank; 6 Central fire station; 7 Janitor's room; 8 Guardroom good distances away from their work units: shopping downtown, playing in parks or visiting relatives and friends who live in other parts of the city. Nonetheless, most unit members centre their lives on the work unit. Frequent travel along mutual pathways and shared activities at common meeting places create plenty of opportunities for people to form neighbourly bonds. In some cases the routines of everyday life are regulated by the use of a public address system, which provides news, announcements, information of upcoming events, music and exercise instructions, at certain times during the day.

The specific configuration of the work unit subtly contributes to the intermingled pattern of work, family and social life. There are crossings between work and home in both spatial and temporal terms. Relatively few activities can claim exclusive use of any particular space in a unit: part of work space may temporarily become social space, while sometimes domestic space may overflow into social space when household activities require it (Bjorklund, 1986, p. 23). As trips between home and work are safe and easy at night, no strict separation exists between work and domestic time. People are frequently assembled in spare time to have work meetings, conduct political study and perform group leisure activities such as sports matches and dancing.

Buildings that house production, residences and community facilities within the work unit differ in height, style and age, but in general they are modern brick and concrete structures designed based on rationalist doctrines (figure 3.10). Except for a few new high-rise buildings, most are walk-ups with up to six floors.

Figure 3.10. A corner of the Research Institute of Agricultural Science, Beijing (photo taken in 2001).

They are orthogonal in shape, with flat roofs and simple mass and lines. Good-size rectangular windows are arranged in a standard manner on the façade, giving the exterior a sense of openness. Architectural details vary over time. Structures built in the 1950s show some influence from classic Chinese and the Soviet Union design (Rowe and Kuan, 2002, pp. 87–106; Lu, 2004). Some constructed before 1955 feature the so-called 'Big Roof style', in which the modern concrete façade is topped with a large tiled roof with traditional Chinese decorative elements (figure 3.11). Some main administrative buildings are composed of a terraced structure dominated by a central tower in the Soviet socialist realistic style (figure 3.12). Both styles were largely abandoned by the mid-1950s for their impractical extravagance. In the years that followed, except for a few important public buildings, construction was reduced to pragmatic designs deprived of any reference to tradition. Only after political guidelines shifted and economic reforms brought prosperity to work units in the late 1970s, did aesthetic sensibility reappear, but generally without resorting to the traditional Chinese style. As the range of possibilities continues to be restricted by the availability of construction funds and local technological limitations, building styles remain relatively homogenous throughout the work unit.

In the case of work units built on developed land, existing structures were seldom destroyed; rather, they were adapted to modern functions: a *yamen* (the local government office) became a modern administration centre, a Confucian temple became a unit social hall, and a traditional courtyard house was divided to accommodate several families. With their origins slowly fading from memory, these buildings no longer have a narrative of their own; instead, they become part of a coherent framework for contemporary life.

Like structures in traditional China, most buildings in the work unit follow a north-south orientation, but the arrangement has a different intention. In traditional China, the southern direction was considered auspicious; a higher-rank figure would sit north and face south, and every important building would have its entrance on the long side facing south, with lesser and lower buildings on the east and west sides (Wheatley, 1971; Wright, 1977). The astrological connotations of the north-south axis are largely lost in contemporary China. The present orientation derives primarily from a pragmatic concern: a westward-facing building would be unsuitable in the winter and summer.

Many work units have a monumental main administration building, which serves as the centre of the work unit space. It may not necessarily be located at the actual geographical centre of the compound; instead, its symbolic importance is achieved via the arrangement of architectural elements (figure 3.13). When the main building is located near the main entrance, the gate opens onto a spacious square with the main building on the other end of the square, facing the gate

Figure 3.11. Designed by Liu Shiying around 1955, the library and main hall of Hunan University in Changsha feature elements taken from local building traditions (photo taken in 2005).

Figure 3.12. Main Building, Tsinghua University, Beijing, competed in 1968 (photo taken in 2005). The design of the building was influenced by the main building of the Moscow State University. Due to limited construction funds, the central Soviet-style tiered tower in earlier plans was replaced with a plain terraced roof.

Figure 3.13. The statue of Mao Zedong was a widely-adopted element in the design of squares before 1976. Tongji University, Shanghai (photo taken in 2001).

(figure 3.12). When the square is not immediately in front of the gate, it is often approached by a broad boulevard with the main building, set at the other end of the square, facing the boulevard. In either case, great emphasis is placed on axiality and the symmetrical design of buildings and landscape. However, the use of perspective here differs subtly from the imperial convention. The layout of traditional Chinese building groups required more than just one vision to create monumentality: '[t]he whole length of the axis is never revealed at once: it does not present a vista but a succession of varied spaces in a related sequence, each one blocked but visibly leading to a further stage' (Boyd, 1962, p. 73). In contrast, the kind of monumentality in the main building group of the work unit is modest. While individuals are invited to take part in similar ritual-like involvement by walking through a series of architectural mini-climaxes such as gates and statues, the procedure remains relatively straightforward. In addition, as the principle of efficiency is the priority, the axiality and symmetrical design remain limited within the scope of the main building group, rarely extending to the whole unit compound.

The floors of the main building and other office buildings consist of closed rooms and corridors. A sign on the door or nearby indicates the function of each room: the head's office, the cashier's office, the boiler room and so on. As the unit compound is the organizational centre not just for its economic function but many facets of social life, a large portion of office space is devoted to the various departments and committees to perform specific functions: the General Services Department (*zongwu ke*), the Housing Department (*fangguan ke*) and the Department of Security (*baowei ke*), to name just a few. These functions are often housed in separate rooms within the same administration building.

Production facilities are housed in large rectangular structures, with internal floor plans and architectural details that vary considerably to meet the particular requirements of production (figure 3.14). In general, the design follows the functionalist principle to achieve maximum economy of time and space: the manufacturing flow determines the floor plan and the floor plan in turn defines the form of the building. The principle is not only applied to the interior space of single buildings, but also extended to the layout of the entire production area to facilitate the supply and distribution flows. Careful consideration is given to proper sanitation, ventilation, lighting and safety appliances. To achieve better working conditions, workshops house functions other than the means of production. The 'life room' (*shenghuo jian*), an element imported from the Soviet Union, is an important component of the workshop plan, which serves a variety of functions, including first-aid stations, shower rooms, locker rooms, nursing rooms, reception rooms and dining rooms (Xie and Zhu, 1956; Sun, 1956). Some of these functions spill over into other structures in the factory (figure 3.15).

Residences include dormitories for single workers and apartments for families, both housed in modern-style buildings in orderly rows. The oldest ones are two to six storeys high with stairwell systems; some newest ones are high-rise buildings equipped with elevators. The design of both dormitories and apartments presents a realistic trade-off between social, utility and housing spaces by externalizing social activities and utilities from housing units. As a number of functions are removed from the private domain and accommodated instead in unit social facilities, the size of residence is reduced significantly.

The design of dormitories is based on the concept that the housing requirements for single employees are less complex and thus space expectations are lower. While centralized common restrooms are provided on each floor, there are no kitchens, dining rooms or shower rooms; people are expected to eat in unit canteens and take showers in public bathhouses (figure 3.16). Each room accommodates four to eight persons and is fitted with bunks. Furniture is provided by the work unit, including desks and chairs in addition to the bunks. Men and women are usually housed in separate dormitory buildings.

Figure 3.14. The working quarter of a beer factory in Gaobei, Fujian, constructed in the 1980s (photo taken in 1993).

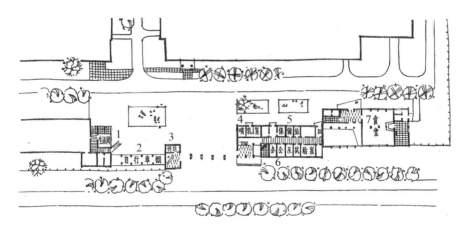

Figure 3.15. The front yard of a factory, published in 1964.
Key: 1. 'Life room'; 2. Bicycle shed; 3. Janitor's room; 4. Nursing room; 5. Clinic; 6. Office and laboratory; 7. Canteen.

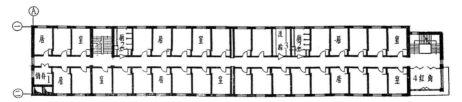

Figure 3.16. The floor plan for a university dormitory, published in 1962.
Key: 1 Storage; 2 Toilet; 3 Washroom; 4 Red corner

Compared to the dormitories, there is greater variety in family housing (figure 3.17, 3.18 and 3.19). Some apartments built in the early years were not unlike the dormitories: they have centralized bathrooms and kitchens shared by several families. Some larger families may be assigned two or three rooms, which are connected by a common corridor. As communal kitchens are inconvenient, families normally set up their own cooking facilities in the corridor. Some apartments built in the 1950s and designed according to the Soviet pattern have larger unit floor space and multiple bedrooms (Lü, Rowe and Zhang, 2001, pp. 108–140). Because of housing scarcity, it is common for two or three households to share one unit. In such cases, limited space sometimes results in heated feuding between families.

A typical multi-storey apartment building has two to four entrances, which are located on the north side so that each unit can have a south-facing balcony which is sunny even in the winter (figure 3.20). Immediately inside the entrance a narrow staircase leads to the upper floors, and each stairwell landing is shared by two or three housing units. Household refuse and personal possessions are sometimes left in the hallway: bicycles are chained to the railings, and vegetables are piled in the corners. Entering the apartment door, one comes first into a small dining room, which also serves as the corridor to other rooms. The kitchen is a separate walled-in room whose basic facilities include a gas burner and a poured-cement sink. The bathroom is in another small room, with a flush toilet and a shower space. A door from one of the inner rooms leads onto a balcony that provides space for laundry and plants. The larger bedroom often serves as a living room for the whole family besides being the master sleeping room. In such cases, the bed is pushed into a corner and a set of sofas is placed in another corner, creating an area for family gatherings and receiving guests. In newer apartment buildings, a more spacious living room is provided for dining and family gatherings, while the bedrooms are relatively small.

The work unit bears certain similarity with the microdistrict (see chapter 2) in terms of overall organization. Like the microdistrict, it occupies a territory bounded by arterial roads with an internal circulation system designed to discourage through traffic. Within this territory, they both support a variety of community facilities and green areas for the exclusive use of their residents. Yet there are some essential differences between the two. The microdistrict performs the single function of residential accommodation, while the work unit is both a unit of production and of consumption, complete with mixed economic, residential, administrative, welfare and political functions. Consequently, while community facilities are given pivotal importance in the layout of the microdistrict, the work unit is centred on the workplace with the main building on a commanding site. As its residents come from different backgrounds and do not have many opportunities to form neighbourly bonds, the microdistrict does not provoke the kind of dense

Figure 3.17. Two-storey apartment buildings in Changsha, Hunan (photo taken in 2005).

Figure 3.18. Five-storey apartment buildings in Beijing (photo taken in 1999)

Figure 3.19. The veranda of an apartment building in Guangzhou (photo taken in 2004).

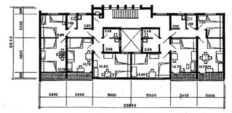

Figure 3.20. A housing design proposal, Shanghai, 1962.

network of human relationship fostered by the work unit. Furthermore, while a microdistrict is pre-planned, the physical environment of the work unit is a result of gradual development and thus allows for a great degree of flexibility in terms of social provision.

Many socio-spatial effects achieved through the peculiar arrangement of the work unit are indeed similar to those of the model company town found in the capitalist society and the Soviet Union (see Chapter 2). Both are characterized by the domination of a single enterprise, the close association of workplace and residence, and the paternalistic policies which extend well beyond the requirements of production (Crawford, 1995). Historically, the emergence of most company towns in the West coincided with the second phase of capitalism, which was characterized by centralized industrial production (*Ibid.*). What may partly explain the similarities between the work unit and the company town is that socialist society shares a number of fundamental characteristics with capitalism of this phase, including the development of heavy industries, the concentration of production, and corporate organization of production. As Lenin once pointed out, the concentration of production in capitalist societies created the economic basis for the development of socialism (Dirlik, 1994, p. 41). Thus, although the work unit and the company town belong to two different societies often seen as oppositional, a similar economic basis – centralized industrial production (in contrast to flexible production under late capitalism) – may account for their similar characteristics. Certainly, unlike the company town, which is often located in an isolated rural location, most work units are situated in urban or suburban areas. As such, they have important implications for the city to which I now turn.

Alternative Urbanism

The characteristic spatiality of the work unit has profound effects on contemporary Chinese society. The work unit provides a safety net through which industrial labour is reproduced, a spatial environment that fosters social exchange, moral bonds and equality, and a social community from which urban residents derive their social identity and sense of belonging. The work-unit-based city displays an urbanism quite distinct from other societies. While some commentators describe the work unit mainly as a repressive institute of state control, I contend that the work unit creates comprehensive urban effects related to community, security, equality, women's rights, employees' rights, welfare and environmental sustainability. Certainly, as I will show below, the work unit has its limits on each of these facets, and its enclosed character has some negative effects upon the city as a whole. Compared with the physical environment, which will last for decades to come once constructed, urbanism has changed dramatically in the past two decades. I shall use the past tense in the following.

Community

The work unit as the focus of urban life resulted in a small community atmosphere lacking in anonymity, a peculiar urban experience not found in other modern cities (Dutton, 1998). A person in the Western modern city, as typified in Edgar Allan Poe's 1840 tale 'The man of the crowd', remains a nameless face in a crowd made up of strangers (Poe, 1986). In contrast, an urbanite in Maoist China was constantly among people who knew him or her well. One experienced warm neighbourliness, but was constantly subject to watchful eyes of the crowd (Henderson and Cohen, 1984). On one hand, when difficulties arose, members of the community pitched in to help; on the other hand, gossip spread quickly when one did anything outside existing norms (*Ibid.*, 1984). As a unit member remarked,

[I]f there's a newcomer in any unit, before long everybody knows his background, history, wage grade, political behavior, whether there are any black marks on his record, what sports he's good at and with whom he does or doesn't get along … A whole range of matters must go through public evaluation, such as wages, bonuses, designation as a progressive worker, being sent out to study, promotions and punishments and allocation of housing and other benefits … Rumors, gossip and nasty remarks are common [too,] and this leads to pointless quarrels, making the relationships between people complicated and tense (Naughton, 1997, p. 181).

The dense network of human relationships and the lack of anonymity inclined many to refer to the work unit as the 'urban village' (Li, 1993). Although the strong sense of community reduced deviance, it inevitably also had side effects such as suffocating interpersonal relations and lack of innovation.

Security and Exclusivity

The work unit provided a safe environment for its residents. With security gates and watchful eyes that prevented outsiders from coming or going unobserved, children could play freely without constant adult attendance. With an internal circulation system that controlled the movement of through traffic past its territory, people could walk or bike on streets safely.

With the high percentage of time spent within their own work unit, people's experiences and contacts outside were relatively few. They often spoke of events happening 'out in society' (*shehui shang*), as if their work unit were entirely separated from the wider world (Lü and Perry, 1997a, p. 8). The limited contact across work units helped to prevent large-scale organized opposition beyond the unit boundary. The numerous protests during the Cultural Revolution, for instance, largely remained 'cellular protests' (*Ibid.*).

'Less urbanism'

The city under Mao, like other socialist cities, appeared 'less of an urban place', to quote Ivan Szelenyi (1993, p. 53), than a typical capitalist city. Szelenzi observes that there was less urban diversity, lower density in inner urban public places and less urban marginality in East European socialist cities (1993, p. 53; 1996, p. 300). The best test case of this was East Berlin, which greatly differed from West Berlin in the aforementioned aspects (Szelenzi, 1993, p. 53).

The enclosed character of the work unit resulted in less choice, social interaction and heterogeneity at the urban level. Georg Simmel, in his analysis of the modern city, contrasts urban space, where density and diversity constantly put the individual in touch with myriad possibilities, to rural space, where individual movement and opportunities are restricted (Simmel, 1964). Simmel characterizes an individual living in a modern city as a mobile subject, moving across the city's social circles and choosing his or her associations to create a particular, individualised social world (Langer, 1984). In the Maoist city, one's social life was largely confined within one's own work unit, which was separated from other parts of the city physically and socially (Lü and Perry, 1997*a*, pp. 11–12). As there was little provision to facilitate interactions in society at large, the urbanite in the Maoist city was restricted to the concentric social pattern centred on the work unit, with few resources available outside this circle.

As strict limits were imposed upon private commercial establishments under Mao, urban residents bought most of their daily essentials from cooperative shops run by the work unit. The streets had fewer shops, restaurants, advertisements, recreational centres and other urban facilities. The social environment of the work unit encouraged socialist collectivism while discouraging social heterogeneity which is central to Wirth's notion of 'urbanism as a way of life' (Wirth, 1938). As the greater 'openness' of private life suppressed behaviour that did not conform to local norms, there was a high level of homogeneity in terms of life styles.

Equality, Residential Segregation and Urban Marginality

A high level of social and spatial equality was maintained within the work unit. The salary difference between managers and workers was not significant enough to create major socioeconomic ramifications, and they worked and lived in more or less similar buildings. To be sure, despite largely homogeneous exteriors, the internal spaces of both office and apartment buildings were differentiated. In office buildings, larger rooms or corner offices were allocated to higher ranking officials. In the case of apartment buildings, the main difference lay in the size and number of rooms of the apartment unit; other subtle differences included the orientation of the apartment unit, the floor on which it was located, and the quality of the building that houses it. Each work unit had a complicated ranking system to assign housing fairly, based on criteria such as rank, job seniority, marital status, family size, ethnic origin (minorities are given priority) and so on. Based on this system, senior workers might be ranked the same as less senior managers. Hence despite the existence of a hierarchical system, the degree of differentiation in terms of living standards remained relatively low within the work unit.

The mechanism of residential segregation in the Maoist city bore little similarity to that found in capitalist cities. Compared with intra-unit differentiation, larger social stratification existed between units in terms of income, welfare and environmental quality. Residential segregation in the Chinese city was most commonly expressed through the separation of different work units, instead of segregating rich, poor and ethnic minorities into distinctive urban areas.

Like other socialist cities, the work-unit-based Maoist city displayed less signs of marginality.[5] The work unit system provided the majority of urban residents with lifetime employment and access to welfare benefits. Supplementary to this system, Residents' Committees created means of subsistence for those not formally employed by work units (Parish and Parish, 1986, chapter 2). In addition to this dual safety network there was strict control of rural migration (Chan, 1994; Wu, 1994). Peasants were kept in their respective villages through a careful coordination of the issue of residential permits (*hukou*) and work permits (Cheng and Selden, 1994). Migrants without correct documents could not survive in the city as basic commodities (e.g., rice, flour, plain cloth, and cooking oil) were rationed in urban areas (*Ibid.*). Consequently, although the city as a whole showed signs of scarcity, fewer extreme expressions of poverty and deviance such as homelessness and crime were found. The orderly Maoist city, devoid of urban ills such as shanty towns and prostitution, was presented as a shining counter-example to the Third World by scholars during the 1970s (Oksenberg, 1973; Weisskopf, 1980).

Women's Rights

The design of the work unit created an institutionally non-sexist environment that supported the activities of employed women and their families. In contemporary China, urban women were expected to have paid employment, while homebound women were the exception. The work unit's integration of production, residence and social services on a manageable scale greatly facilitated the functioning of two-worker families. Public kitchens and canteens offered alternatives to cooking at home, nurseries within the unit compound reduced the time spent in commuting, and nursing rooms near workshops helped mothers to get back to work.

The Maoist city therefore contrasts sharply to the Western capitalist city in this regard. The latter is recognized as fundamentally dependent on the subordination of women by a vigorous feminist critique since the 1970s (Sandercock and Forsyth, 1992). As a result of the gender-based planning under capitalism, social childcare is rarely available near office centres; the transportation pattern assumes the woman as an available full-time driver; and the whole idea of suburb is indeed based on the assumption of the self-reliant home with full-time operator – the woman.[6]

Nevertheless, residual patriarchal authority survived in Chinese domestic space; women were almost invariably expected to spend more time on housework and childcare than men (figure 3.21). Women's double burden of work and domestic responsibilities sometimes results in household crisis (Wolf, 1985). In response to women's particular needs, every work unit has a women's committee which deals with a broad range of women's concerns and family disputes.

Discipline vs. Employees' Rights

While the modern capitalist city is based on contractual relationships between individual subjects mediated by the market, the Maoist urban society was founded on a collective labour's 'organized dependence' on the work unit. Walder's famous study reveals that as the paternalism of the work unit penetrated various aspects of workers' lives, the latter were subject to the patronage of unit leaders (1986). Many commentators point out that discipline within the work unit relied not only on the presence of unit Party leaders and workshop managers but also upon the mutual surveillance among workers (Rofel, 1992; Bray, 2005, p. 166). Watchful eyes put pressure upon colleagues so that there was less chance of malingering or lateness (Henderson and Cohen, 1984).

Yet the managing powers and disciplinary effects of the work unit were nonetheless limited. In fact, there was widespread acknowledgment among the Chinese urban reformers that the work unit system promoted inefficiency and lack of discipline among workers. The reasons for this were multiple. First and most importantly, the guarantee of permanent employment granted employees much power to resist efficient management. Hence when the Western ways of industrial discipline were introduced in the late 1970s, advocates of enterprise reform vigorously called for removing lifetime job security (Solinger, 2002).

Second, the operational logic following the ideals of the Maoist 'mass line' created unique labour relations within the work unit (Lee, 1991). Unit cadres were required to remain close to the employees, while workers were encouraged to participate in management. As a consequence, the power of managers was

Figure 3.21. A 1961 photograph entitled 'After work' published in People's Pictorial (*Renmin huabao*), a major publication that disseminated images of national progress.

significantly weakened. Third, as David Bray rightfully points out, the spatial arrangement of the work unit was 'ill suited to the creation of disciplined and individuated worker subjects' (2005, p. 166). The close link between living and working space bred socialist collectivism rather than the logic of individual-oriented labour. The lack of clear boundary between productive activity and everyday life served to increase employees' powers to resist the discipline of workplace management.

Welfare

As mentioned earlier, due to a lack of a society-wide welfare system, a wide range of welfare programmes were organized via the work unit. The unit trade union was and still is the key agent to perform various welfare functions. Following the Soviet model, the trade union in China plays a different role from the trade union in capitalist society (Pravda and Ruble, 1986). Based on the assumption that under socialism there was no need for the trade union to protect workers against the interests of the capitalist, the trade union was reconceptualized as the link between the party and the working class (Brown, 1966). Although the trade union was initially designed as an extension of the Party leadership in China (*Renmin ribao*, 1950a), in practice the party leadership was taken over by the unit party branch, while the trade union was mainly in charge of managing workers' welfare (*Renmin ribao*, 1957f; Lee, 1989).

Following the 1951 national policy 'Labour insurance regulations', the Labour Insurance Fund was raised (3 per cent of monthly salary) to provide the payment of medical expenses, disability pensions, funeral costs and financial support for the families of workers killed in the workplace, retirement pensions and maternity leave (Bray, 2005, pp. 104–105). The work unit offered additional funding for other benefits such as medical expenses for injuries and illness and maternity care. The unit trade union managed 70 per cent of the Labour Insurance Fund and other resources provided by the work unit for welfare programmes. Through the unit trade union's role in managing many facets of everyday life meticulously on a daily basis (such as providing assistance to workers in need and organizing group leisure activities), urban workers were effectively enmeshed within a comprehensive safety net.

Environmental Sustainability

The distinctive mixed land-use pattern of the work unit had important environmental significance. The close association of workplace, residence and social facilities greatly reduced the need for urban residents to travel beyond their unit compound. Such an urban form depended little on the provision of an extensive and expensive public transport system. As Clifton Pannell observed in the late 1970s, major Chinese cities such as Shanghai and Beijing had a very small number of buses and other public transport vehicles: the number for both cities was around 2,200 in 1977, much less than other Western cities of similar sizes (Pannell, 1977, pp. 161–162). Without any private cars, the principal modes of circulation at the time were bicycling and walking. Energy consumption was also reduced through shared facilities such as canteens and public bathhouses. It is indeed an incredible environmental achievement to have an urban system based on minimum energy costs without generating serious dysfunctions in economic and social organization.

Despite a certain similarity the Maoist city bore with the Soviet city in terms of collectivism, 'less urbanism', enterprise-based welfare systems and so on (Bater, 1980; Szelenyi, 1993, 1996; Sil, 1997; Straus, 1997a, 1997b), it differed from the latter in several aspects. First, despite planners' desire to reduce the distance between work and home, production and residence remained unattached in the Soviet city (French, 1995). Even in a company town, the two were separated by greenbelts rather than mingled together (Castillo, 2003). Second, although housing in the Soviet Union was often built by industrial ministries as part of the construction of a new factory, unlike China, the housing was usually turned over to Soviet municipal authorities within six months after the construction was completed (Sawers, 1978, p. 355). Third, the Soviet residential district was usually larger than a Chinese work unit, and comprised residents from different enterprises (Bater, 1980; French, 1995). As such, although it was held that residential design should foster a sense of neighbourliness in early Soviet planning thought (as represented in the 1920s communal housing experiments and the subsequent adoption of the microdistrict), the objective was not achieved. A 1970 study found that inhabitants in a Soviet residential district knew 'only 5 to 10 of their neighbours by sight, 3 to 5 by name, and almost nothing about where they work or about their character' (Sawers, 1978, pp. 351–352). Fourth, due to the separation between work and residence and because of weather conditions, the Soviet urban system relied more on the provision of extensive public transport systems than the Chinese system (Straus, 1997b, pp. 148–154).[7] From these perspectives, work-unit-based urbanism was indeed an alternative both to capitalist and to Soviet urbanism.

Change and Continuity in the Reform Era

Changes brought by economic reforms since 1978 have been accompanied by enormous transformations of urban China. The work unit has gradually declined as the fundamental socio-spatial unit of the Chinese city. This section provides a brief account of some of the most salient developments in the social and physical environment of the work unit.

The effects of reforms until the mid-1990s strengthened the role of work units in some aspects (Naughton, 1996, 1997). Fiscal decentralization, for example, has given work units increased economic autonomy in regard to decisions on investment and resource allocation. More and better consumption facilities such as high-rise apartment buildings, convenience shops and children's play grounds within work units were built after the reforms (figures 3.22 and 3.23). The urban

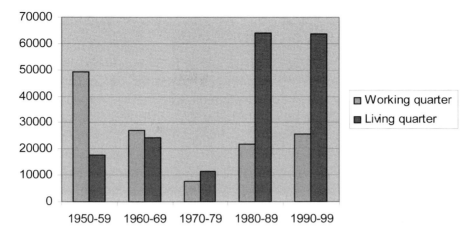

Figure 3.22. Floor space constructed in the working and living quarters at the General Institute of Iron and Steel Research, Beijing, 1950–1999 (in square metres). (*Source*: The Basic Construction and Planning Department, the General Institute of Iron and Steel Research, Beijing)

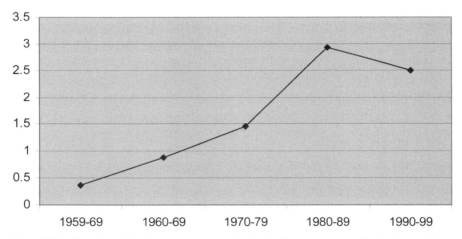

Figure 3.23. The ratio of the floor space constructed in the living quarter to that in the working quarter at the General Institute of Iron and Steel Research, Beijing, 1950–1999 (*Source*: The Basic Construction and Planning Department, the General Institute of Iron and Steel Research, Beijing)

reforms aiming to increase efficiency and re-commodify labour have given more managerial autonomy to unit managers to hire, dismiss and discipline staff (Walder, 1989). Certainly, the industrial restructuring since 1992 has weakened the role of state units in the national economy; some, especially those in heavy industry, lose their competitiveness and become insolvent.[8] Their workers are laid off and become new urban poor after the reforms (Solinger, 2002).

Figure 3.24. The former workshop of the Central Documentary Filmmaker was turned into a disco bar, Beijing (photo taken in 1999).

The shift from state ownership of land and its free administrative allocation to paid transfer of land-use rights while state ownership is retained has important implications for the work unit (Wu and Yeh, 1997). The land value of some urban districts, especially those close to the inner city, has increased dramatically (Wu, 2002*a*). Work units located in these districts convert part or all of their land to commercial or other uses (figure 3.24). A most common practice is to build stores and office buildings in areas near streets and rent or sell them to private firms (Bray, 2005, p. 170). As residential development became increasingly profitable, some work units transferred their land-use rights to real-estate companies to generate additional income. In some cases, the work units, often the ones that generate severe pollution, are relocated as a whole to remote suburban areas (Yin, Shen and Zhao, 2005). The land price difference between the old and new locations allows them to upgrade their workshops and other facilities. Some work units that perform poorly under a market economy but situated in favourable locations convert themselves into real estate companies. Workshops are torn down to make way for new commercial or residential buildings. Some former unit members are included as part of the new companies while the rest are laid off or retire early (*Ibid.*).

Housing reforms have brought mixed effects to the work unit. On one hand, as the urban housing market provides other housing options, some better-off households move out from their unit apartments to private residential estates. On the other hand, the work unit plays an ongoing role in housing development and management. Although the key objective of housing reforms is to encourage urban residents to purchase their housing, the low cash salary that most unit members receive would not allow them to do so. In response to the problem, the work unit continues to provide subsidized housing for those who cannot afford to pay for 'commodity housing' (*shangpin fang*) at market prices (Wang and Murie, 1996; Bian, *et al.* 1997; Wang, 1999). Different from the past, existing or new housing units of the work unit are sold to members at prices lower than market prices. Such purchases only provide the buyers part ownership rights while the work unit holds the rest, so the housing units cannot be sold freely. The work unit also manages the 'housing accumulation fund' (*zhufang gongjijin*) that requires each employee to contribute five per cent of his or her salary for housing development (Bray, 2005, pp. 174–175). The fund is often used to finance housing construction organized by the work unit.

Social ramifications have intensified after the reforms. The proof is the new residential landscape (figure 3.25): people are sorted according to their income into commodity housing ranging from affordable housing to luxury villas, housing in unit compounds and old neighbourhoods, to migrant enclaves on the edge of the city (Huang, 2005; Hu and Kaplan, 2001). The economic performance of individual work units more than ever influences their capacity in housing and other social provisions. Profitable units are able to invest in new housing and social facilities,

Figure 3.25. The new residential landscape of Guangzhou (photo taken in 2005). Apartment buildings constructed in different periods display distinct styles.

and sometimes buy housing units from the market and then sell them to their employees. Less successful units have limited capacity to offer housing and other benefits for their members, which places them at a disadvantaged position in regard to competing for human resources. The reforms also generate a sharp differentiation within the same work unit. Within the same work unit, some sub-units may perform much better than others. Some members may receive a lucrative income from their highly successful sub-unit, while others may still live on a modest salary.

Accelerating marketization has resulted in an increasing mobility of capital and labour across the borders of the work unit. Some work units transform themselves into commercial companies listed on the stock market, some collaborate with other private companies to develop new projects, and still others lease part of their offices or laboratories to foreign firms. The flows of capital are accompanied with the flows of people. Some members leave their unit to work in the rapidly expanding private sector. Many live comfortably outside of the work unit system, while others adopt the 'one family, two systems' strategy (Leng, 1992). That is, one joins the private sector to seek better economic opportunities, while one's spouse remains in the state unit so that the family can enjoy various welfare programmes provided by the unit (Bray, 2005, p. 169). Meanwhile, rural migrants flood into the previously exclusive work unit and take over the most low paying service jobs (Solinger, 1997).

The central government has sought to divest the work unit from their social responsibilities and encourage them to open up their community facilities for outsiders' use. As a result, social services within the work unit have become increasingly market-oriented. Canteens are subcontracted to individuals or private companies, the management of unit housing is taken over by newly established estate management companies (*wuye guanli gongsi*), and guesthouses and bathhouses are open to the general public (chapter 7). Meanwhile, unit residents no longer depend solely on their work units for social needs (Tang and Parish, 2000). Society-wide health insurance and pension systems have been established. A variety of consumption options are now made available by the city: shopping malls, billiard parlours, beauty shops, video theatres, disco bars and all kinds of clubs. Diverse urban places provide new opportunities for social interactions. As a result, the work unit no longer serves as the focus of everyday life for many; heterogeneous lifestyles mushroom both within and outside the unit compounds.

While the work unit is adapting to the new opportunities brought by the reforms, some of its features are reproduced in private companies and new residential developments. Corinna-Barbara Francis's study of Beijing's high-tech sector reveals that paternalistic approaches to management similar to those employed by the work unit are adopted by private firms in Haidian District

(Francis, 1996). Studies show that similar characteristics in management practices and spatial arrangements can be drawn between the work unit and the rising 'gated communities' in reform China (Wu, 2005; Huang, 2005; Bray, 2005, pp. 181–190). A survey by the Chinese Research Centre reveals that the work unit is deeply embedded in cultural norms and expectations as well as social practices (Li, Wang and Li, 1996). Therefore, despite a radical change in market practices, the work unit will continue to serve as an important template for urban development.

Notes

1. During the pre-reform era, the government allocated 95 per cent of first jobs in urban areas; once one was assigned to a specific work unit, job changes were difficult (Naughton, 1997, pp. 171–174).
2. The writing of this section is based on my fieldwork in Beijing, Wuhan, Guanzhou, Shanghai, Xiamen and Gaobei in 2000, a survey of 15 work units conducted in Beijing in 2000–2001, my own experience of living and working with in a work unit, and related publications. The survey was conducted with the help of my research assistant Gai Shijie. Survey questions included the years in which different living facilities within the work unit were constructed and people's attitudes toward unti-based consumption provision.
3. To be sure, when new work units were created in remote rural areas, such as the 'Third Front' enterprises, more social facilities were provided from the very beginning because of a lack of existing urban infrastructure (Naughton, 1988).
4. For a detailed account of the development of a single work unit, see You (2000).
5. Robert Park considers the existence of marginality as one of the most central features of urbanism in both 'positive' and 'negative' senses. On one hand, the fact that urbanites are more likely to be marginal leads to greater creativity. On the other hand, urban marginality results in more deviance such as crime and prostitution (Park, 1928; Perlman, 1976, pp. 98–99).
6. I owe this account to Manuel Castells's lecture series on 'Comparative Urban Policies', 1997, University of California, Berkeley.
7. Poor transportation negatively affected urban functions during the early period of Soviet building. Workers at Novogireevo, for example, had to walk in the dark 'through the woods in groups of ten for protection against hooligans' up until 1935 (Straus, 1997b, p. 149).
8. The national survey in 1996 showed that the share of state units in total industrial output was 28.5 per cent, the share of collective units (including rural enterprises) 39.4 per cent, and the share of other types of enterprises 32.1 per cent (Li and Li, 2000, p. 22).

Chapter Four

The Socialist Production of Space: Planning, Urban Contradictions and the Politics of Consumption in Beijing, 1949–1965

In quiet and untroubled times, it seems to every administrator that it is only by his efforts that the whole population under his rule is kept going, and in this consciousness of being indispensable every administrator finds the chief reward of his labour and efforts … But as soon as a storm arises and the sea begins to heave and the ship to move, such a delusion is no longer possible. The ship moves independently with its own enormous motion, the boat hook no longer reaches the moving vessel, and suddenly the administrator, instead of appearing a ruler and a source of power, becomes an insignificant, useless, feeble man.

Leo Tolstoy, 1865–1869 (1976), *War and Peace*

In his book *The Urban Question* (1977), Manuel Castells offers an insightful account of the rise of collective consumption in capitalist society. He argues that, although the capitalist system must secure the adequate reproduction of labour power as a prerequisite of continued production, individual capitalist producers find it less profitable to invest in crucial consumption facilities such as housing, schools and health facilities. As the potential for a crisis in social provision is inherent in the nature of the capitalist mode of production, it falls to the state to intervene in the sphere of consumption. Yet the more the state assumes responsibility for social provision, the more the problem of collective consumption becomes politicized. A reduction at the level of provision necessarily leads to social struggles in capitalist welfare society.

Castells's influential work has resulted in a vast new body of literature in urban analysis (Saunders, 1986; Ball, 1986). Inevitably, questions arise regarding the logic of consumption provision in socialist society. By eradicating the capitalist class, the socialist state became the sole agent of capital. Claiming that it appropriated the surplus value for the benefit of the whole population, the state assumed the responsibility of social provision. How did this structural difference result in the different rationale of collective consumption in socialist society in contrast to capitalist society? What were the problems generated by the forms and purposes of state intervention in the sphere of consumption under socialism? And how was urban space produced under the socialist logic of provision?

There have been considerable efforts to understand consumption provision in socialist society, but most work stops at the level of generalizations and focuses on the former Soviet Union and East European socialist countries (Buzlyakov, 1973; Pahl, 1977; Magagna, 1989). This chapter explores the dynamics of provision under Chinese socialism in a concrete local setting. Based on first-hand archival materials, I examine the conflicted relationship between the state, work units and planners in the construction of essential consumption facilities in Beijing between 1949 and 1965 (covering the period after the socialist revolution and before the Cultural Revolution).[1] I argue that the overlapping role of the socialist state in production and consumption did not result in the disappearance of contradictions in social provision. Instead, as the socialist state strove to achieve the fastest possible industrial growth, new conflicts were generated between the needs of accumulation and the necessity of labour reproduction. Political pressure from both the newly enfranchised workers and the state forced work units to take on the responsibility of consumption provision.

The chapter will show that, as little state investment was allocated to non-productive construction, the building of living facilities within work units was often accomplished through construction outside the state approved plan, resource hoarding and exchanges via informal channels. I analyse the rationale behind work-unit-based provision by accepting two insights provided in studies of the dynamics of state socialism: soft budget and shortage economy. Although the two concepts are provided by the scholars of East European socialist countries, as this study will show, they are also valid in the context of Maoist China. By revealing the significance of the two mechanisms in urban processes, I justify the argument that the socialist mode of production plays a fundamental role in the production of the built environment.

As the regulators of the urban spatial order, planners made every effort to stop illegal construction. To achieve their objectives, they strove to convert the vertically controlled urban growth system into a horizontally coordinated one. Yet their attempts were effectively ignored, due to weak planning powers and the lack of effective means of regulation. The resulting Chinese urban form in no way matched the planning ideals planners were taught to cherish, lacking as it did clear functional zoning, greenbelts and integrated residential districts. The work unit gradually developed into the basic unit of collective consumption complete with essential living facilities. Its peculiar spatial form contributed to the reproduction of social relations under the socialist mode of domination of everyday life.

I next turn to the issues surrounding production, consumption and scarcity. This is followed by a description of uncontrolled urban construction in the city of Beijing, an analysis of the work-unit-based consumption provision, and an account of planners' intentions and practices to create a spatial order. The chapter closes with an assessment of the political implications of consumption provision under Chinese socialism in comparison with those in welfare capitalist society as formulated by Castells.

Production, Consumption and Scarcity

How to achieve rapid industrialization with scarce resources is a common problem faced by newly established socialist countries. At the end of the second volume of *Das Capital*, Marx (1867, 1976) disaggregates an economy into two departments: Department I produces fixed and circulating constant capital, use values destined for productive consumption; Department II produces use values for individual consumption, necessities for workers and luxuries for the bourgeoisie. Marx maintains that the quantities of inputs and outputs in the two departments should be in the right proportions if accumulation is to take place smoothly. Due to the 'accumulation-for-accumulation's-sake' nature of capitalism, however, the production of Department I often increases faster than that of Department II in such a system. This formulation has long attracted people for different purposes, including the former Soviet leader Joseph Stalin. To achieve maximum accumulation of capital for industrialization, Stalin interpreted Marx's scheme as: in order to realize expanded reproduction, the production of Department I should be given priority over the production of Department II (Yang, 1987, pp. 27–34). Despite a vigorous debate devoted to this deduction during the 1920s, it remained the key theory to justify the Soviet state's high accumulation and selected growth policy under Stalin.

When the Chinese communist leaders set about building a new society, they imported from the Soviet Union not only a highly centralized political and economic system, but also the Stalinist interpretation of production and consumption. Almost immediately following the founding of the People's Republic, production was associated with development while consumption was associated with waste and bourgeoisie lifestyles. Cities, related to consumption and colonialism, were considered evil and corrupting. Shanghai, for example, was depicted as 'a parasitic city … where consumption is greater than production'

(Gaulton, 1981, p. 46). A campaign to convert the 'cities of consumption' into the 'cities of production' was launched in 1949.

Planners believed that the tertiary sectors were a wasteful use of resources; the city should transfer most of its manpower and assets to industrial development. A predominance of productive activities (e.g., industry, construction and transport) over consumer activities (e.g., wholesale and retailing, finance and catering) was established. Beijing, the national capital, was set as an example of the city suppressing its consumptive roles (*Dangdai zhongguo congshu bianjibu*, 1989, pp. 411–412). An initial reduction of establishments and employment in commerce and services was achieved in the city through the collectivization programme of 1955. Between 1958 and 1960, a greater reduction was made: in 1960 alone, the number of establishments in commerce dropped by 78 per cent and those employed by 22 per cent (Sit, 1995, p. 149). The old imperial capital was transformed into a major industrial base (table 4.1). By 1965, the city's total industrial output reached 5,917 million RMB yuan, 35 times that of 1949 (*Beijingshi tongjiju*, 1999, p. 161).

A new productive/non-productive binary was established in urban construction. State investment was tilted in favour of productive construction – the erection of structures directly related to production – and biased against non-productive construction, that is structures used to render services. The total industrial investment in Beijing reached 4.01 billion RMB yuan between 1950 and 1965, accounting for 36 per cent of all investment in the city (*Beijingshi tongjiju*, 1999, p. 161). Housing was categorized as non-productive construction; as such, its priority and share of state investment remained relatively low (table 4.2). Construction of floor space allocated for production, compared to residential and service uses stayed at a ratio of 1:1.12 during 1953–1957 when the normal ratio should be 1:3; it

Table 4.1. The share of industrial output in total output in Beijing, 1952–1965

Year	The share of industrial output
1952	45.05
1953	40.52
1954	39.97
1955	41.68
1956	40.74
1957	41.90
1958	54.25
1959	57.40
1960	63.09
1961	59.76
1962	59.26
1963	60.30
1964	60.76
1965	62.17

Source: Beijingshi tongjiju, 1999, p. 15

Table 4.2. Distribution of capital construction investment in Beijing, 1949–1965.

Construction period	Productive construction investment %	Non-productive construction investment	
		Total %	Housing %
1949–1952	54.5	45.5	9.1
1953–1957	51.6	48.4	15.6
1958–1962	69.3	30.7	5.9
1963–1965	62.8	37.2	12.2

Source: Beijingshi tongjiju, 1999, p. 97.

dropped even lower to 1:0.9 after 1958 (Sit, 1995, pp. 208–210). Other crucial social facilities, such as schools and shops, also received low priority in state investment (*Beijingshi tongjiju,* 1999, pp. 98–99).

Industrial expansion caused a dramatic growth in urban population. Between 1949 and 1965, the city's population increased from 2.09 million to 7.87 million (*Beijingshi tongjiju,* 1999, p. 49). Rapid urban growth and biased investment policies together created immense scarcity of crucial consumption facilities (*Renmin ribao,* 1957c). According to a 1963 report, new construction in suburban Beijing was concentrated on productive structures; there was a constant shortage of housing and facilities in these areas (*Beijingshi dang'an guan,* hereafter BDG, 1963a). In Guanxiang District, one of Beijing's western suburbs, for example:

… the district is comprised of 18 factories, 4 storage buildings, 10 colleges, 9 cadre and Communist Party schools, 17 scientific institutes, and 110 administration and design institutes... The ratio between production space and housing is currently 1:1, far below the standard 1:3 … The situation of commercial and public services … is worse: the current ratio between housing and services in the area is 40:1, while in the inner city the ratio is 16:1. (*Ibid.*)[2]

To be sure, between 1949 and 1965, the total housing floor space increased from 13.54 to 30.52 million square metres (table 4.3).[3] Most new factories and institutions built apartment buildings for their workers.[4] Yet as enterprises grew faster than the original plans, the existing housing stock was constantly insufficient to meet the demand (*Renmin ribao,* 1957o). Per capita housing floor space decreased from 4.75 square metres in 1949 to 3.68 in 1965. Housing shortage was so appalling that residents described it as the city's 'malignant tumour' (ZSKYZD, 1989, p. 637). The scarcity of crucial living facilities negatively affected urban functions. A 1956 document reported that some workers in Beijing had to get up at four o'clock in the morning and walk two miles to buy groceries (BDG, 1956a). To go shopping or take in a movie, one had to travel across the city to Wangfujing, the old commercial district of Beijing. In some areas, children walked for more than two hours to attend school (*Ibid.*).

Meanwhile, newspapers and magazines frequently featured representations

Table 4.3. Housing in Beijing, 1949–1965.

Year	Total housing floor space ($m^2 \times 10^6$)	Per capita housing floor space (m^2)
1949	13.54	4.75
1950	13.69	4.90
1951	14.02	4.45
1952	15.09	4.49
1953	16.03	3.76
1954	17.10	3.70
1955	18.93	3.88
1956	20.55	3.76
1957	22.18	3.70
1958	24.50	3.89
1959	25.17	3.42
1960	26.28	3.24
1961	27.34	3.49
1962	27.99	3.67
1963	28.73	3.66
1964	29.55	3.67
1965	30.52	3.68

Source: Beijingshi tongjiju, 1999.

that celebrated the national progress in modernization and the happy life under socialism (figure 4.1). *People's Pictorial* (*Renmin huabao*) published many 'before and after' photographs to prove the superiority of the new society. In an illustration captioned 'The past and present of Xichengwai', for example, pictures of one of Beijing's suburbs contrasted the erstwhile dire roads lined with shacks of the pre-1949 era, with the tree-lined boulevards and block after block of new workers' appartment buildings of the present. A 1950 *People's Daily* article detailed new proletarian life in one of the model factories (*Renmin ribao*, 1950*b*). Workers lived in brand new dormitory buildings and ate at factory canteens which provided plenty of choice: ordinary home-made meals at Hall 1, rice and side dishes at Hall 2, and noodles and wine at Hall 3. At the end of the day, workers engaged in diverse leisure activities: dancing at the Worker's Club, playing basketball at the athletic field, or reading in the unit library (*Ibid.*). The propaganda conjured up a society where every aspect of workers' lives would be taken care of by the state (figure 4.2). Yet reality in no way matched the life imagined for the world of triumphant socialism. The disparity between the paucity experienced in everyday life and the idealized image of material well-being only intensified the feeling of scarcity.

Construction outside the Plan

The staggering amount of construction without permit – 'illegal construction' (*weizhang jianzhu*) – plagued the City Planning Bureau of Beijing throughout the

Figure 4.1. 'The past and present of Xichengwai', Beijing, 1959. Similar 'old versus new' photographs were published extensively in the 1950s as testimony to the success of nation building.

1950s and 1960s (BDG, 1954*a*, 1956*b*, 1957*a*, 1958, 1959*a*, 1960*a*, 1961*a*, 1963*a*, 1964*a*). It was reported, for example, that 339 work units built illegal construction projects between 1956 and 1959 (BDG, 1959*a*), 190,000 square metres were built in 1960 (BDG, 1961a) and 27,000 square metres by 208 work units in 1963 (BDG, 1964*a*). Many work units were stopped several times by the planning bureau, only to restart construction again later (1956*b*). A 1956 report offers a vivid account of the state of chaos:

Work units vied with each other to build on vacant land without getting permits in the [Hepingli] area... On 18 August the Bureau of Construction Technology erected an apartment complex of 361.5 square metres; thereafter the Ministry of Geology built 24 apartment units and a garage of 806 square metres. Immediately following, the Ministry of Labour completed 18 apartment units, and are now in the process of building 8 more. With knowledge of other work units' construction projects, the Ministry of Forestry reproached us [the planning bureau] for rejecting their application for permission to build a nursery last year while allowing other work units to build apartments in the area. (BDG, 1956*g*)

In addition to construction without permit, many work units cheated by reporting small, redeveloped and temporary construction projects while instead building large, new and permanent structures (BDG, 1957*c*, 1957*d*, 1960*b*, 1960*c*). In 1956 alone, more than 400 work units built so-called 'small structures' (*lingxing jianzhu*) with floor space totalling 3.63 million square metres, of which only 64,000 square metres were in fact small structures – defined by the planning bureau as structures of less than 100 square metres (BDG, 1957*c*). Still others applied for

Figure 4.2. A modern-style workers' convalescent home, 1959.

'quotas for small construction' several times and then pooled them together to build larger projects (*Ibid.*).

Notably, most illegal construction projects were housing and other living facilities such as nurseries, canteens, public bathhouses and social halls. According to a 1956 report, workshops accounted for only 1.8 per cent of the total floor space of illegal construction, while apartment and office buildings accounted for 80.4 per cent (BDG, 1956*d*). 1959 saw a total of 436,704 square metres of illegal construction, of which 96,969 square metres were workshops and storage space, 42,534 square metres offices, 196,579 square metres apartment units, and 100,622 square metres other living facilities (BDG, 1959*a*). In 1963 productive construction constituted of only 26 per cent of the total illegal construction, while the remaining 74 per cent consisted of non-productive construction (BDG, 1964*a*).

Lacking in coordination, construction outside the approved plan resulted in an uneven distribution of services and a mixed land-use pattern within the city. As each work unit built its own offices, housing and welfare facilities, some urban areas were over-provided while others lacked sufficient basic living facilities (BDG, 1956*a*). Within a small area of the Nanyingfang district, for instance, five work units built seven boiler rooms and chimneys, but none of them built other needed facilities in the area (*Ibid.*). Illegal construction projects often brought about changes to the land uses prescribed in master plans (BDG, 1960*a*).

As the gatekeeper of the spatial order in the city, planners made every effort to stop construction outside the plan, which generated much friction between the planning department and work units. Planning reports on the handling of illegal construction cases reveal a polyphony of contention. For example, the planning bureau tried to stop three work units conducting unapproved construction in the Hepingli area in August 1956 (BDG, 1957e). The State Bureau of Construction Technology (SBCT) built a 360 square metre apartment building without permit. The planning bureau demanded that SBCT stop construction and write a 'self-criticism'. SBCT nonetheless continued with the project and built another 300 square metre apartment building. When the planning bureau again requested they desist, Xu, the department chief of SBCT, replied, 'It is definitely impossible to discontinue this project, unless the municipal government gives us housing' (Ibid.). Later, in a phone negotiation, Xu said: 'We won't discontinue construction unless you bring the head of the planning bureau along to talk with the mayor' (Ibid.). He closed the conversation by saying: 'We will continue to build' (Ibid.).

Similarly, a 1959 document recorded various expressions of discontent towards the planning bureau: 'It is bureaucratic to force us to get building approval from the planning bureau'; 'To demolish [a building] is wasteful'; 'A self-criticism is just a self-criticism. It will not affect our construction project'; 'We have built without permit in the past and at present; and we will continue to do so in the future' (BDG, 1959a).

Women played an active role in pushing for the construction of welfare facilities. Almost immediately after the 1949 revolution, women, most of whom

Figure 4.3. Photograph entitled 'Going to work in the morning', showing the new lifestyle of working women, 1960.

had been homebound, were urged to work on an equal level with men. The wife/mother was considered a positive part of the work force (figure 4.3). New mothers were encouraged to go back to work after maternity leave of 54 days (MacQueen, 1977). The changing role of women created an urgent demand for nurseries and kindergartens. The scarcity of childcare facilities at the municipal level forced work units to build their own. Lacking enough state quotas for non-productive construction, such facilities were often built without official approval. Much conflict and strife was generated as the planning bureau tried to turn down any illegal project once identified as such. The Ministry of Labour, for example, built a nursery without permit in 1956, and the structure was demolished after repeated warnings from the planning bureau (BDG, 1957e). Soon afterwards the planning bureau received a letter sent from the ministry, jointly signed by 'a group of mothers'. The letter said: 'The planning bureau has ulterior motivations: its plan is to plan people to death!' (*Ibid*.) The letter warned that mothers were going to write to newspaper editors in revenge.

The Work Unit and the Socialist System

As we have seen, many work units responded to the scarcity of essential living facilities by building them as illegal construction projects outside the state plan. This section asks two key questions: Why did the work units do this? And how did they manage to accomplish this? I address these questions from the perspectives of power relations and the control and allocation of resources. I argue that the transfer of responsibility for provision from the state to the work unit offered the initial impetus for unit leaders to take up workers' welfare, while 'soft budget constraints' as formulated by Kornai (1979, 1980, 1992) shaped the rationale of unit-based provision behaviour. In terms of resource allocation, I argue that the financial system that allowed work units to tap into capital flow and to hoard resources, and the existence of the second (informal) economy provided the conditions for the construction of projects outside the state plan. I shall illustrate each of these aspects in turn.

The Transfer of the Responsibility for Consumption Provision

New scarcity in provision produced by the policy of high accumulation reshaped relations between the state, the work unit and workers. Much political strife was caused by the lack of crucial living facilities during the 1950s. *People's Daily* reported that unhappy workers did not just grumble but publicly expressed their dissatisfaction through diverse forms of protest: strikes, petitions, letters to newspaper editors, and disobedience and opposition to unit leaders (*Renmin ribao*,

1956*b*, 1957*b*, 1957*g*, 1957*h*, 1957*l*). Facing the political pressure caused by urban scarcity, the central state responded by establishing a new ethic through public propaganda which required unit leaders to be responsible for their employees' welfare (*Renmin ribao*, 1956*a*, 1956*c*, 1957*b*, 1957*i*). A 1956 article entitled 'Take better care of workers' lives', for instance, blamed unit party leadership for their indifferent attitude towards the woes of workers (*Renmin ribao*, 1956*c*). Adopting bureaucratic work styles and methods, the article stated, some leaders seldom visited workers or discussed problems with them, while others recognized the problems yet made no effort to improve workers' living conditions (*Ibid.*). Another 1957 article urged unit leaders to keep the welfare of workers in mind despite the adoption of frugality policy (*Renmin ribao*, 1957*i*).

By requiring work unit leaders to take care of their employees, the state established itself as a representative of the 'public interest', while the anger of disgruntled workers over poor living conditions was directed towards the corporate group to which they belonged. Permanent employment granted workers enough power to confront unit leaders in regard to personal problems (*Renmin ribao*, 1957*o*). The mobilization politics fostered by Maoist populism, such as the rectification movements and the Hundred Flowers Movement (1956–1957), exerted further pressure on unit leaders. Managers who incurred the greatest popular indignation might be removed from office by higher levels of authority (*Renmin ribao*, 1957*e*). Meanwhile, unit-based welfare policies were established, step by step, by the state to strengthen the social function of the work unit institutionally (Yang and Zhou, 1999; Bray, 2005, chapter 5).

Political pressure from both workers and administrative levels above them forced unit leaders to make huge efforts to provide necessary means of consumption. At times they took up workers' interests against state management. The rationale can be best illustrated by the words of a housing manager of a sub-unit of the Ministry of Electric Power (BDG, 1957*f*). When the manager was accused by the Beijing Planning Bureau of undertaking illegal construction in 1957, he responded:

As our work unit expands, there is not enough housing for distribution. We have encountered great difficulty, especially with the newspapers' recent demand that requires us to solve our workers' personal problems. Our employees raised more than 2,800 suggestions and criticisms, 90 per cent of which were about housing. What should we do under such circumstances? The state would not approve the construction quota, nor would you [the planning bureau] issue us the building permit. All we could do, therefore, was build without approval. We understand that our mistake is serious; we hope you'll be considerate regarding our case. (*Ibid.*)

This paragraph not only illustrates the conflict generated by the ambiguous position of the socialist state in the sphere of consumption, but also sheds light on worker-manager relations. As the state's systemic preference lay on maximum accumulation, it strove to keep the cost of labour reproduction as low as possible. To alleviate political strife caused by housing scarcity, the state pushed the work unit toward the fulfilment of the responsibility of consumption provision. The new ethic the state established consolidated the political consciousness of workers regarding their right to essential means of consumption on one hand, and directed their demands toward the work unit they belonged to on the other. The unit manager was torn between being responsible to the interests of his workers and being caught overreaching supervision. Eventually, pressures from the newly enfranchised workers forced the manager to step beyond the bounds of state regulations to build housing as illegal construction. The transfer of responsibility for provision from the state to the work unit hence resulted in collusion between the manager and his workers.

Soft Budget

Consumption provision by the work unit represented serious liabilities including low return on investment and periodic maintenance expenses. 'Soft budget constraints' as formulated by Kornai explained the rationale of unit-based provision despite these disadvantages. Kornai, a long-term observer of the Hungarian economy, suggests that the lack of efficiency of a socialist firm is due to the existence of 'the softening of the budget constraint' (Kornai, 1979, 1980, 1992). Under pressure from the unbridled competition of capitalism, an enterprise is aware that its survival and growth depend on profitability, and thus its expenses are strictly limited by budgetary constraint. In the socialist economic system, in contrast, if an enterprise suffers financial losses, the state will cover it sooner or later. Therefore the enterprise can go beyond the currently available or reasonably expected financial resources without much risk, which often leads to thoughtless investment initiatives that harm efficiency.

A 1956 confrontation between a unit manager and the planning bureau illustrates that Kornai's insights are equally valid in the context of Maoist socialism. The Third Bureau of the Ministry of Geology built a garage near the planned road in Hepingli without obtaining a permit from the planning bureau in 1956 (BDG, 1957e). Soon after completion, the garage was demolished at the request of the planning bureau, resulting in a loss of 160,000 RMB yuan. The unit manager was asked to write a 'self-criticism' to guarantee against future violations. Yet in the August of the same year, the work unit built two more projects without permits: a garage larger than the demolished one and an apartment building. Gao, a unit administrative officer, said to the planning bureau:

Our actions were decided by fairly responsible cadres. The fine [you put on us] simply means that money [from the state] was transferred back [to the state]. And we don't care to write another self-criticism. [If you want to] put someone into prison please send our head administrator Liu. We need housing ... we have no alternatives. (*Ibid.*)

This episode provides a vivid example of the indifferent attitude of the work unit toward financial penalties. Work unit revenues were to be submitted to the state anyway; suffering a loss or paying a fine was like robbing one hand, to pay the other. Hence, without the internal disciplinary mechanisms generally characteristic of enterprises under capitalism, work units in principle could exceed budget constraints to meet employees' consumption needs without any serious consequences, as the state would eventually take over the losses.

The statement that the unit leader was ready to go to prison illustrates the way in which the manager was willing to defend workers' interests against state power. After all, managers were not impersonal representatives of state interests. They were real people living in the work unit themselves, sharing with their workers the hard reality of everyday life. The logic of soft budget and 'soft' administrative management (with 'self-criticism' as an inadequate means of discipline), together encouraged the managers to take decisions that benefited their work unit as a 'we' community. The provision role of the work unit thus served as a significant impetus to internal interest and corporate autonomy.

Capital Flow, Resource Hoarding and the Second Economy

Decisions on construction investment were made by three agencies under the jurisdiction of the State Council: the State Planning Commission, the State Economic Commission and the State Construction Commission (Kwok, 1973, pp. 84–87).[5] Construction investment was distributed by the three agencies through central ministries and local governments to individual work units. In principle, state investment targeted specific projects and the implementation of annual plans was under close supervision. Yet in reality, it was possible for individual work units to skim a portion of state investment for other purposes (Naughton, 1997, p. 174). In addition, with a pricing system biased against agriculture, many enterprises were highly profitable. In 1965, for instance, the surplus created by each worker was more than four times the value of his total wages (*Ibid.*). Although technically most surpluses should be transferred to the state, work units had initial control of their own profits. Indeed, it had been a vexing issue for the central state that a great number of work units had pocketed part of their profit for their own use since the early 1950s (Lü and Perry, 1997*b*, p. 10). Despite a series of state investigations into enterprise revenues, such corruption was never effectively stopped; the 'small coffers' of individual work units continued to grow (*Ibid.*).

Major building materials such as steel and cement were brought under centralized control in 1952. The Ministry of Building Materials was established in 1956 to manage their distribution (Chao, 1968). Work units were required to submit applications to the respective 'supply bureau' in order to receive materials for construction. As the application process was time-consuming, it was common for work units to apply for much larger quantities of materials than they needed in order to protect themselves from the risk of being unable to complete a project because of lack of materials. Stockpiles built up in 1953 for this purpose amounted to 30 per cent of the actual yearly consumption of building materials for the construction sector as a whole (*Ibid.*, pp. 144–146). Even in 1956, when serious material shortages halted many construction projects, sizable amounts of unused reserves were held by work units. An incomplete 1957 statistic revealed that 112,600 tons of structural steel, 244,000 cubic metres of timber, and 23,000 tons of cement were stockpiled by work units in nineteen provinces and cities (*Renmin ribao*, 1957d). The hoarding of these materials made the construction of consumption projects outside the state plan possible. A 1961 document, for example, reported that the Nonferrous Metal Research Institute appropriated building materials initially intended for workshop construction to build housing and offices, which included 192 tons of cement, 63 tons of steel, and 970,000 bricks (BDG, 1961a).

Apart from the stockpiling of construction materials, land hoarding also provided favourable conditions for illegal construction. Under state ownership, land was allocated by the local government to work units through administrative methods. Because land was free, work units tended to ask for as much land as possible. During the 1950s, the state tried hard to curb land waste caused by land hoarding, but the tendency continued due to the lack of effective regulations (BDG, 1956c, 1957g, 1961b; *Renmin ribao*, 1957a, 1957e, 1957m). Much of the extra land taken by work units was empty during the early period of their development; built-up areas accounted for less than one-fifth of the land occupied by many work units (*Renmin ribao*, 1957a). The availability of vacant land near workplace allowed work units to build their own set of consumption facilities over time.

The hoarding behaviour was a common feature of socialist enterprises. Kornai considers the socialist system supply-constrained as opposed to demand-constrained capitalism. As the expansionist tendency and investment hunger were inherent in the centrally-planned economy, resource hoarding was a systemic flaw of the socialist system. The result of hoarding was what Kornai (1980) terms 'shortage economy', in which sufficient resources actually existed, but not where they were needed. Shortages provoked a variety of strategies for enterprises to acquire resources from outside the official system of distribution, hence the rise of the second economy. The activities under the second economy ranged from 'black market' exchanges to corruption in distributive networks (Verdery, 1991). Reports show that it was common for work units to barter with each other to obtain needed resources (*Renmin ribao*, 1957d; ZSKYZD, 1998, pp. 740–744). Part of these bartered materials were used for illegal construction (BDG, 1961a).

Between Planning Ideal and Urban Reality

A number of master plans were produced for Beijing in the 1950s. Chinese socialist planners worked together with Soviet specialists to rationalize the previous imperial capital according to modern urban planning principles. In its most significant manifesto, *The Athens Charter*, CIAM defines the keys to city planning as encapsulated in the four functions: housing, work, recreation and traffic. Although Chinese socialist planners usually refrained from quoting CIAM, planning models imported from the Soviet Union had much in common with CIAM planning principles. Planners envisioned a city which would be divided into a number of urban functions, each of which would be subdivided, rationalized and assembled into coherent functional zones. A master plan would connect these zones together, ensuring that each would perform its function in harmony with the others.

The 1953 master plan of Beijing, for example, adopted functional zoning to divide heterogeneous urban activities into exclusive functional zones. Industrial zones were dispersed in suburbs, while new residential areas were located between the old city and new industrial zones (Sit, 1995, pp. 92–97). These homogeneous zones of activities were separated by greenbelts and structured by a network of ring roads supplemented by radial sub-arteries. In the 1957 master plan, following the Russian model, the principle of limited journey to work was established, and the microdistrict was introduced to organize residential areas. Each microdistrict was to be 30–60 hectares with 10,000–20,000 residents (*Ibid.*, p. 97).

It did not take long for planners to realize that the fulfilment of these planning ideals would require a radical restructuring of the urban system. The centrally-planned socialist economy prescribed a vertically-controlled urban growth system. Much of construction investment was project-specific, and was distributed by the central state through ministries to individual work units, while municipalities received only a small share of investment for urban development (Gong and Chen, 1994; Wu, 1999, p. 207). The result was a decentralized pattern of urban growth: each work unit developed its own construction project, over which the municipal government had little control.

The need to build a horizontally coordinated urban system in order to reshape Beijing according to modern planning ideals had been recognized since the early 1950s. A 1954 document issued by the Beijing Municipal Committee, for example, reported that scattered urban growth resulted in a chaotic urbanscape with dispersed construction sites and poorly arranged cultural and welfare facilities (BDG, 1954*a*). It suggested that individual work units should not build any non-productive structure within the production quarter except small ones such as garages, canteens and public toilets. Instead, the city should set up a few key construction areas; all housing and office buildings should be centrally planned, designed and constructed within these key areas. To achieve this goal, the document proposed that construction funds for housing and office buildings should be collected from individual work units. A chief unit should be established to manage construction investment, carry out unitary construction and redistribute buildings to work units (*Ibid.*).

Uncontrolled urban growth was a major worry of the central state. In his 1955 speech 'Several issues in current basic construction', Bo Yibo, the then director of the State Construction Commission, demanded work units to build according to the city's master plan (ZSKYZD, 1998, pp. 778–781). He suggested that offices, housing and public facilities should be planned and constructed by related municipal departments. The 'six-unification' (*liutong*) principle was raised in the State Council's 1956 resolution on the construction of new industrial districts and towns (*Ibid.*, p. 789). In order to create an economic and viable urban infrastructure, the resolution requested housing and socio-cultural facilities to be put under unitary 'planning, designing, construction, distribution, adjustment and management' (*Ibid.*). The resolution also requested cities to be managed by local municipalities.

Throughout the 1950s and 1960s, the 'six-unification' principle was addressed repeatedly in numerous planning documents, but it was never successfully implemented. Individual work units preferred building their own housing and facilities. A 1956 planning report, for instance, complained that there were far too many units managing urban construction (BDG, 1956*f*). It reported that there were over 500 construction units in 1954; in 1955 the number dropped to 250 as a result of the implementation of a new policy which required construction to be managed by the respective municipal departments, but 1956 saw the number increase again to more than 300. The document urged that construction should be brought under centralized management to change the uncontrolled state of urban growth.

The ideal model for residential development for planners was a combination of the principle of functional zoning, the close association of work and residence, and unitary neighbourhood planning. As articulated in a 1955 document, residence should be separated from the production quarter, neighbouring work units should share a unitarily designed living quarter, and welfare and cultural facilities should be planned along with housing to form integrated neighbourhoods (BDG, 1955). Many 'new villages' were proposed according to this model, but only a small number were built. A 1956 document reported that, although more than 1.7 million square metres had been constructed by April 1956 in the Guangxiang area of western suburban Beijing, only two integrated residential districts –

Baiwanzhuang and Sanlihe – were successfully built, which accounted for one-eighth of the total new construction floor space in the area (BDG, 1956a).

The same document reported that residential development proposals made by the planning department largely remained on paper. For instance, the department planned a residential district in the area of Xinjiekouwai in the early 1950s, but the three work units occupying the land could not afford the construction at that time, nor did they allow other work units to use their land to build. As a result, the plan was abandoned (Ibid.). The idea of setting up key construction areas also proved difficult to execute. In 1954, for example, the planning department mobilized more than thirty work units to participate in a construction plan in the Guangbailu area, which would have enabled housing and office buildings to be planned and built in a coordinated way (Ibid.). Initially eighteen work units agreed to take part, but many subsequently withdrew. In the end, only seven units joined the construction plan. In the following year, planners set up another ambitious plan to develop Nanheyuan into a key construction area, but despite their best efforts, only one work unit agreed to participate and eventually only one building was erected in the area. (Ibid.)

From the late 1950s. planners aspired to achieve a new spatial order and an even distribution of scarce consumption facilities in the city by replacing scattered living quarters within individual work units with unitarily planned microdistricts (chapter 2). However, several factors prevented the realization of their ideas. Construction investment was channelled through all-powerful vertical sectoral lines, over which the planning department had little control. The department operated in an environment lacking effective legal procedures to execute its intentions; administrative measures were simply too weak to bring decentralized urban growth and illegal construction to an end. Furthermore, the central state oscillated between the intention to crack down on spatial disorder and the willingness to tolerate demands necessitated by labour reproduction.

On one hand, the state continued to condemn the unruly situation of urban construction and to request individual work units to follow planning regulations (ZSKYZD, 1998, p. 798). On the other hand, as the state supported the idea of unit-based provision, it was somewhat sympathetic towards the fact that some living facilities were built by work units as illegal construction projects. At times, the Beijing Planning Bureau was dismissed by the state for being too strict and bureaucratic, and for not considering workers' 'real needs'. In a 1956 work plan, for example, the planning department was forced to slam its own bureaucratic and authoritative attitude in handling work units that conducted illegal construction (BDG, 1956h). Another document of the same year reported that, at the request of the Beijing Municipal People's Committee, the department wrote a self-criticism and refunded fines to the units that built without a permit (BDG, 1956i).

The Chinese state was sufficiently pragmatic not to follow planning orthodoxies blindly, but to adapt to the changing urban reality. Dense, self-contained communities were favoured as they helped to minimize human flows and thus reduced the demand for massive investments in large and extensive public transport systems. The principle of the close association between work and home was stressed, while the idea of strict segregation of land use was disputed in the June 1958 master plan of Beijing (Sit, 1995, p. 98). Institutional support for unit-based social provision was gradually established by the central state. A 1952 document showed that the Factory Head Foundation (*changzhang jijing*) was established to support the construction of welfare facilities, although investment from this foundation was far below what was required if a comprehensive welfare system was to be built (ZSKYZD, 1989, p. 629). The book *Zhongguo danwei zhidu* (The Chinese Work Unit System) lists a series of state welfare policies closely related to the work-unit-based provision established during the 1950s (Yang and Zhou, 1999, pp. 54–59).

Urban planning turned out to be a feeble intermediate element under Chinese socialism, unable to cast a new spatial order according to the profession's own preferences. With the arrival of the Cultural Revolution (1966–1976), the city's master plan was suspended in 1967, and the Beijing Planning Bureau was dismantled in 1968 and not re-established until 1972 (Sit, 1995, p. 205). Beijing was in a period of planning anarchy; a great deal of piece-meal urban development was carried out by individual work units. By 1989, work units owned 90 per cent of urban public housing, while only 10 per cent was controlled by the municipal government (Zhongguo chengshi jianshe nianjian bianweihui, 1989).

Power, Space and Everyday Life

In both capitalist and socialist societies, labour must be reproduced, but this necessity is threatened by the dynamics of accumulation under the respective mode of production. The capitalist free market system allows individuals and enterprises to occupy equal footing in exchange, but as Marx points out, 'exchange value already in itself implies compulsion over the individual' (Marx, 1973, p. 248). Such a compulsion comes from competition: capitalists are free to dispose the surplus they appropriate but those who accumulate slowly face the danger of being pushed out of business by those who accumulate faster. Unbridled competition among enterprises results in a reluctance to invest in less profitable spheres including the provision of crucial consumption facilities, which endangers labour reproduction and thus the continuing production of surplus value. According to Castells (1977), as private capital has shown a marked inability to produce crucial social facilities, it falls to the state to intervene in the reproduction of labour power. In the process the state assumes a dual function: while its structurally-defined role is to maintain the relations of capitalist domination, it achieves this by responding to the power exerted by different classes. The substitution of bureaucratic criteria for the market, however, turned the principle of 'allocation according to the capacity to pay' into 'allocation according to need'. With increased state intervention in the sphere of collective consumption, 'the entire urban perspective becomes politicized', which has given rise to an upsurge of urban movements in welfare capitalist society.

Under Chinese socialism, the state set up national goals, controlled the means of production, and regulated the accumulation and distribution of capital and surplus value. The organization of production and consumption overlapped under the socialist mode of production, but the conflicts relating to social provision did not disappear. With a strong drive to catch up with the more advanced countries, the Chinese state strove to achieve maximum accumulation of capital for industrialization, which created a fundamental contradiction between the needs of capital accumulation and the necessity of labour reproduction. In comparison with welfare capitalist society, an opposite process took place in the sphere of consumption under Chinese socialism: the responsibility for social provision was transferred from the state to individual work units in the face of political strife caused by urban scarcity.

Due to the lack of the competitive mechanisms characteristic of capitalism, work units were willing to develop essential means of consumption for their own workers despite low return on investment and other liabilities. The redistribution system was so designed that it was possible for work units to switch a portion of capital from production to consumption via both formal and informal channels. Planners worked hard to reverse the development of the self-contained work unit by consistently stressing coordinated urban growth, but they were unable to correct the all-powerful tendency created by the system.

While initially designed as a unit of production, the work unit gradually developed into the basic unit of collective consumption. The peculiar form of provision, as this chapter reveals, was not a result of abstract structural requirements, but an outcome of the struggles between social agents (the central state, the municipality, planners, unit leaders, workers) at a specific stage of Chinese socialism. Each element – personal consumption, political action and state intervention – created its own dynamics under the historically constituted condition of urban scarcity, and it was the interactions between these elements that gave rise to the unique configuration of the work unit. To paraphrase Lefèbvre 1991a), the space of the work unit was therefore not an innocent geometric form but infused with the logic of Chinese socialism.

The cellular pattern of collective consumption has important political implications for contemporary Chinese society. First, the work unit came to serve as a 'power container' that facilitated the construction and maintenance of the socialist order. As in capitalist society, consumption provision became increasingly politicized under state socialism once the principle of 'allocation according to need' was established. In response to the consequent social conflicts, the state offloaded the responsibility of consumption provision on to individual work units. Social grief generated by the scarcity of necessities became encapsulated within individual work units while leaving the basic relations of political domination intact. The state appeared as the representative of 'public interest' in the sphere of consumption; contradictions between needs of accumulation and the necessity of reproduction were fought at the unit level rather than on a society-wide basis. With this new structure of power relations, a socialist urban system was stabilized despite the continuing presence of scarcity.

Second, the work unit as an integrated unit of everyday life contributed to the reproduction of social relations. Castells (1977) points out that the welfare state dominates in the management of everyday life through its intervention in the sphere of collective consumption. A salient feature of the work unit is its dual function in organizing both production and consumption. This overlapping role facilitated an all-embracing socialist mode of domination of everyday life. The mingling of work and home allowed the interplay of diverse socialist means for disciplining labour, relying on a combination of ideological appeal, moral imperative and cultural norms (chapter 3; Dutton, 1992; Bray, 2005). Workers came to depend on their unit not only for remunerative work but also for a whole array of needs and desires (Walder, 1986; Li and Li, 2000, chapter 4). The enclosed space of the work unit served as the general frame of reference for social life – within it the various competitions, accusations and struggles could be performed, while the frame itself belonged to the domain of silent complicity beyond any contestation.

Work-unit-based collective consumption nonetheless generated a new set of contradictions within the system. Work units' access to resources varied considerably according to their administrative and sectoral status in the national hierarchy. As each work unit developed consumption facilities for the exclusive use of its own members, the result was an uneven and fragmented welfare system. Furthermore, the switch of provision responsibility from the state to the work unit pushed the latter toward corporate autonomy. As we have seen, unit managers' upholding of internal interests undermined their predominant loyalty to the administrative levels above. To satisfy workers' needs, the work unit paid the increasing cost of labour reproduction, which was achieved by diverting capital from the production to consumption circuit. As a result, the more the work unit assumed the responsibility for the production and maintenance of consumption facilities, the more it became inefficient in extracting surplus value. While individual work units could go beyond budget constraints without much risk, the state suffered from the tendency for the rate of accumulation to fall.

Notes

1. I also conducted archival study in Shanghai and Wuhan in 2000. The post-1949 archival materials made available to the public are highly selective in each archive. I selected Beijing for the case study due to the availability of a large number of planning reports. Cities, of course, differed from each other in many respects. There were, for example, more central work units than local units in Beijing than in other cities; Beijing, provincial capital cities and key industrial cities were relatively resource-rich compared with other Chinese cities. Nonetheless, as newspaper articles, published documents (e.g. ZSKYZD, 1989, 1998) and other publications show, there was a great degree of commonality shared by cities under Mao in terms of the shortage of housing and other living facilities, the uncoordinated pattern of urban growth, and planning deficiency. This chapter presents the beginnings of a framework to understand the production of space under Chinese socialism based on these existing materials.
2. All quotations from archival documents in this book are my translation.
3. To ensure that urban housing was affordable to all, the state adopted a low rent policy for public housing. In 1958 the municipality of Beijing set the average monthly rental for residential housing at 0.27 RMB yuan per square metre. In 1966, the rent was further decreased to 0.24 RMB yuan per square metre (Sit, 1995, pp. 206–207). The state also put strict controls over private housing so that rental prices fell in line with the general low-rent situation. In 1958, a policy was adopted in Beijing which required that renting of all private property should be the prerogative of the government (*Ibid.*). Because the costs of maintenance were often higher than rent income, many landlords were unwilling to lease their property. The discouragement of private provision hence contributed to housing scarcity.
4. During the early 1950s, single workers or those who married but moved to the city alone were the majority of the total working force. When the state planned residential buildings for new work units, it followed a quota in which married workers only accounted for 60 per cent of all workers (*Renmin ribao*, 1957o). As single workers got married and married workers brought their families to the city, the demand for family housing was gradually increased (*Ibid.*).
5. The State Planning Commission was responsible for drafting national economic plans, including integration, revision and appraisal of long-term plans and annual plans from ministries as well as those of provincial, local and municipal governments. The State Economic Commission managed the short-term plans and coordinated between the planning departments within the ministries and bureaus. The State Construction Commission controlled national investment programmes, including new construction and redevelopment projects (Kwok, 1973, p. 84–86).

Chapter Five

Modernity as Utopia: Planning the People's Commune, 1958–1960

You simply cannot make an omelette without breaking eggs, as a whole line of modernist thinkers from Goethe to Mao have noted. The literary archetype of such a dilemma is ... Goethe's *Faust*. An epic hero prepared to destroy religious myths, traditional values, and customary ways of life in order to build a brave new world out of the ashes of the old, Faust is, in the end, a tragic figure.

David Harvey, 1989, *The Condition of Postmodernity*

'[T]he establishment of people's communes ... is the fundamental policy to guide the peasants to accelerate socialist construction, complete the building of socialism ahead of time and carry out the gradual transition to communism' (Lethbridge, 1963, p. 72). This statement, made in the resolution adopted by the Chinese Communist Party (CCP) Politburo meeting in August 1958, became the keynote for the subsequent development of the people's commune movement. The Party claimed that the commune was to be a new organizational form which integrated industry, agriculture, trade, education and military affairs. The commune movement aimed to improve production forces, eliminate urban-rural distinctions, promote collective living, and free women from the drudgery of home life (Zhonggong zhongyang wenxian yanjiushi, hereafter ZZWY, 1995, pp. 598–623).

Concurrent with sweeping institutional changes, the state mobilized planners, architects and students in spatial disciplines to make planning proposals for the newly established communes. Designers boldly experimented with modernist design between 1958 and 1960. The countless proposals they produced represented a complete negation of the existing rural life world. Scattered, small villages were reordered into concentrated, large residential clusters. In place of diverse vernacular dwellings, modernist structures were arranged in a rigidly stipulated order. Yet despite the energy and enthusiasm instilled in these plans, they rarely progressed from paper. A series of agricultural disasters and other factors resulted in a severe famine, which claimed millions of lives between 1959 and 1961. The state decided to retreat and shift the emphasis of development from industry to agriculture in 1961.

Today, with China back on track in the sober quest of modernization, the commune movement has been dismissed by both the party leadership and researchers of contemporary China as a historical aberration. This chapter is an attempt to come to terms with the complex relationship between the commune movement and Chinese modernity at the moment of the demise of revolutionary visions. I approach the movement not as an isolated event in the turmoil of early Chinese socialist development, but as a project to articulate an alternative modernity that had much in common with modernist programmes in other parts of the world. In particular, I explore an intriguing aspect of Third World modernism – the 'utopianization' of modernity – by looking into the curious combination of modernist and utopian elements in commune design.

Utopia and Modernity in the Third World Context

From backward-looking, naïve fantasies of the Golden Age, to the futuristic prospect of the Millennium, the land of Utopia is simultaneously an indefinitely remote place and a place of ideal perfection. The ambiguity of utopia is indeed already implicit in Sir Thomas More's coinage of the term in his 1515 book *Utopia*: *ou-topos*, 'nowhere', and *eu-topos*, 'somewhere good' (Hansot, 1974, p. 2). The *Shorter Oxford English Dictionary*, tracing the initial reference back to More, defines utopia as 'a place, state, or condition ideally perfect in respect of laws, customs and conditions' or 'an impossibly ideal scheme, especially for social improvement'. The double meaning of utopia suggests its ambiguous relationship with history. While history is the imperfect reality that men are in the process of creating, utopia is the perfect, yet futile future that men hope for (Meisner, 1982, p. 3). Thus, for thinkers like Marx and Engels, utopia is defined largely in terms of its negative function of obstructing the revolution (Levitas, 1990, chapter 1).

Utopia may not be able to bring about change directly, but it certainly plays an important role in disrupting the taken-for-granted nature of the present and in pushing people to think about an alternative future. In his book, *The Principle of Hope*, the German philosopher Ernst Bloch coins the notion of the 'Not Yet', which carries the meaning of something that is not *yet* but is expected, stressing a future presence, and also something that is still *not*, stressing an absence in the present (Bloch, 1986). For Bloch, the futurology of possibilities embraces 'the growing realization of the realizing element', instructs people to will and desire better, and may eventually effect emancipation (*Ibid.*, p. 209).

The Not Yet, however, has a different connotation within a Third World historical context. Dipesh Chakrabarty (2000, p. 8) considers colonial historicism to be the colonizers' way of saying 'not yet' to non-European peoples, who were forced to wait until they became 'civilized enough to rule themselves'. This 'psychological violence', according to Franz Fanon, drove the colonized to believe that the values and institutions of the metropolitan power are superior to their own, generating a sense of self-hatred: 'The look that the native turns on the settler's town is a look of lust, a look of envy; it expresses his dreams of possession – all manner of possession...' (1968, p. 39). After independence, despite the end of direct colonial rule, the vision of an evolutionary history sustained. Admitting that all nations were heading for the same destination and that some people arrived earlier than others, the Not Yet was built into Third World modernity and profoundly shaped visions of the kind of world people would build if they were free from the difficulties of reality.

Therefore, the imaginary 'waiting room' did not disappear after independence; instead, the acute self-awareness of the temporal lag developed into a nationalistic aspiration for modernization. As Bloch has described, the Not Yet in a Third World context was a combination of absence and anterior presence, longing and potential satisfaction, and anguish of scarcity and hope of fulfilment. Yet unlike most modern Western utopias that serve as critiques on industrial modernity, the latter was the dominant objective of Third World utopias. An all-encompassing project of modernization was not only at the top of national agenda but also the collective, state-controlled dream. If utopia is the 'expression of the desire for a better way of being and living' (Levitas, 1990, p. 8), industrial modernity was turned into this better way of being in Third World countries. The numerous blueprints sparked by official utopianism in these countries often did not go beyond what had already happened or was happening in the developed world: abundance, industrialization, electricity and automation. It was precisely because modernization had not happened, but was yet to come, that potential existed to employ the vision to 'teach desire to desire, to desire better, to desire more, and above all to desire in a different way' (Thompson, 1977, p. 791). This vision of modernity was, therefore, not simply an end, but a process. I argue that this utopianization of modernity is an important dimension of Third World modernism.

Chinese modernity was at once a socialist and a Third World one, hence the quest for an alternative future modernity was even more thoroughly entangled in the complex relationship between developmentalist drives and revolutionary aspirations. In his insightful book *Seeing Like a State*, James Scott (1998, p. 90) defines 'high modernism' as 'a particularly sweeping vision of how the benefits of technical and scientific progress might be applied – usually through the state – in every field of human activity'. With the close alliance between modernism and state power within a socialist context, the proliferation of high modernist faith was particularly favoured. Planners, architects and technicians strived to 'use state power to bring about huge, utopian changes in people's work habits, living patterns, moral conduct and worldview' (*Ibid.*, p. 5). Seeing the past as an impediment to the realization of an ideal future, high modernism determined to create a legible and ultimately controllable order out of messy reality through scientific, authoritarian state planning. In this respect, the Chinese people's commune movement can be conceived of as a concrete manifestation of the high modernist vision. Built on fantasies of industrial and social modernity, commune modernism was directed by a faith in the possibility of overcoming the past to create a brand new world. Like many high modernist experiments in other parts of the world, however, the mass utopia only left a history of disasters in its wake. The sections that follow will provide a historical account of how the tragedy came about.

The Rise of People's Communes

China's political atmosphere changed rapidly in 1958. The significant success of the first Five-Year Plan (1953–1957) gave the state the confidence to believe that spectacular economic growth was possible (ZZWY, 1995, pp. 431–439). An ambitious plan for 1958–1962 was launched, which aimed for an overall increase of 75 per cent, in both industrial and agricultural production, and a 50 per cent increase in national income by the end of the plan (Hsu, 2000, p. 654). In early February 1958, the National People's Congress announced the 'Great Leap Forward' Movement for the next three years to create an intensive and urgent work environment. Overtaking Britain within 15 years in the production of steel and other major industrial products became the official goal (Su, 1985, p. 219).

A piecemeal amalgamation of agricultural producers' cooperatives was launched by local leaders in various parts of China amid the frantic drive towards the Great Leap. Several cadres in Suiping, Henan, took the first step towards communization by forming a federation of 27 Advanced Agricultural Producers' Cooperatives (Kang, 1998, pp. 12–15).[1] In an inspection tour in early August 1958, the Party leader Mao Zedong praised this new move and decided to push it further. A resolution was adopted at the CCP's enlarged politburo meeting in Beidaihe, calling for the formation of people's communes in rural areas. The resolution declared two primary objectives for the movement: 'The all-round, continuous leap forward in China's agricultural production; and the ever-rising political consciousness of the 500 million peasants' (Lethbridge, 1963, p. 71). Official approval gave a forceful push to the movement. By September 1958, 23,397 rural communes had been established in 27 provinces, embracing 90.4 per cent of rural households (Song, 2002, p. 177). After some successful communes were established in several major cities, the Party decided in early 1960 that the urban commune served a useful economic purpose, and that it was possible to carry out its development on a larger scale (Luard, 1960).[2] In April 1960, it was reported that the total membership of urban communes reached 20 million (Salaff, 1967).

The motivations behind the movement were multiple.[3] The commune movement was conceived with deep ideological roots. While the Soviet leader Nikita Khrushchev criticized Mao for being to radical when he visited Beijing in summer 1958, Mao, in announcing the establishment of the communes, maintained that the Chinese were moving ahead of Russia in becoming communist (Kang, 1998, pp. 20–22). The commune aimed to revolutionize traditional social institutions by collectivizing family life. Communal services such as public canteens, nurseries, kindergartens, and public homes for the aged were considered essential to achieve these goals (ZZWY, 1995, pp. 599, 615–616). The range of such establishments varied from commune to commune, but the operation of public canteens was widely adopted (figure 5.1). The system of supplying 'free meals' to commune members through public canteens not only aimed to free women from housework, but was also considered an essential step towards implementing the principle of distribution according to one's need (*Ibid.*, pp. 517–522, 604–606). By introducing industry into rural areas and establishing similar functions for the countryside and the city, the leadership hoped that the urban–rural differences could be reduced (*Ibid.*, p. 582).

The commune functioned as an efficient means to facilitate state taxation and mobilize surplus rural labour in irrigation and other agricultural construction works. Chinese agricultural doctrine moved towards collectivization step by step.[4] Shortly after the 1949 revolution, land was distributed to peasants, which helped to break up the traditional social stratification (Pye, 1984, p. 264). The Cooperative initiated in 1954 required member households to pool land together while allowing each member to retain ownership. The Collective in 1956–1957 introduced the principle of property amalgamation; with the abolition of private ownership of land, a member's reward was totally dependent on his labour. By abolishing the last vestiges of private ownership, the commune system was another step to achieve fuller collectivization, through which the state acquired a higher level of control over rural labour and farm products (ZZWY, 1995, p. 608).

Within a Cold War context, each commune was considered a military unit, which organized adults into militia and put them under military training (*Ibid.*, pp. 618–620). This greatly helped to strengthen the collectivization of rural life. A Party magazine depicted the new life style in the Chaoying commune in Hunan:

At daybreak, bells ring and whistles blow for assembly... In about a quarter of an hour the peasants line up. At the command of company and squad commanders, the teams march

Figure 5.1. Peasants eating
in the canteen, 1961.

to the fields, holding flags. Here, one no longer sees peasants in groups of two or three, smoking and going slowly and leisurely to the fields. What one hears are the sounds of measured steps and marching songs. The desultory living habits which have been with the peasants for thousands of years are gone forever. (quoted in Lethbridge, 1963, p. 84)

'The Education of Desire'

Radical institutional changes necessarily involve the creation of newly desired objects and desiring subjects. The utopian vision may be denounced by some as escapist; for others it '[embodies] in the forms of fantasy alternative values sketched in an alternative way of life' (Thompson, 1955, 1976, p. 790). E.P. Thompson points out that:

in such an adventure two things happen: our habitual values (the 'commonsense' of bourgeois society) are thrown into disarray. And we enter Utopia's proper and new-found space: *the education of desire. (Ibid.)*

Utopia hence represents a broadening of aspirations in terms of human fulfilment. This education of desire motivates individuals to pursue a better future by turning the abstract elements of an alternative society into the concrete.

The immediate problem for the CCP leaders was how to project an attractive vision for the new establishment. Two historical commune experiments were cited: the Paris Commune of 1871, and the peasant communes in the Soviet Union in the 1930s. Elements of previous works on ideal society were employed to facilitate new social imaginings. A finely phrased passage from Marx's *The German Ideology* became the most quoted passage in official publications, in which Marx exclaimed that the communist society would be a world in which 'nobody has one exclusive sphere of activity but each can become accomplished in any branch he wishes' (Hsu, 2000, p. 587). Mao drew upon the late Qing reformer Kang Youwei's work, *Datong shu* (The Book of Universal Commonwealth) to characterize the commune as *da* (grand) and *gong* (public) (Kang, 1998, p. 21). In *Datong shu*, Kang (1900, 1994) depicted a perfect world in which there was no private ownership while public hospitals, welfare, free education and homes for the aged were provided for all. Kang also suggested the abolition of the family paradigm and the emancipation of women from servitude in the kitchen. Some of these elements were reflected in commune organization (Chi, 1967, pp. 62–78).

Soon, the commune movement produced its own utopian visions. Tan Zhenling, the Minister of Agriculture, gave a vivid illustration of how people would live if visions came to fruition:

[W]hat does Communism mean?... First, taking good food and not merely eating one's fill. At each meal one enjoys a meat diet, eating chicken, pork, fish or eggs...

Second, clothing. Everything required is available. Clothing of various designs and styles, not a mass of black garments or a mass of blue outfits. After working hours, people will wear silk, satin and woollen suits...

Third, housing. Housing is brought up to the standard of modern cities. What should be modernized? People's communes. Central heating is provided in the north and air-conditioning in the south. All will live in [high-rises]. Needless to say, there are electric lights, telephones, piped water, receiving sets and TV...

... Communism means this: food, clothing, housing, transportation, cultural entertainment, science institutes, and physical culture. The sum total of these [mean] Communism. (quoted from MacFarquhar, 1983, p. 84)

What is remarkable about this utopian vision is its attempt to equate abundance and modern conveniences with what communism had to offer to humankind. Most of its elements were amenities already common in advanced capitalist societies but were now presented as objects of desire for commune dreamers.

The commune movement ushered in a new era of rural aspiration. Sparked by official optimism, numerous artistic works were produced by peasants, depicting desired changes. Poetry competitions were held in villages, new folk songs were performed, and *dazibao*, the 'big character posters', were employed to publicize poems and proposals (Mao, 1971, pp. 499–500). It was reported that in Zhayashan People's Commune, peasant poets produced more than 30,000 poems within one year (Kang, 1998, pp. 241–242). In countless folksongs, poems and posters, peasants expressed their fervent yearning for prosperity and modernization. In an artistic rendering of a commune in south China, for example, modern factories were proudly juxtaposed in harmony with vernacular architecture (figure 5.2). A 1958 poster depicted a happy peasant holding a plate full of cotton, vegetables and fruits (Yang, 1958). Some lyrics, furthermore, reflected the official rhetoric of development (Kang, 1998, p. 198; my translation):

Peasants are driving tractors
Food and cotton are heaped in mounds
Standing on the mountain looking west
Little Britain is nowhere to be found

As photographs of factories, bridges, dams and power plants frequently appeared in official propaganda publications to demonstrate the industrial and technological accomplishments of the new nation, they became recurring themes in rural visions (figure 5.3). One example is representative of countless others (*Ibid.*, p. 215; my translation):

There are nine silver dragons that cross the garden
Pounding to produce electric power in the village's southern corner
For sixty-six huge factories
And ninety-nine huge workshops.
To the east of the village, geese and ducks fill the reservoir
To the west, cattle and sheep ramble on the mountain
The heaven and earth, the mountain and the river
Are as beautiful as brocade
In a happy life with boundless joy.

As in the early period of the Western industrial revolution, there was an aestheticized fetishism of machinery (Marx, 1994). A 1958 report of a commune in Jiangxi Province took 'the hum of blowers, the panting of gasoline engines, the honking of heavily-laden lorries, and the bellowing of oxen hauling ore and coal' as welcoming signs of social improvement (Spence, 1990, p. 580). Although electrification had been realized in Chinese cities, most rural villages were still lit with kerosene lamps. Electric lamps, together with other modern facilities such as telephones, were symbols of ideal life for peasants. 'Up and down the building, electric lamps and telephones' (*loushang louxia, diandeng dianhua*) was a most popular catchphrase of the day. Modern-style housing became the new paradigm in rural fantasies. A planning illustration by peasants, for instance, depicted the commune as a huge walled town (figure 5.4). Within the town, modernist, multi-storey flats sat side by side existing village pitch-roofed, single-storey buildings.

Figure 5.2. Vernacular architecture of a riverside village in south China juxtaposed with smokestacks and modern buildings, representing the new rural aspirations, 1961.

Rural utopian dreamers aspired to possess electricity, machinery and modern architecture, things that were available in the city but had not yet developed in the countryside. The city was invoked as an object of comparison, as Zhou Libo expressed through the words of a village official in his famous novel *Great Changes in a Mountain Village* (1958):

It'll be soon, we won't have to wait for ten or even five years. Then we'll use some of the co-operative's accumulated funds to buy a lorry and when you women go to the theatre in the town, you can ride a lorry. With electric light, telephones, lorries and tractors we shall live more comfortably than they do in the city, because we have the beautiful landscape and [fresh] air. (quoted from Becker, 1996, p. 61)

Figure 5.3. Illustrations representing the ideal rural life, 1958.

Figure 5.4. Plan for Xiefang Production Team, Suicheng People's Commune, Henan, 1958.

The Spatial Revolution

Generations of dreamers found their utopias in ideal physical forms, which led
Lewis Mumford to go so far as to claim that 'the first utopia was the city itself'
(1973, p. 3). The Chinese leadership certainly held the same conviction. In
the autumn of 1958, the state ordered urban-based planners and architects to
'go down' to the countryside and work with local peasants to plan commune
residential clusters. Professors and students of architecture, urban planning and
geography were also mobilized to create commune design proposals (figure 5.5).
The Geography Department of Beijing Normal University, for example, sent work
teams to eight provinces, including Inner Mongolia, Shandong, Henan, Sicuan,
Ganshu, Hubei, Guangxi and Fujian (*Dili zhishi*, 1959, p. 84). Within one month,
these work teams, each consisting of two to three members, completed planning
for 16 communes, wrote 24 guidebooks, and produced 160 drawings (*Ibid.*).

To raise the political consciousness of peasants and increase agricultural output, socialist planners believed that traditional rural settlements should be revolutionized through a fundamental reorganization of the physical environment. Elements from the neighbourhood unit concept and the microdistrict schema were taken to plan the commune as a combination of economic activities, civic administration and residences. A new discursive formation of the 'residential cluster' (*jumin dian*) soon became prevalent and fuelled new visions for rural planning (Pei, Liu and Shen, 1958; Wang and Cheng, 1959; Wu, 1959). Planners held that scattered, undersized villages should be reordered into concentrated, large quarters according to modern neighbourhood planning and design

Figure 5.5. Designers and commune cadres discussing the planning of Xiangfang People's Commune, Ha'erbin, 1960.

principles, with the residential cluster as the basic unit (figure 5.6). Proper links between the agricultural field, the industrial area and the residential quarter were stressed, and efforts were made to integrate social facilities and parks. Based on commune planning experiences in north-east China, for example, Wang Shuoke and Chen Jingqi (1959) proposed that population size should be between 4,000 and 10,000, based on factors such as population density, geography and production scale. Their article established a number of principles for site selection and development scale, and suggested four types of residential clusters: the central town (3,000–100,000 residents) complete with social, cultural and educational facilities; the satellite residential cluster (10,000–15,000 residents), accommodating major agricultural and industrial production; the specialized residential cluster (3,000–4,000 residents) for small production units such as pastures and orchards; and the work station (300–400 residents) for resting and storage (figure 5.7). Wu Luoshan (1959) proposed the establishment of proper links between agricultural land, residential quarters, social services and green spaces. The influence of Ebenezer Howard's garden city idea was evident.

The distribution of residential clusters was based on the optimum distances between central residential clusters and satellite clusters (figure 5.8). Similar to the microdistrict, the organization of community facilities within each residential cluster was based on the 'service radii' of the facilities and the number of residents they served (Liaoningsheng jiansheting, 1958). Nurseries, kindergartens, primary schools, social halls, canteens, sports fields and gardens were arranged

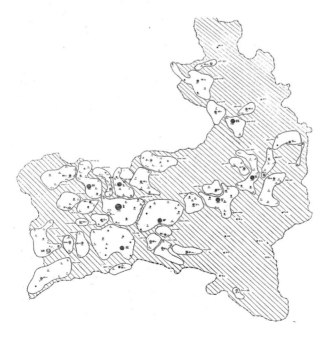

Figure 5.6. A diagram showing how to combine scattered, small villages into large residential clusters based on commune planning experiences from northeast China, 1959.

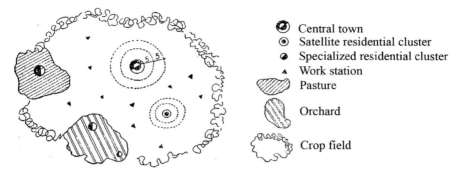

Figure 5.7. Different types of residential cluster, 1959.

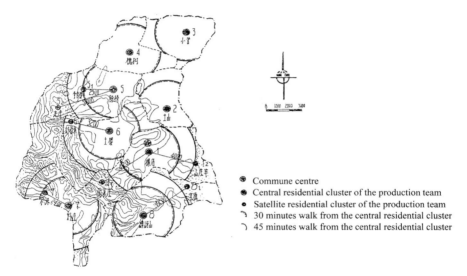

Figure 5.8. The distribution of residential clusters, Satellite People's Commune, Suiping, Henan, 1958. The commune consisted of 238 villages laid out on 214 square kilometres of land. The selection of locations for central residential clusters was based on the optimum distances between central and satellite residential clusters.

within easy walking distance (figure 5.9). However, unlike the microdistrict, which was purely residential, the residential cluster was to be a multifunctional unit that integrated industry, agriculture, trade, education and military. The scale and content of commune planning was hence close to those of regional planning. The plan for Xiaozhan Commune in Tianjin is a case in point (Tianjin daxue jianzhuxi, 1958). The commune occupied an area of 2 million *mu* (134,000 hectares), encompassing a population of 60,000 and 19 villages (figure 5.10). The commune plan reorganized the population into seven residential clusters. The central residential cluster, situated at the site of the existing town, was the

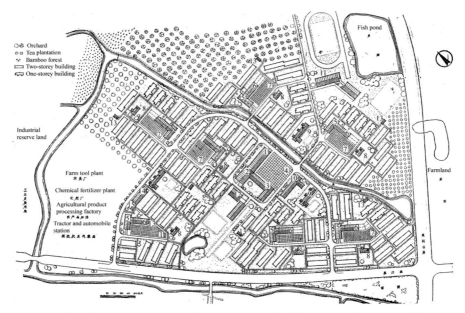

Figure 5.9. Site plan of a 'new village' for a commune of 1,208 residents, Shanghai, 1958. *Key*: 1 Administrative office; 2 Club; 3 Department store; 4 Central Square; 5 Canteen and attached services; 6 Storage; 7 Sunning ground; 8 Nursery; 9 Kindergarten; 10 Clinic; 11 Middle school; 12 Primary school; 13 Toilet; 14 Bathhouse; 15 Sewing workshop

commune's political, economic, cultural, and administrative centre. Regardless of the original locations of existing villages, six residential clusters were placed near the intersection of major highways, each accommodating several neighbourhoods. In the plan for the Southwest Settlement, for example, an 'L' shaped territory was divided into five neighbourhoods, each of which was about 5 acres and consisted of 1,000 residents belonging to two production teams. The per capita land-use standard was set at 40 square metres, slightly higher than that used in the city (35 square metres). One canteen was provided for every 500 residents, two nurseries and one kindergarten for each neighbourhood, and two neighbourhoods shared one primary school (figure 5.11). Each residential cluster had a park, a community centre and an industrial district.

Modern neighbourhood planning principles were sometimes adapted to new functional requirements; a target range, for example, was incorporated into many design proposals as peasants were to be organized into commune militias (*Ibid.*). In keeping with the goal of collectivizing rural life, some designers adopted radical standards to weaken the family unit and free women from the drudgery of housework. Families were to be separated and housed in different buildings or apartment units (figure 5.12). Except married couples, adults were assigned into

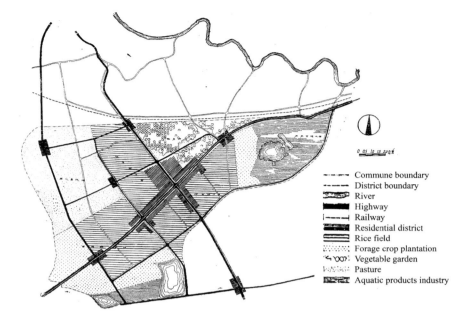

Commune boundary
District boundary
River
Highway
Railway
Residential district
Rice field
Forage crop plantation
Vegetable garden
Pasture
Aquatic products industry

Figure 5.10. Master plan of Xiaozhan People's Commune, Tianjin, 1958.

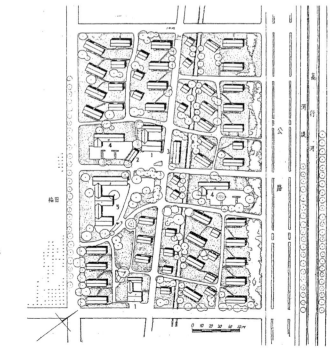

Figure 5.11.
Neighbourhood site
plan, Xiaozhan People's
Commune, Tianjin.
Key: 1 Canteen and
club; 2 Office and post
office; 3 Shops and
library; 4 Nursery; 5
Kindergarten.

dormitory rooms where three to four persons of the same sex shared the same space (Wang *et al.*, 1958). Aged people stayed in retirement homes, and young children boarded at kindergartens or residential schools. All were expected to eat in public canteens (figure 5.13). In a housing proposal for Suicheng People's Commune, for example, kitchens and living rooms were abolished from the floor plans, while shared restrooms were provided on each floor (figure 5.14) (*Ibid.*).

Like modernist projects elsewhere, the design of the commune followed what James Scott typifies as the logic of high modernism, in which certain visual symbols were employed as an abbreviated sign of order and efficiency (Scott, 1998). Instead of making use of existing structures, commune planners preferred a complete redevelopment of rural residential clusters at whatever cost. Local architectural motifs and built forms were ignored; production, livelihood, and education activities were housed in orthogonal, modernist buildings laid out in orderly rows. The plan made for Suiping Commune is particularly revealing about planners' 'quasi-religious faith in a visual sign or representation of order' (*Ibid.*, p. 114). The site was dominated by a grand, symmetrical main building group; a spacious square was laid in front of the main building to strengthen its central status (Huanan gongxueyuan jianzhuxi, 1958). On both sides of the main building

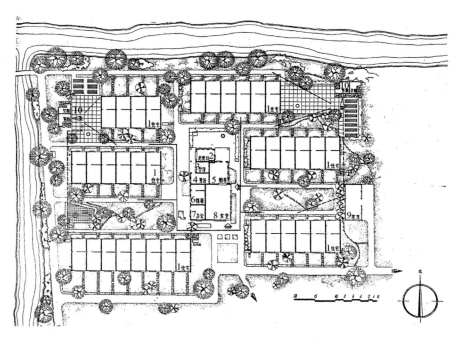

Figure 5.12. Neighbourhood plan, Vanguard Cooperative Farm, Shanghai, 1958.
Key: 1 Housing; 2 Stove; 3 Women's bathroom; 4 Men's bathroom; 5 Kitchen; 6 Storeroom; 7 Office; 8 Canteen; 9 Storage; 10 Toilet

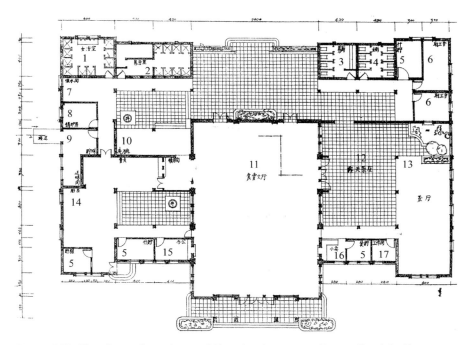

Figure 5.13. The floor plan of a multifunctional canteen, Panyu People's Commune, Guangdong, 1959.
Key: 1 Women's bathroom; 2 Men's bathroom; 3 Men's toilet; 4 Women's toilet; 5 Storage; 6 Staff housing; 7 Water storage; 8 Boiler room; 9 Coal storage; 10 Washroom; 11 Dining hall; 12 Tea garden; 13 Teahouse; 14 Kitchen; 15 Office; 16 Shop; 17 Workshop

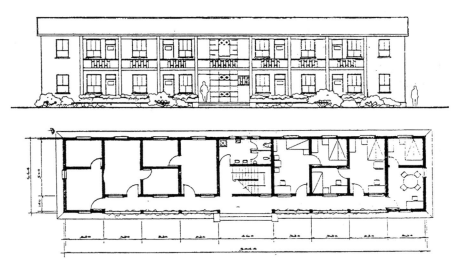

Figure 5.14. The proposal for the apartment building, Suicheng People's Commune, Xushui, Hebei, 1958.

group, minor buildings were arranged along the orderly, rectangular street grid (figure 5.15). Although Suiping Commune was located in Henan Province of northern China, and although under no circumstances would palm trees grow there, two were casually included by the designers. This visual element thus subtly revealed the designer's logic: the commune plan was based on the professionals' own aesthetic preferences rather than local particularities.

Commune proposals represented a complete negation of traditional rural life in many aspects (figure 5.16). Traditional villages were replaced by modern residential clusters. Previous focal points for rural life (ancestral halls, temples, local markets and so on) gave way to modern institutions (collective canteens, schools, co-op shops and so on). Vernacular dwellings that provided shelter for extended kin were abandoned; their various functions were divided into separated institutes. Communal food, laundry and nurseries were provided to free women from traditional divisions of labour. In every way, the commune schema hoped to proclaim the end of the peasantry, its institutions and its long-established way of life.

Despite the energy and enthusiasm instilled in countless rural utopias and commune proposals, they remained castles in the air. The inept economic policies of the Great Leap Forward and the commune movement ignored technological and physical constraints; workers and peasants were called upon to work shift after shift with little rest. It soon became apparent that the communes neither increased individual income nor raised the level of satisfaction obtained from working (Lethbridge, 1963, pp. 121–122). The egalitarianism adopted by the commune system resulted in slacking off at work. Meanwhile, in 1960, the Soviet Union not only withdrew its technicians and terminated its aid to China, but also imposed pressure for repayment of debts (Liu and Wu, 1986, p. 265).

The combined effects of these factors and agricultural disasters resulted in a severe famine, which claimed millions of lives between 1959 and 1961 (Becker, 1996, pp. 266–274). At the January 1961 Ninth Plenum, the state decided to retreat, shifting the emphasis of development from industry to agriculture. The concept of private plots was reintroduced; peasants were again allowed to grow vegetables and raise livestock (Pye, 1984, pp. 247, 250). The state also retreated on commune organization, shifting accounting down to the level of the production brigade, and decision-making on work to the production team (*Ibid.*, p. 248). Although the commune continued to exist formally, its image as the revolutionary organizational form gradually faded.

The leadership, seriously demoralized, considered planning impractical. The state announced at the 1960 national planning meeting that urban planning practice should be suspended for three years (Tongji University *et al.*, 1981, pp. 24–25). Planning departments were dismantled, planners were forced to find jobs

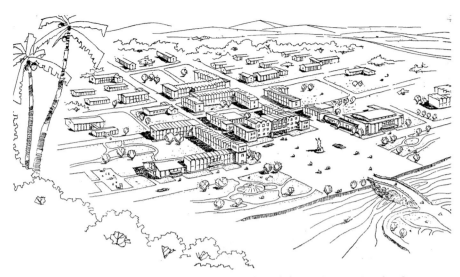

Figure 5.15. Perspective drawing for the central residential cluster, Suiping People's Commune, Henan, 1958.

Figure 5.16. In place of vernacular buildings, cookie-cutter modernist structures were arranged in orderly rows. The planning model for a rural commune, 1959.

in other professions, and universities were forced to eliminate their Departments of Urban Planning (*Ibid.*).

Third World Modernism and Its Discontents

The commune movement was a grand mass utopia. Zygmunt Bauman characterizes utopia as a peculiar human mode of existence 'founded on a unique phenomenon of the future, as a mode of time qualitatively distinct from the past in the sense of being not entirely determined' (Bauman, 1976, p. 11). In the twentieth century, the desire for social forms that transcended existing structures was often expressed through mass utopias, in which immense human power was mobilized by state power to realize collective dreams (Buck-Morss, 2000, p. ix–xi). Like the actions of fictional character Faust, the commune movement, sponsored by the state, was able to drive the whole population 'to extremes of organization, pain, and exhaustion in order to master nature and create a new landscape, a sublime spiritual achievement that contains the potentiality for human liberation from want and need' (Harvey, 1989, p. 16). Yet in contrast to generations of utopian dreamers who raised their eyes high above the level of current reality, the goals set for the Chinese commune schemas were quite modest in their penchant for singling out industrial modernity as the most desirable change.

The commune movement took place in an era when social engineers and planners had a firm belief in progress through rationalization projects on a huge scale. Whether it was in the planning of the modernist city Brasilia in the late 1950s, or the compulsory 'villagization' project in Tanzania in the 1960s, social reformers shared the same faith in the improvement of existing patterns of development and human settlement via radical social rearrangements (Scott, 1998). Driven by their technical conviction and sense of planned beauty, designers tended to substitute visual order for real life and paid little attention to the actual effects of their interventions. In this regard, the commune movement was not an isolated historical aberration but a forceful attempt to achieve a deeper modernity that had much in common with modernist programmes in other parts of the world.

The construction of mass utopias did not result in a coherent national space, but was characterized by fragmentation within the space it created. The state hoped for rapid industrialization, a revolutionized countryside, and expanded state power. Peasants yearned for an ideal modern life, resplendent with everything they most keenly longed for: prosperity, electricity, education and so on. Designers aspired to create a powerful rational order in rural China by applying scientific planning principles and modernist aesthetic cannons. While all three parties shared the same faith in a fuller modernity, the discrepancy between these aspirations produced deep contradictions in the implementation of utopian dreams.

The planning proposals for the communes, for example, shared quite a few spatial features of the work unit: the close association of work and residence, the extensive provision of social facilities, and the rationalist spatial layout and architectural style of the buildings. Had the commune proposals been realized, the countryside might have achieved a spatial structure similar to that of the city. Yet most commune proposals required opening new land and constructing new buildings from scratch outside of existing village sites. Such plans were enormously expensive. As the state's economic development effort concentrated on industry, there was little hope that it would direct limited resources to such projects. In fact, while agriculture accounted for more than half of the country's net material product in the 1950s, it only received 7.1–10.5 per cent of total state capital investment between 1953 and 1959 (Chan, 1994, p. 62). Therefore, the planning proposals for the rural communes rarely progressed from paper; the city remained what the countryside was not.

Although the state believed that comprehensive collectivization would result in increased agricultural production, in reality it eliminated the motivation that had kept Chinese peasants producing as much as they could in the past. The countryside used to be in equilibrium with customary cycles of activities and modes of distribution, but the establishment of the communes destroyed the known patterns. Chinese peasants were transformed from hard-working farmers into far less efficient ones (Lethbridge, 1963, p. 121). The grand celebration of modernity hence only intensified some of the most tragic contradictions of modernization. Among others, what made the reality of the Chinese commune movement even more tragic than the Faustian tragedy was the landscape of extreme scarcity it created: millions of people lost their lives because of hunger (Becker, 1996, pp. 266–274). If scarcity was an inherited wound of Third World modernity, further modernization only made it deeper. While the commune movement uncompromisingly pushed individuals to seek a better future, the historically constituted condition of scarcity limited the possibility that the desire for modernity could ever really be fulfilled. In the end, the disruptive forces that the modernist experimentation brought about turned the same people into its victims.

To be sure, the commune movement did trigger some social and spatial changes. The emphasis on the combination of agricultural and industrial production introduced to the countryside small plants that produced simple industrial products for local use. The new bureaucracy developed during the commune movement established rural statistics networks and the concept of economic and physical planning as a scientific way of managing local growth.[5] Popular campaigns to promote hygiene, physical training, education and literacy were carried out on an ambitious scale.[6] In the city, the establishment of urban communes introduced small workshops and social services into old neighbourhoods, which strengthened the mixed land-use pattern in these areas (Salaff, 1967). A new emphasis on agriculture and self-reliance after the 1959–1961 food crisis led to a higher level of urban self-sufficiency.

Rethinking Modernist Architecture

The failure of the commune plan forced Chinese architects to re-examine the issue of architectural modernism. Modernist architecture, first introduced to China in the late 1920s, gradually gained popularity in the 1930s (Zou, 2001, chapters 1 and 2). Meanwhile, a group of foreign and native architects devoted considerable effort to exploring the adaptation of the Chinese style into modern buildings (Cody, 2001; Lai, 2005). In the early 1950s, revivalist architecture was dominant under the influence of the Soviet idea 'Socialist Realism', while the modernist style, considered empty, cold and bourgeois, fell into disrepute (Rowe and Kuan, 2002, pp. 87–106). The Chinese architects' experimentation with Socialist Realist architecture, however, was soon suspended. The austerity policy adopted in 1955 decisively changed the balance of power between revivalist and modernist architecture. As buildings with large roofs and traditional ornaments were condemned as wasteful, professionals came to agree that Western modernist architecture could serve both capitalism and socialism, the bourgeois and the proletariat (Lu, 2004). During the commune movement, however, although architects were eager to apply modernist design to rural development, the country was short of steel and concrete. By 1962, when the country was recovering from the extreme disruptions, there were attempts to mobilize architects to design new rural houses with the idea of 'walking on two legs', a combination of both modern and traditional methods, being emphasized (Beijingshi jianzhu shejiyuan, 1962; Li and Li, 1963).

In the December 1962 'Rural Housing Design' symposium, architects discussed the applicability of concrete structures in the countryside and recognized the need to adapt design to the realities of available materials, technology and skills (Zou, 2001, p. 284). As a comprehensive survey of local building traditions was launched, the early 1960s saw a sudden expansion in knowledge of vernacular dwellings in different parts of the country. At the same time when reports on various vernacular dwelling types were published in China's *Architectural Journal* (e.g., Wang, 1962; Zhang, *et al.*, 1963), the same journal also began extensive coverage of architecture from Third World countries. The 1963 issues included architecture in Indonesia, Cambodia, Burma, Cuba, North Korea, Vietnam and Albania, while the 1964 issues added Egypt, Mexico, Ghana, Guinea and Syria to the list. Unlike typical Western representations of Third World architecture, these articles focused on the newly developed modernist architecture of these countries rather than their traditional structures. Authors paid particular attention to how developing countries adapted modernist buildings to local geography, climate and culture (e.g., Dong, 1963; Yin, 1964; Wei, 1964).

A new conceptual distinction was made between the modernism of the West and that of the Third World. While Western architectural modernism was gradually normalized and established as part of universal knowledge in the late 1950s, it once again became a subject of intellectual contention. This conceptual twist is reflected in a 1964 article titled 'A Review of Ten Buildings in the West', which depicted the works of 'master architects' in Western countries (including Le Corbusier, Louis Kahn, Frank Lloyd Wright and Eero Saarinen, among others) as 'chaotic', 'ugly' and 'sick' (Wu, 1964). The narratives of Third World modernism, in contrast, were filled with praise for the achievements that had been made in architectural modernization. Occasionally, a 'sameness' was drawn between building practices in these countries and those in China. 'Sotto porticos' (*qilou*) in Cambodia, for instance, were associated with similar arrangements in the city of Guangzhou (Cheng, 1963).[7] The varied interpretations of modernist architecture in these countries, along with China's own local traditions, together gave rise to a new vision of Third World modernism (Lu, 2004).

Notes

1. Several cadres working in Suiping county of Henan province took the first step towards communization by forming a federation of 27 Advanced Agricultural Producers' Cooperatives, in which the management of the resources of previous cooperatives was taken over by a committee chosen democratically by the peasants. The new organization was initially called the 'Zhayashan Collective Farm' and later renamed 'Satellite Commune' (Kang, 1998, pp. 12–15).
2. When the *Beidaihe Resolution* announced the formation of the people's commune, only the establishment of communes in the countryside was mentioned; there was no reference to the urban communes.
3. For a comprehensive list of Chinese-language materials on various aspects of the people's commune, see, Ma (1982).
4. The Chinese leaders certainly shared Stalin's faith in collectivization; the purpose, as Stalin stated in May 1928, was 'to transfer from small, backward, and fragmented peasant farms to consolidated, big, public farms, provided with machines, equipped with the data of science, and capable of producing the greatest quantity of grain for the market' (Scott, 1998, p. 209).
5. See, for example, *Tongji gongzuo* (1958); *Jihua yu tongji* (1960); *Jihua yu tongji* (1958).
6. For more Chinese journal articles in this regard, see, Ma (1982).
7. 'Sotto portico' refers to the street-side building with upper floor(s) projecting out to provide a covered walkway on the ground level.

The Latency of Tradition: On the Vicissitudes of Walls[1]

> Tancred [the hero of the epic 'Jerusalem Liberated'] unwittingly kills his beloved Clorinda in a duel while she is disguised in the armour of an enemy knight. After her burial he makes his way into a strange magic forest which strikes the Crusaders' army with terror. He slashes with his sword at a tall tree; but blood streams from the cut and the voice of Clorinda, whose soul is imprisoned in the tree, is heard complaining that he has wounded his beloved once again.
>
> Sigmund Freud, 1955, *Beyond the Pleasure Principle*

In 1989 the world witnessed some of the most dramatic events of the twentieth century: in May portions of the Iron Curtain were demolished in Hungary; in November the Berlin Wall was breached; and in December the Romanian leader Nicolai Ceausescu was tried and executed. The dizziness and disorientation brought by the downfall of Communism in Eastern Europe produced various visions of future political and social trends, among which what might be termed the 'triumph-of-capitalist-democracy' scenario echoed frequently through Western discourse. Notable among this genre of commentary was Francis Fukuyama's argument concerning 'the end of history' (1992). Fukuyama claimed that with the disintegration of socialist regimes there remained no legitimate alternative to market capitalism and liberal democracy. With the expansion of the latter as the final, universal form of political-economic structure for all human societies, 'history', understood as the contest between ideologies, was over (*Ibid.*).

The actual developments of the past decade, however, contest such an assumption. The disintegration of socialist regimes and their opening up to market capitalism have not automatically led to the formation of homogeneous social spaces. Instead, longstanding and problematic tendencies within these societies have been exacerbated: military dictatorships, ethnic conflicts and other modes of social domination, to name just a few (Rubin and Snyder, 1998). What has happened in post-socialist societies of Eastern Europe has by no means been unique. In other parts of the world, where analysts of globalization once assumed that the homogenization of culture would reduce the possibilities for local alternatives, there has been an upsurge of localisms and religious movements (Castells, 2004).

As 'pasts' which had long been relegated as 'backward' and 'behind' have been resurrected in different parts of the world, it seems that conflicts over modernity articulated as part of the Cold-War antagonism between socialist and capitalist models have been replaced with a surge of diverse cultural claims (Dirlik, 2002). It is within this context of radical change that the question of tradition has become more pressing than ever. Has the passing of the era of Cold War ironically brought the return of multiple traditions with rival claims on the future? Does the resurgence of traditions hold the potential for viable alternative rationalities? Or does it just temporarily postpone an inevitable historical trend in which (as Fukuyama and others have argued) sooner or later all nations will join the march of progress, following the models of 'advanced societies'?

In this chapter, I shall venture a preliminary reading of some possible trajectories of tradition through a case study of the making and unmaking of the wall-building tradition in contemporary China. By doing this, my aim is to boost appreciation of the vitality and transformability of tradition in our time. 'Tradition' in its barest sense, to quote Edward Shils, means 'simply a traditum; it is anything which is transmitted or handed down from the past to the present' (Shils, 1981, p. 12). This examination of the persistence of the wall as a building typology in China emphasizes 'tradition' in a fast-changing society as constantly constructed and deconstructed in a perpetual flux of historical practices. I argue that it is in this ongoing process that the same tradition may be appropriated, rehistoricized and transplanted. With a capacity to renew itself, tradition may be held back temporarily during periods of political and social change, but rarely does it die off completely. Instead, it tends to reappear in new guises in new contexts.

In this chapter I describe this tendency as involving 'the latency of tradition'. My use of the term 'latency' is specifically inspired by the writings of Sigmund Freud (1939, 1967) in *Moses and Monotheism*. Thus, I preface the discussion of Chinese wall-building with a brief introduction to some of Freud's ideas and their implications for current approaches to tradition in the built environment.

Tradition and History

In *Moses and Monotheism*, Freud offers an explanation of the history of the Jews from the perspective of a psychoanalyst. At the beginning of his book, he claims that Moses was not a captive Hebrew but an Egyptian. And although Moses led the Hebrews from Egypt to Canaan to preserve their withering monotheism, he was later murdered by the Hebrews in a rebellion. According to Freud, both this traumatic event and the Mosaic religion were repressed following the moment of the murder. Yet they returned later to constitute the essence of Jewish history, as the religion of Moses was assimilated into a new Jewish monotheism, and the founder of the latter was also named Moses. The dualities, writes Freud, 'are necessary consequences of the first: one section of the people passed through what may properly be termed a traumatic experience which the other was spared' (*Ibid.*, pp. 64–65). In this way, the repressed was never truly forgotten; it returned by taking the form of reappearance.

Freud notes that there is a latency period between the repression of the trauma and the return of the repressed. In the section entitled 'Latency period and tradition', he gives an example of a train accident to illustrate the dynamics of trauma,

It may happen that someone gets away, apparently unharmed, from the spot where he has suffered a shocking accident, for instance a train collision. In the course of the following weeks, however, he develops a series of grave psychical and motor symptoms, which can be ascribed only to his shock or whatever else happened at the time of the accident. He has developed a 'traumatic neurosis'. (*Ibid.*, p. 85)

In spite of the fundamental difference in the two cases – the problem of the traumatic neurosis and the history of Jewish monotheism – Freud finds a correspondence between them: that is, the latency of the shocking event curiously resonates with the belatedness of the Jew's traumatic experience. Thus, the murder and the repression of Moses and his religion could not be understood at the moment they occurred, but could only be truly assimilated when they returned after the 'latency period'.

Freud contrasts the role of tradition during the latency period with that of written history. According to him, written history itself is an engine of repression, through which unpleasant traumatic experiences are denied and original events are distorted. In contrast, tradition is less subject to distorting influences, hence '[w]hat has been deleted or altered in the written version might quite well have been preserved uninjured in the tradition' (*Ibid.*). It is here, Freud claims, that the history of the Jewish religion finds its explanation:

the facts which the so-called official written history purposely tried to suppress were in reality never lost. The knowledge of them survived in traditions which were kept alive among the people. (*Ibid.*, p. 86)

In other words, traditions store and pass on the repressed even without people being conscious of it. Thus, as time goes by, some traditions may grow more and more powerful, and ultimately allow the return of the repressed as a force strong enough to influence decisively the thought and activity of the people. '[T]he religion of Moses', Freud thereby proclaims, 'exercised influence on the Jewish people only when it had become a tradition' (*Ibid.*, p. 64).

Despite its roots in psychoanalysis, I believe that Freud's formulation of history and tradition is inspiring as an alternative way of seeing tradition. In modernist thinking, events are considered to be moving forward irreversibly, and historical time is divided into lineally developed periods (Chakrabarty, 1997). From the nineteenth century on, with the spread of colonialism, such a Western pattern of temporality reordered the spatial relationships of people and things into evolutionary series (*Ibid.*). Societies and artefacts that are 'less progressed' were termed traditional, in contrast to those considered modern. Freud's view, however, proposes that the past is constantly contained in the present as repeated flashbacks and, among other things, this provides a way to circumvent the progressive bias in modernist historicism. Here, the past always rests upon the present, competes with the present, and at times thrusts forward to shape the future.

This alternative way of seeing the past and the present invites us to rethink the relationship between tradition and modernity, not as being connected in a unilinear evolutionary link, but as living equally in the present. Certainly, what should be immediately pointed out is that while, epistemologically, the two may coexist equally within a common temporality, they occupy unequal positions in the current world power geometry (Majid, 2000). Thus, it is modernity that continues to dominate, and provides an arena for tradition to contest. Yet we should also bear in mind that the shift from industrial modernization to globalization has brought new contradictions and ambivalences onto the scene. If the boundaries between tradition and modernity used to be clear, the new global condition has rendered the borders vague, porous and subject to crossings from both sides. It is with this ambiguity that both modernity and tradition have become contested terrains where more voices than ever before demand a hearing.

With this understanding of tradition in mind, I now turn to the story of wall-building in China. In the following section, I provide a brief history of traditional wall-construction practice. In subsequent sections I give an account of how the practice of city wall-building was overturned in the 1950s; how a new tradition of work-unit wall-building emerged in the 1960s; and how the reform era has brought new twists to the story. The final section provides a discussion of the implications of this study for the understanding of tradition and modernity.

Walls in Traditional China

Walled enclosures were among the most basic features of the traditional Chinese landscape (Boyd, 1962. p. 49). Walls not only physically bounded various kinds of space – cities, villages, gardens, temples, houses – they also symbolized the manner of classification in an ordered Chinese environment. The variety and significance of walls is evident from the number of words in Chinese describing their different forms and meanings. To take just a few examples, high walls around courtyards were called *qiang*, implying something used to shield oneself; house walls and part walls were called, *bi*, connoting something that warded off and resisted the wind and cold; and low walls were called, *yuan*, suggesting something one leaned on and thus took as protection (Xu, 2000, p. 197).

In particular, the importance of the city wall transcended that of other types of wall. Symbolizing authority, order and security, the wall was so central to the Chinese idea of a city that the traditional words for city and wall were identical, the character *cheng* standing for both (Wheatley, 1971, p. 221). The city wall and the local centre of imperial administration were also institutionally and conceptually inseparable; thus an unwalled urban centre was almost as inconceivable as a house without a roof. Like city walls in many other societies, those in China were built essentially to protect the city against invasions and peasant rebellion. Before the introduction of modern artillery, Chinese city walls, which were ordinarily surrounded by a moat, were almost indestructible. Their solidity made any attempt to breach them difficult, and their height, ranging from 5 to 15 metres, made scaling them hazardous (Chang, 1977). Further, the walls around many riverine Chinese cities had the additional function of defence against floods, which were a major menace in lowland areas (*Ibid.*, p. 79).

Besides these practical functions, the Chinese elite also attached rich symbolic meaning to city walls from Zhou times (256 BC to around the eleventh century). For the earliest city, the construction of the walls signified the establishment and maintenance of an order that could be kept in accord with the ideal order of the cosmos. Such symbolism conformed to political circumstances, as individual states struggled against each other for power. Under the socio-political conditions of imperial China, the symbolic emphasis shifted. The city was no longer treated as the centre of the cosmos; rather it was the loyalty of the region to the emperor in his imperial capital, and to the social order it established, that mattered most (Xu, 2000, pp. 240–241).

The Mongols interrupted this tradition, however, and few walled cities were constructed during the Yuan dynasty (1280–1368), whose Mongol founders, pastoral in origin, were unsympathetic to the wall-building tradition (Chang, 1977). In order to display their power, at one time the Mongols forbade the building of city walls throughout China. Thus, during the thirteenth and early fourteenth centuries walls that pre-dated the Mongol conquest deteriorated and, by the time the Mongols were finally overthrown, they needed repair. The first half of the Ming dynasty (1368–1644) witnessed the advent of 'the great age of Chinese wall-building'. This had the 'psychological function of reaffirming the presence of the Chinese state', and re-established proper social order after a century of Mongol rule (Mote, 1977, p. 137). Perhaps because of this new significance, while early city walls had simply consisted of pounded earth ramparts, Ming engineers faced them with bricks, ceramic blocks, or stones.

Intensive wall construction continued into the Qing dynasty (1644–1911), the last dynasty of imperial China, and a new function for city walls arose under the specific social circumstances of this period. The Manchus, in the wake of their conquest of China in the seventeenth century, were concerned to preserve the ethnic identity and military prowess of their troops stationed at key places. To this end, they appropriated for exclusive Manchu residence entire sections within the walls of many cities, and sometimes built a partial internal wall to create a separate enclosed Manchu quarter. In a few instances they even built a completely separate enclosure within a short [...]

four such twin cities were created [...]
to achieve ethnic segregation (Ch [...]

Another type of wall within [...]
Since Zhou times, city plannin [...]
divided into wards, both for sym [...]
This led to a pattern of distinct re [...]
exclusively occupied by local g [...]
separated by streets (Xu, 2000, p. [...]
(581–618) and the early Tang dyn [...]
on daily life in the city. For exam [...]
into large enclosed wards by ext [...]
were confined to the interior of t [...]
junctions of major avenues (Yan [...]
main streets were devoid of com [...]
to the city's fortress-like East and [...]

It was during the late Tang and the early Southern Song periods that this strictly controlled ward system began to collapse. As the autocratic grip of the Sui emperors was replaced by a bureaucracy of scholar-officials, the enclosed marketplaces and walled residential wards were gradually replaced with a more open street system (Heng, 1999, chapters 4 and 5). This period coincided with the growth of commercial suburbs outside the city gates, caused by the intensification of a market economy, itself a result of urbanization, and a slackening of commercial controls and urban regulations (*Ibid.*).

Because all traffic to and from a sector of the city's hinterland had to be channelled through the city gates, the areas immediately outside them became favoured sites for markets and businesses. By the nineteenth century, suburban development outside at least one gate was common in many walled cities in China, and in some cases, such built-up areas outside the walls even exceeded those within the walls (Chang, 1977, p. 99). Concern for the security of these suburbs sometimes led to the construction of a second, outer wall to encompass all or part of this suburban area. But in many cases, no attempt was made to enclose the commercial suburbs. In fact, some researchers of Chinese history maintain that cities in late imperial China were largely open institutions, and they claim that the basic political, social and cultural divisions, unlike those of the premodern European city, were between classes and occupations rather than between the city and the countryside (Skinner, 1977b). As F.W. Mote states in his study of Nanjing during the early Ming:

Neither the city wall nor the actual limits of the suburban concentration marked the city off from the countryside in architectural terms. Nor did style of dress, patterns of eating and drinking, means of transportation, or any other obvious aspect of daily life display characteristic dichotomies between urban and rural. (Mote, 1977, p. 116)

Such a continuum was physically manifest in the fact that urban areas were not spatially separated by walls from rural areas during the late imperial period.

The Fall of the City Wall

Historically, the meanings and functions of the city wall went through various shifts under the tide of social and political transformation. Yet spiritually, to traditional Chinese thinking, the city wall represented what was constant in the vicissitudes of life. In many poems and articles, writers portrayed city walls as part of the timeless universe, in contrast to the incessant changes in the world. One example is a story told by Tao Qian (c. 372–427 A.D.) in his *Soushen houji* (1981). In the story, Ding Lingwei turns into an immortal crane after studying the *dao* of immortality for a millennium. When he flies back to his home place he laments the transience of human life, singing 'city walls are as ever but people are not the same' (Xu, 2000, p. 126).

This sense of eternity attached to the city wall, however, melted into air with the advent of a new socialist era. When the Chinese Civil War finally ended in 1949, socialist leaders were left with the task of rebuilding war-ravaged Chinese cities. Although there was no shared sense of what exactly constituted a socialist urban environment, many agreed that in order to create a world reflecting the modern life imagined for the new society, some heritage would have to be abandoned. Such was the case of the Chinese city wall. While walls were once the most important symbol of the city, upon consolidation of socialist control in 1949, their utility was immediately called into question. Because of its importance, the city wall of Beijing serves as a focus for this discussion.

Beijing was a city of walls within walls. It had both outer walls (the traditional walls of the Chinese city) and inner walls (the walls of the Tartar City). Within the inner walls were the walls of the Imperial City, and within these were the rust-red walls of the Forbidden City (figure 6.1). The main city, accommodated within the inner walls, was initially constructed in the Yuan dynasty and revised in the Ming era (Farmer, 1976). These walls measured 6,650 metres east–west, and 5,350 metres north–south, and had nine gates (Sit, 1995, chapter 3). The outer walls were added in the mid-sixteenth century to accommodate the prosperous southern commercial suburb. While the plan for these outer walls was that they were to circumscribe the whole city, due to a shortage of funds, only the southern outer area was actually enclosed, so the new walls were shaped like a cap adjoining the main city. During the Qing dynasty, the conquering Manchus drove most of the native population from the main city into this southern suburb surrounded by outer walls. For this reason, the inner city came to be known as the Manchu or Tartar city, and the outer city, the Chinese city (*Ibid.*). Osvald Sirén described the beauty of the inner city walls and their attached gate-towers in *The Walls and Gates of Peking* (figure 6.2):

Of all the great buildings of Peking there is none which can compare with the walls of the Tartar city in monumental grandeur. At first sight they may not be as attractive to the eye as the palaces, temples, and shop-fronts of those highly coloured and picturesquely composed wooden structures which still line the old streets or hide behind the walls, but after a longer acquaintance with this vast city, they become the most impressive monuments – enormous in their extension and dominating everything by their quiet forceful rhythm... The corner towers, massive and fortresslike, form a magnificent finale of the whole composition. (Sirén, 1924, pp. 34–35)

The destruction of city walls, however, had already begun when Sirén was conducting his research in the early twentieth century (Zhang, 2003, pp. 318–320). With the fall of the Qing dynasty in 1911, Beijing was no longer an imperial capital but the site for the competing ambitions of rival warlords. With no authority to protect its precious legacy, traditional shop-fronts and courtyards were destroyed every year to make room for new buildings. A few parts of the pink wall around the Imperial city were torn down in order to construct electric streetcar lines. Observing this destruction, Sirén asked at the end of his book: 'How long will they still remain, these wonderful walls and gates, these silent records of Peking's most beautiful and glorious past?' (Sirén, 1924, p. 219).

If changes began during the Republican period, their pace increased dramatically after 1949. Beijing was made the national capital in 1949, and the city government proclaimed that the guiding principle for urban construction was 'to serve the masses, to serve production, and to serve the Central Government' (Sit, 1995, p. 91). In the years that followed, Beijing entered an era of rapid

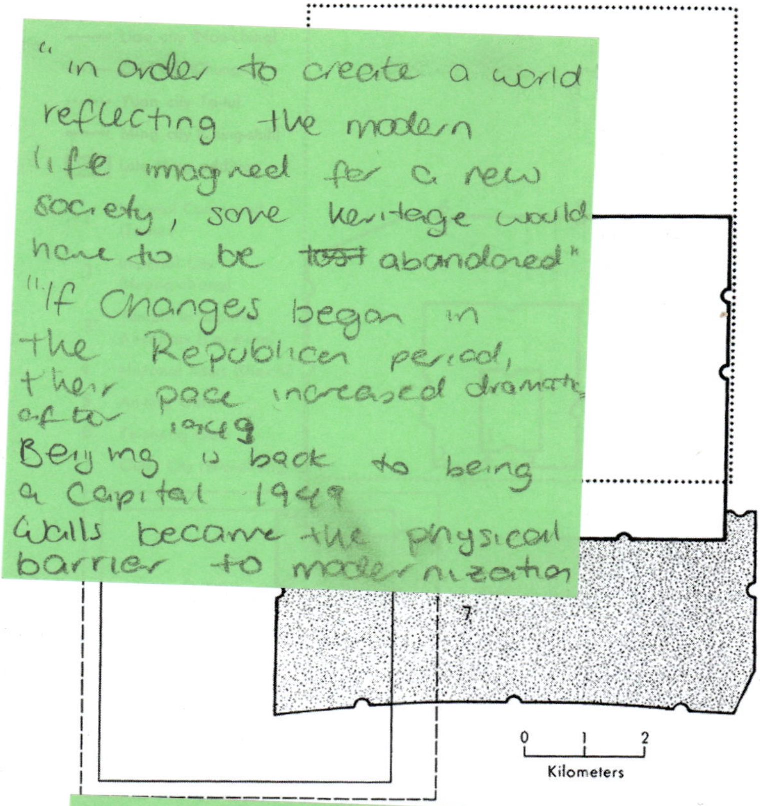

Figure 6.1. … rent dynasties.

"in order to create a world reflecting the modern life imagined for a new society, some heritage would have to be ~~lost~~ abandoned"
"If changes began in the Republican period, their pace increased dramatically after 1949
Beijing is back to being a capital 1949
Walls became the physical barrier to modernization

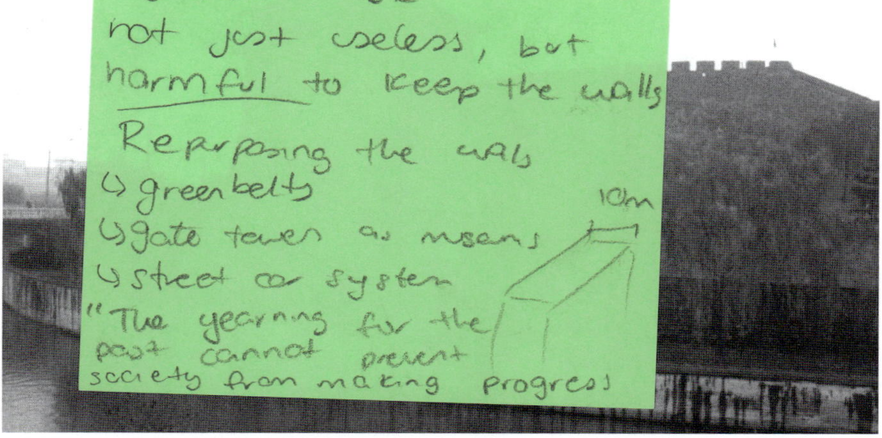

Figure 6.2. The gate tower on Beijing's city walls.

Ideologically, walls represented imperial hierarchy
- It had now finished its historical task
not just useless, but harmful to keep the walls
Repurposing the walls
↳ greenbelts
↳ gate tower as museums
↳ street car system
10m
"The yearning for the past cannot prevent society from making progress

development, and the demand for all types of buildings multiplied. While walls were torn down in places such as Guangzhou before 1949, the city of Beijing was still very much confined by its walls, which were now considered by many to be a physical and symbolic barrier to modernization. For planners eager to shape the city into a modern, socialist capital, the issue of how to deal with the walls became a central concern. There was a great divergence of views as to whether to demolish or preserve them.

One group argued that the city walls should be torn down for both political and economic reasons. Ideologically, they argued, city walls were a relic of ancient emperors, a symbol of the 'feudal' tradition, and a sign of division between urban residents and peasants (BDG, 1953). Practically, this group maintained that the city wall was an ancient defence work that had now finished its 'historical task'. In the new age of socialist development, the persistence of the city wall blocked traffic, wasted land and limited urban development (Wang, 2003, p. 200). Hence, it was not only useless but also harmful to keep the walls.

The other group, however, insisted that it would be a big mistake to demolish the city's great heritage; they argued that the walls should be preserved and put to modern use. Various ways of doing this were proposed: some suggested building a high-speed streetcar system on the walls; others proposed remodelling the gate towers into museums; still others imagined connecting the city walls and their adjacent areas into greenbelts (*Ibid.*). The last idea was supported vigorously by the architectural historian Liang Sicheng, who wrote extensively on the preservation of Beijing's cultural legacy during the early 1950s. Liang (1986, p. 46) suggested in a 1950 article that the city walls and moats should be redeveloped into a 'three-dimensional' park (figure 6.3). With a width of more than 10 metres, the top of the walls would provide a perfect place for people to stroll and enjoy distant views of the city. Dozens of gate towers could be refurbished into reading rooms or teahouses. By diverting water from the Yongding river, the moats would allow people to go fishing in the summer and skating in the winter (*Ibid.*).

Yet Liang's proposals for the city walls, together with his other ideas on historical conservation, were dismissed as nostalgia in the mighty torrent of socialist development surging forward at the time (Chen, 2005). During an era in which historical materialism achieved near total supremacy, most decision-makers judged plans in accordance with their imagined role in 'the progress of social history'. Thus, Hua Nangui, one of the key petitioners on many urban construction issues, considered the removal of the city walls inevitable due to '[t]he evolution rule of society' (Hua, 1956). He maintained that 'the yearning for the past cannot prevent society from making progress' (*Ibid.*).

While debate about the city wall still reverberated in the general public, its piecemeal demolition had already begun, conducted by individual work units

Figure 6.3. Liang Sicheng's proposal to redevelop Beijing's city walls into a public park.

(BDG, 1957*h*). One reason was that there was a constant scarcity of construction materials in the early 1950s (Chao, 1968). As many construction projects were interrupted by inadequate supplies of new materials, the city walls became an alternative source of bricks and earth. Thus, in December 1956, the Beijing Planning Bureau reported how the city walls were being excavated by individual work units in a chaotic way (BDG, 1956*e*; 1957*j*). Some demolished the inner walls, and some tore down the outer walls; those who only needed earth inside the facing left crushed bricks all around, and those who only needed bricks peeled the brick facing off the walls and left the inner earth standing alone (BDG, 1956*e*). The bricks and earth taken by work units were used for all kinds of projects. The planning bureau even received requests from some suburban agricultural production unit leaders who intended to use the bricks to build pigsties (BDG, 1957*l*).

As the brick facing of most parts of the walls was removed, the soil began to wash away in the rain, threatening collapse anytime (BDG, 1957*i*; 1957*b*). By 1959 the outer walls had been demolished except the part on the south of Tiantan, and the inner walls had been partly dismantled (BDG, 1959*b*). Under these circumstances, the municipality decided that the remaining city walls should be removed completely (BDG, 1959*e*). Thus eventually, the city of Beijing burst through its walled enclosure and burgeoned outwards in every direction.[2] Except for a few segments, in the place of the city walls today, one finds wide, well-paved boulevards. Only the names of the old city gates remain, now nothing more than picturesque reminders of a legendary past.

The Rise of the Unit Wall

Ironically, while the city walls were being torn down, new walls were being constructed around individual work units throughout Beijing. Initially, such new wall-building projects were held in check. During the 1950s most work units were without walls; and for those that needed some kind of physical confinement, more often than not only barbed wire entanglements or wattle walls, were erected. Many work units started to build permanent walls in the 1960s, but even then such behaviour was not encouraged by planners. To ensure that major construction projects within the national plan would not be interrupted by inadequate supplies of materials, the planning department kept strict control over the consumption of building materials by minor projects. As wall building was considered a waste of resources which were already in short supply, the Beijing Planning Bureau was generally reluctant to approve the wall-construction projects by work units, except in the case of crucial institutions such as military-related units and schools. The application procedure for such projects was complicated and time-consuming. Successful applicants had to demonstrate that they had a reliable source of building materials for the project and to justify the absolute necessity for the walls (BDG, 1964b).

In order to obtain endorsement, each work unit tried hard to show its special circumstance in the application. Some stressed that they would only use building materials of substandard quality or bricks made of waste materials. In order to build walls with a length of 850 metres, for example, the College of Nationality claimed that it devised a method for making cinder bricks out of coal (*Ibid.*, p. 45). Because brick was one of the construction materials that was in constant short supply, in early May of the same year, the municipal government of Beijing issued a circular which required that no further brick walls be constructed. In response to this constraint, some work units requested permission to build fences instead (BDG, 1964d).

Despite the strict control from the planning department and the municipal government, work units were nonetheless eager to build walls. During the short time between 22 May and 23 July 1964 alone, 51 work units submitted wall-construction applications to the Beijing Planning Bureau (BDG, 1964b). The main reason for this wall-building enthusiasm was concern for security. The application submitted by the Chinese Science Council, for example, described the difficulties in maintaining safety in its residential district without walls:

Because there are no walls, it is impossible to manage the unit. Access is available in all directions; people are free to come and go; and vendors are hawking everywhere. This has not only been disturbing, it has also created safety concerns. According to an incomplete estimation, there were 11 cases of burglary in 1963... (BDG, 1964f)

Most newly established work units at this time were located in suburban areas, and there was tension between the units and the neighbouring peasants. Unit leaders considered the tradition of building security walls that separated their territories from the rural hinterlands the only solution to the conflict. According to the application submitted by Miyun Hydraulic Power Plant in 1964, for example, peasants not only herded pigs and sheep in the plant's working and residential areas, but they also developed family vegetable plots within the unit (BDG, 1964e). Another application submitted by the Fifth Branch of the Automobile Repair Factory detailed the conflicts between the unit and its neighbours (BDG, 1964g). Located on the former site of Shiye Timber Factory, the factory was sandwiched between two residential districts, while bordering the Taiyanggong People's Commune on the other side. Factory leaders complained that because of the ineffective management of the previous tenant, residents in the vicinity had developed the habit of coming to the factory to pick up leftover materials. When the factory tried to bring the practice to an end, local peasants were upset and spread complaints everywhere. In addition, while the previous tenant allowed more than 300 households in the vicinity to share electricity with it, factory managers decided to cut off the supply (Ibid.). The sudden power failure caused great 'misunderstanding' among the locals; on two occasions, hundreds of people gathered at the factory to protest. The crises were later solved with the assistance of the Public Security Bureau and the Electricity Provision Bureau. Yet the relationship between the factory and local residents had turned sour. Consequently, when unit leaders decided to build a new power distribution house, they considered walls the only way to protect factory property (Ibid.).

Second to the security function, unit walls played an important role in defining boundaries. In particular, this had to do with an urban property rights system adopted in China that was not ordinarily found in market economies. Soon after the founding of the People's Republic, most privately owned urban land was confiscated by the state (Yang et al., 1992). Socialist reform of private industries and businesses, launched in 1956, further changed the ownership of private real estate by instituting 'joint state-private ownership' and state management of leases. By 1958, the bulk of urban land had been converted to state ownership, and profit and rent on land had disappeared from the Chinese economy (Ibid.).

However, while it was clear that urban land in China belonged to the state, what remained vague was the relationship between the state and the urban land user. The question of whether the requisitioned land was the property of an urban land user or remained the property of the state was never clarified in government documents or theoretical writings. In effect, those who used the land would manage the land, but there was no legal protection for users' rights. As a result, although there was no time limit set for the use of land, the state might take the land back from the work units at any time. During the 1950s, for example, because the General Institute of Iron and Steel Research needed room to expand, the state required its neighbouring work unit, the Research Institute of Agricultural Science, to yield its experimental farmland. As it had taken several years to develop that farmland, the action caused a great loss for the latter. Without explicit legal protection, therefore, walls became an important means of safeguarding land use rights.

While it was always desirable to acquire as much land as possible, work units generally had little say in the urban land disposition process. Without a market mechanism, initial land disposition was a matter of administrative allocation under the state investment plan. In other words, when an investment plan was approved, the application for land was simultaneously approved, and the local government would determine land allocation according to a ratio between the construction project and its land-use area. In this disposition process, the government played a determining role, while the direct users of land had little influence. Thus, once a work unit was set up, even if the unit had the incentive to expand its production capaci[ty], [it] could not acquire land freely. I[f] investment plans were approve[d] (Yang et al., 1992, chapter 2).

Under these circumstances, [walls and] boundaries became the preferre[d ...] this strategy appears in a docu[ment ...] schools (BDG, 1965). In 1964 th[e ...] building projects by primary an[d ...] projects that had been complete[d ...] boundaries (Ibid.). The walls con[s...] University, for example, enclose[d ...] the east, south and west. Its nort[h ...] plan, would have circled 6 a[cres ...] neighbouring production team.

As the unit wall gradually became the norm, the wall was once again an essential part of Chinese life. Indeed, when a new work unit was established, a perimeter wall was often the first structure built. Today, every work unit is a walled enclosure or a cluster of several walled enclosures. The wall creates a clear separation of the unit from its surroundings, a visible expression of place identity, and a boundary protecting its property from outsiders (figure 6.4).

Walls in an Era of Reform

In 1978 the Chinese Communist Party leadership launched a series of reform programmes to move the country from a planned to a market economy. Foreign investment and joint ventures were introduced, alternative forms of profit-making enterprises and means of industrial growth were established, while previously suppressed cultural activities were rehabilitated. Among many, the rebuilding of city walls has become one of the most profound ironies of the present reform era. While Beijing was developed as an industrial city under Mao, after the initiation of the Open Door policy the economy of the city was redirected towards the development of tourism and service industries. Local value systems and self-perceptions were affected by the resumption of tourism, the return of the Chinese diaspora, and the development of international trade and cultural exchange.

With the growing awareness of its position in the global hierarchy, the Beijing municipality realized that the development of an urban identity was central to its ability to compete for global flows of tourists and capital. Traditional architectural elements were now appreciated for their value as exotic visitor attractions and an important source of symbolic capital (Broudehoux, 2004). Thus, while the city wall was considered the symbol of the old society and a hindrance to urban modernization during the 1950s, today the city government acknowledged that its demolition was short sighted. A mile-long segment of the wall, on Beijing's old south-east corner, was re-erected, and officials said that more sections might be restored in the future (*Economist*, 2002).

In addition, with rapid commercialization, the state considered some aspects of the socialist landscape to be barriers to the new economic and social life; the enclosed work unit compound is one of them. In previous decades, individual work units developed social facilities within their walled territories for the exclusive use of their members. As emerging market forces opened up new opportunities for private-sector employment, the cellular pattern of collective consumption became less viable.

The scarcity of urban facilities for the general public was aggravated by the arrival of a large number of rural migrants. Unrestricted rural migration was forbidden under Mao's rule in order to maintain a neat socialist urban order devoid of such urban ills as unemployment and hunger (Cheng and Selden, 1994). In the reform era, as the state recognized the contribution that cheap peasant labour could make to invigorating city economies, the decades-old prohibition on rural migration was gradually relaxed. Within a few years of the initiation of economic reforms, millions of peasants left their rural hinterlands to seek employment and business opportunities in cities. Yet the unprecedented arrival of massive numbers of peasants brought many problems to the cities, one of which was a drain on already scarce public resources.

As the shortage of [...] increasingly felt in the city, the state encouraged work units [...]ities. In July 2001 the municipal [...] once-exclusive work units t[...]uded cultural and educatio[...]tional facilities (sports field[...] living facilities (canteens, pu[...]itories.

Most work units, [...] In fact, many of ther[...]egulate human and goods t[...]d social instability brought [...]g work unit's newsletter, f[...] had in recent years becom[...]ning all around and strang[...]s of new regulations to cor[...]ity (Ren, 1996, p. 4). My survey o[...]continued importance of unit walls: 14 out of the 15 interviewees (m[...]t officials) stressed that unit walls were necessary; only one of them considered walls useless and harmful.[3]

The unit wall has been emulated by newly developed private office complexes and residential districts. Rapid real estate development has greatly transformed the urban landscape in the past two decades: luxury hotels, high-rise office buildings, and large-scale [...] everywhere in Chinese cities. [...]lly changed patterns of hou[...]ization, new real estate dev[...]the previous era. A signific[...]l boundaries through walls. [...]le, is entirely surrounded by [...]ivate security (figure 6.5). In [...]entrance gate (which reads [...], and step off the bicycle w[...]pically found at work unit[...]condominium, persons passi[...] identification procedures, v[...]

Planned a[...]lential projects are large in [...]h as nurseries and community clubs. Similar to those o[...]e facilities are

---

Handwritten note (top):

Mile-long portion of the wall was rebuilt and plans are on to build more

Cellular pattern of work units became less viable

Rural exodus to the city

Private-sector employment

State encouraged work units to allow peasants to use their facilities

Handwritten note (bottom):

2. Defining Boundaries

Joint state-private ownership blurred the line between what was the state's and what was the land owner's

'Safeguarding land use rights'

Wall gives 'place identity and a boundary'

'Open door policy'

& Beijing as a tourist city

Strong urban identity → Tourism

Figure 6.4. The wall and gate define the unit boundaries, Beijing (photo taken in 2005).

Figure 6.5. The guarded gate of a luxury condominium complex, Beijing (photo taken in 2003).

protected by walls and controlled gates, giving no access to outsiders. Indeed, the security systems of these new microdistricts are more sophisticated than their socialist counterparts. For instance, in promotional literature, many residential developments built on the urban fringe boast 24 hour policing and high-tech alarm systems. When I asked a real estate developer why his projects should be so intensively fortified, he responded by telling me stories of their construction.[4] Many of the projects in suburban areas were located on agricultural land acquired from local peasants, and the great economic benefits gained by developers often fostered a sense of relative deprivation among peasants. As a result, conflicts often erupted between peasants and builders, which not only frequently forced the latter to change their development strategies, but also, at times, led to violent encounters. Had these developments not fortressed themselves behind walls, the developer concluded, it would 'not be safe' to live in them.

As Piper Gaubatz has rightly pointed out, a new urban environment is developing around functionally specialized nodes of commerce, finance and trade in reform China (Gaubatz, 1995; 2005). The cellular landscape of the Maoist city, however, would not disappear easily. Instead, as the tradition of building security walls, together with other features characteristic of the socialist city, continues to shape urban construction, a hybrid landscape is in the making, combining both the marks of the past and the imprints of present development trends.

Concluding Remarks

In the story with which this chapter began, Clorinda, killed and buried by Tancred, was able to turn up again in front of her beloved, though in the form of a sorrowful voice crying out from a tree. In a somewhat similar manner, the vignettes I have outlined above suggest that, while the 'wall' as a traditional Chinese building typology was officially condemned at certain times, it has a tendency to return over and over again under new social conditions. Like Clorinda, the wall-building tradition did not return as a pure repetition; instead, it re-emerged under new guises in response to different contexts. With the past constantly *present* in the immediate present, the history, rather than representing a series of events unfolding progressively through time, is a case of dynamic repetition.

In his book *The End of History and the Last Man*, Fukuyama (1992) presents a world history in which the power of science, the free market, and democracy slowly obliges one nation after another to reshape itself. With the passing of communism, all nations with distinctive pasts will now necessarily reach for a common 'liberal democracy'. As a result, Fukuyama believes, all major problems have now been solved; we are facing a world in which struggle over major world issues has ended.

Arriving at a time of disorientation in the face of new historical conditions, Fukuyama's thesis has been well received in popular, post-Cold War political discourse in the West. Yet, in light of the relationship between past and present framed above, I contend that such a view ignores the role of tradition in the making of history, and thus is far from an accurate account of reality.[4] Traditional characteristics of nations do not disappear easily. Some may be held back temporarily during times of political and social change, but like the traumatic experience in Freud's account, after a latency period, these traditions may resurrect themselves under new conditions, and once again actively participate in shaping, for better or worse, distinctive presents. Therefore, if in Fukuyama's vision, a quietus has currently descended on history's long storm, I suggest instead that the debris that has been smashed by the previous storm is more than just a residue: it holds the potential to bring about another storm.

Notes

1. An earlier version of this chapter appeared in AlSayyad, N. (ed.) (2004) *The End of Tradition?* London: Routledge.
2. For a list of the dates of the demolition of different parts of the Beijing city walls, see the Appendix in Zhang (2003).
3. The survey was conducted in Beijing in 2000–2001. See chapter 3, note 2 for more details.
4. Interview by the author in Beijing, 11 January 2000.
5. Fukuyama's thesis has been criticized by many from different perspectives. Adopting a conservative culturalist approach, for example, Samuel Huntington (1996) conceptualizes an impending 'clash of civilizations' to secure a post-Cold War world order. Unlike Fukuyama, Huntington depicts the world as having moved during the twentieth century from nation-state conflict to ideological conflict, and finally to cultural conflict. The civilizational groups are now doomed to conflict in the new global space in which 'local politics is the politics of ethnicity; global politics is the politics of civilizations' (*Ibid.*, p. 28). From a different perspective, Robert Kaplan (1994, 2000) argues that, while part of the globe is inhabited by Fukuyama's Last Man savouring the offerings of modernity, a large part of the world's population continues to be 'stuck in history', condemned to a life of poverty. Although the media continues to attribute riots and other struggles to cultural and ethnic conflict, such depictions are often a chimera that hides the actual cause of conflict: the competition for scarce resources. Kaplan's argument echoes other studies on the effects of environmental stress (e.g. Homer-Dixon, 1991, 1999; Ophuls and Boyan, 1992).

Chapter Seven

The New Frontier: Urban Space and Everyday Practice in the Reform Era

If space as a whole has become the place where reproduction of the relations of production is located, it has also become the terrain for a vast confrontation...

Henri Lefèbvre, 1976, *The Survival of Capitalism*

In 1978 the Chinese leadership initiated the course of partial reform, 'feeling for stones to cross a river by taking one step and looking for the next', to use Deng Xiaoping's phrase. Experimenting with a few 'special economic zones' on its coastal border, China has gradually shifted from a centrally planned economy to 'a market economy with Chinese characteristics'. The state sector is shrinking, while private enterprises are growing rapidly (Nee, 1996; Logan, 2002). Production driven by the needs of the market has replaced the previous focus on the development of heavy industry (Ma and Wu, 2005a). With political controls lessening, previously suppressed consumption and cultural activities are booming (Davis *et al.*, 1995; Davis, 2000). Fiscal decentralization, the rise of the land-leasing market and municipal entrepreneurship have changed the processes of the production of urban space (Wu, 1997; Gaubatz, 2005), while the relaxation of regulations over rural migration allows a large number of peasants to move into the city (Solinger, 1999; Zhang, 2001; Friedmann, 2005, chapter 4).

How has the work unit responded to these major economic and social shifts? In what ways has its former enclosed space been altered by the restructuring process? And to what extent has the pattern of daily life within the unit compound been affected by the changes taking place in the city? A study of everyday practice within a work unit presented in this chapter reveals a microcosm of China's urban transition in the reform era. As a participant in, and observer of, many aspects of daily life in SRI, a work unit in Beijing, I witnessed a multitude of changes during my time there.[1] I observed, for instance, some of the unit walls were breached by stores and restaurants; a nightclub run by a Taiwanese businessman sat side by side with the public canteen; and numerous advertisements bombarded one's senses from roadside billboards. I heard some unit members applaud new choices opened up by commercial interests while others complained that market processes caused inequality. Party members still attended the political study sessions regularly, though more often than not the issues generating the most enthusiasm had to do with the amount of yearly bonuses. While rural migrants felt fortunate to be able to work in the city, their presence unavoidably clashed with some aspects of the previously exclusive work unit space.

This chapter focuses on the transition of the work unit from an enclosed entity to a more fluid space and the conflicts generated by this process.[2] Following Henri Lefèbvre (1991*b*), I maintain that the small realities of everyday life hold the forces that may reshape the social tapestry from the bottom up.[3] Below I present an ethnographical account of three selected episodes which reflected a correlation between large social processes and mundane human experiences. First, the takeover of work unit space by the expanding private sector for the realization of profit resulted in a confrontation between the use and exchange value of space. This is illustrated by the efforts of a group of work unit members to obtain a place to exercise, as their former leisure space was taken for commercial uses. Second, rural migrants created new identities and lifestyles as they strived to survive in the work unit while existing entirely outside its provisioning system. This is shown through a description of the life and daily routine of a housemaid from the countryside of Anhui Province, and the way in which her perceptions and experiences of space helped to shape her self-image in the city. Third, although the institutional barriers that prohibited unrestricted rural-to-urban migration were eroding, the social and cultural boundaries between urban residents and rural migrants remained, and were indeed reinvented. As I will show below, this is evident in the views on social disorder and the use of urban space expressed by work unit members and rural migrants.

The Frictions of Space

Located in north-western Beijing, the SRI was founded as one of the key research institutes in 1951. In the following decades, it gradually grew from a small 'urban village' with only tens of employees and a few buildings to a well-equipped unit of about 2,000 members, with research, administrative and living facilities closely situated within three neighbouring walled compounds. As one of the resource-rich units, the SRI provided its members housing and a variety of community services which included a kindergarten, a clinic, a library, a public bathhouse, canteens, sports fields and convenience shops. After two decades of reform, many of its social functions remained, yet the thread holding them together started to decay.

Before the reform, like other work units, the SRI was required to turn over most of its revenues to the state, which in turn redistributed money and scarce goods to the SRI according to the central plan. With the introduction of a market economy, while the SRI was still required to hand over part of its profits to the state as taxes, it enjoyed more financial freedom than before. This greatly enhanced its capacity to provide more consumption facilities for employees. Its recent construction and redevelopment projects included a number of high-rise apartment buildings, two supermarkets and a post office.

The SRI's new management system required its sub-units to pay their share of state taxes and to provide salaries to their own employees. The shift resulted in uneven development within the SRI. A few sub-units were so lucrative that they became companies selling stocks on the stock market, while the less successful ones struggled to cover their employees' salaries by renting their office space to private companies. One sub-unit, for example, leased its chemical laboratories to a Korean firm, and another rented a three-storey office complex to a stock broking company. Some unit canteens were converted into restaurants open to the general public. Attracted by higher salaries and more opportunities for personal development, some members left the SRI and joined private companies. Some, while still remaining in the unit, established firms that were closely connected with the private sector. Many people owned mobile phones and had internet access at home. Those most successful bought their own cars. As people frequently travelled beyond the unit compound for career, business and pleasure purposes, the once closely bounded work unit space became increasingly permeable.

Under Mao's rule, leisure activities often took the form of group action in the name of 'collectivism' (Wang, 1995). Unit members were organized to dance, have team sport events, and do standardized exercises (*guangbo tichao*) broadcast over loudspeakers (Brownell, 1995). In the reform era, as political controls relaxed, leisure options multiplied (Friedmann, 2005, chapter 5). A vibrant fitness culture developed within the SRI. People enthusiastically adopted various kinds of Chinese and Western style dance, and traditional regimen exercises and martial arts (e.g., *taiji*, *qigong*, and sword-handling), as ways of training. During my stay in the SRI, I was struck by the zeal with which people danced (figure 7.1). Three major squares of the unit were occupied by dance groups from 7.30 pm to 9.30 pm every night in the summer. The coarse ground hardly bothered people who ardently danced the rumba, waltz and fox-trot. Because females outnumbered males, many women danced with each other. This certainly was not by choice:

as one woman told me, 'I hope more men [will] join us, so I don't have to always perform the male steps (*tiao nanbu*)'.[4] Disco dancing, no longer confined to strobe-lit halls for the young, was taken up as a daily fitness technique for those in search of health, healing and longevity. Senior unit members demonstrated deftly on the square their newly forged dance routines – 'old-people disco' (*laonian disike*) – swaying, rocking and stretching their arms and legs.

Gone were the days when the Chinese spent most of their waking hours on group activities, but their disposition, as Pierre Bourdieu notes, was difficult to change because the *habitus* was unconsciously formed through long-term discipline: 'it goes without saying because it comes without saying' (Bourdieu, 1977, p. 94).[5] When there was a lack of choice in their leisure activities, people's disposition could be particularly durable. Most dance enthusiasts were senior unit employees and housewives. While bars and night clubs mushroomed in the city, the main patrons of these new recreational establishments were those who had become wealthy in the new economy and the younger generation. For many old residents of the SRI, these were considered establishments of 'high consumption' (*gao xiaofei*), far beyond their financial means; they sought cheaper ways of amusement instead. Influenced by the collectivist culture of the previous era, these often took the form of group activities.

Fitness and other leisure activities generated new group identities among unit residents. People distinguished themselves by joining different activity groups: technicians mostly belonged to the Western-style dance groups, while housewives

Figure 7.1. Dance in the nearby park (photo taken in 2000).

were often found in the *yangge* groups. The *yangge*, once a popular folk dance in rural north China, was transformed into a 'loyalty dance' to express loyalty to Mao during the Cultural Revolution. It was striking to see the 'loyalty dance' of Maoist time revive as a form of recreation devoid of any political meaning. Because its dancers wore brightly coloured clothes, had their faces heavily powdered, and were accompanied by the din of, often very noisy, clashing gongs and cymbals, *yangge* was considered by some to be 'low-class' (*di cengci*). This did not prevent dancers from enjoying it. In fact, some enjoyed dancing so much that they would dance whenever possible. As one woman confided to me, 'I wish I could escape the duty of cooking dinner, so I could come out to dance earlier'.[6] Booming leisure activities also contributed to the emergence of avowedly autonomous associations in the unit. While the state forbade the formation of any kind of voluntary groups during the first three decades after 1949, the situation had changed greatly. By the year 2000, the SRI had around a dozen registered voluntary or semi-voluntary societies, most of which were recreational groups, such as the 'Calligraphy Association', '*Taiji* Association' and 'Dance Association'.

As Dell Upton (1991, p. 197) points out, 'Once introduced into the landscape, the identity of a building and the intentions of its makers are dissolved within confusing patterns of human perception, imagination, and use... This process of creation goes on long after the crew leaves the site'. The sweeping craze for fitness transformed a variety of previously unclaimed spaces within the unit – the entry halls of some office buildings, squares, gardens, or simply small paved areas – into meaningful places for pleasure and interaction. When I tentatively asked one of my informants, Chang, a senior chemical engineer and a dance enthusiast, to draw me a map showing the general layout of the unit and the places where certain leisure activities took place, she produced an elaborate one. Chang not only illustrated the locations of various community facilities on the map, including two canteens, a small library, a clinic, a public bathhouse, a kindergarten and a guesthouse, but she also marked every apartment building within the unit. While there were many open lots in the three districts, only the open spaces in front of the three main office buildings were labelled 'squares'. This was because, Chang told me, 'Although we do exercises elsewhere in the unit, only the three squares are spacious enough for group activities'.[7] All three squares were intensively used. People performed *taiji* in the morning from 6 am to 7 am on the North Square, and danced from 7.30 pm to 9.30 pm at the same place at night. Similarly, on the South Square, people played *taiji* in the morning while others performed *mulan quan*, another popular traditional Chinese martial art, at the middle part of the square, and danced in the area to the east of the Main Building at night. The three squares were the places where people not only exercised together, but also gossiped, exchanged dance techniques and made gathering arrangements.

The rise of new opportunities for people to manipulate work unit space for their own purposes, however, was paralleled by the rapid dissolution of welfare facilities. As the urban reforms deepened, the SRI sought ways to redevelop welfare facilities into moneymaking operations, which was often accomplished at the expense of members' social needs. Among others, the loss of the social hall invoked the deepest grief. In January 1995, the SRI leaders decided to rent the structure to a firm owned by a 'Taiwan boss' at a price of 25 million RMB yuan (USD$3 million) for 10 years; the latter planned to redevelop the building into an 'Entertainment Palace'.[8] A 1995 unit newsletter article described this as a reasonable move:

Our unit is facing a financial dilemma due to the decrease of state investment and the increase of retired members ... in 1994, the unit spent more than 5 million RMB yuan on pensions. The figure is still swelling because the number of retired members will increase to 1,700 in the next five years. To support research, production and living costs, the only choice is to deepen the reforms, adjust to the market, and develop new businesses... Under these circumstances, the question is how to take full advantage of existing territorial advantages, adjust the distribution of resources and realize the full potential of real estate property. (Zong, 1995)

A dance enthusiast, however, considered the loss of the social hall a disaster:

The social hall used to be a place where we danced, played ping-pong and had gala celebrations. It is too bad that we cannot use it any more. We certainly enjoy dancing outdoors during the summer, but it is too cold to dance outside in the winter.[9]

Disappointed dancers turned to the unit trade union (*gonghui*) for solutions. As in the past, the trade union continued to manage welfare affairs within the unit; its various functions ranged from orchestrating social events to providing assistance to infirm persons. But its power was diminishing in the reform era. When the union asked two unit canteens for help, the negotiations turned out to be difficult. The canteens were contracted to individuals in the early 1990s. While they still provided cheap meals for unit members, major profits were generated from business with the general public, for whom they remained open until midnight. As a result, the canteens were no longer readily available for unit members' group activities. It was after many rounds of negotiation that the canteen managers agreed that the union could use the halls once a month.

The agreement, however, turned out to be short-lived. It came to an end in early 2000, when the canteen managers claimed that the accommodation of the events had a negative effect upon their business because of the regular displacement of furniture and monthly closure. Dancers were forced to turn to the trade union again, and the latter, after several failed ventures, turned to the unit library for help. The library agreed that dancers could use its reading room for group activities when it was closed on Tuesday mornings. As the available time was limited and the room was too small to dance, dancers were unhappy with the terms of the agreement. They wanted the leased social hall returned for their use after the current tenancy expired. But that would require a wait of another 5 years. A member of the Dance Association commented on the uncertain future: 'Now our unit won't do anything if it can't make money. Who knows if we could get it back in 2005?'[10] And she was right: when I revisited the SRI in 2005, I noticed that the structure, though no longer the 'Entertainment Palace', now housed a Sichuan cuisine restaurant.

Living on the Edge

According to a senior unit resident, until 1975 no peddlers were allowed to enter the unit. Starting with a few vendors in the late 1970s, rural migrants gradually took over most service jobs (newspaper delivery, street-sweeping, street-vending and baby-sitting) within the unit. The unit stores, which once held a monopoly, now had to compete with small shops run by peasants (figure 7.2).

Although rural migrants had become a part of urban daily life, they were, to a large degree, invisible. When asked if they knew where migrants lived, few unit members could answer. For them, migrants came and went without a trace, as if from nowhere. Some simply assumed that they lived somewhere in the suburbs where rents were cheap. Contrary to the speculation, however, many migrants working in the unit lived close by. Those contracted to the work unit as elevator operators often lived in the basements of unit apartment buildings, and some lived in rentals just a street away from the SRI, hidden behind the walls of private courtyard houses (*siheyuan*). Walking through the narrow, unpaved back alleys, which were barely noticeable from the busy main streets, one would soon reach the single-storey, traditional courtyard houses. Entering any of them, one would find a yard crowded with small brick huts built on every corner of the compound. In the narrow space between the huts, tricycles, garbage bags and piles of cabbages littered the ground, and lines of hanging laundry stretched chaotically between huts (figure 7.3).

The compound was quiet during the daytime; except for mothers with small babies, most residents were gone to work. Only at day's end was the courtyard filled with the sounds and smells of life: cooking, children playing and the exchange of neighbourly greetings. In warm weather, the doors of most huts remained open at dusk. The low and narrow wooden doors, which could be difficult for larger people to enter, provided entrance to the small rooms inside the huts. Rooms in these huts ranged from 8 to 12 square metres; they had hard-packed earth floors, unpainted walls and tiled roofs. Each of the rooms typically accommodated a family of four to six; cooking, eating, sleeping and entertaining

Figure 7.2. Shops run by peasants compete with unit stores (photo taken in 1999).

Figure 7.3. A courtyard that provides rentals for peasants (photo taken in 2000).

all taking place within this small area. The substandard living conditions were close to what one would typically find in a Third World slum.

I was brought to the compound by my informant, Aunt Wang, a maid from Anhui Province. She lived in one of these huts with her family: her husband, a sanitation worker; her eighteen-year-old son, a temporary worker hired by the SRI; and her sixteen-year-old nephew, a leather jacket street-vendor. In their 11 square metre room, they had one bunk bed (the lower level for the couple and the upper one for the son), one small single bed (for the nephew), one table, three chairs, a charcoal stove, an aluminium pot and other small utensils. The ceiling and walls of the room were covered with *Beijing Youth Daily* (*Beijing qingnian bao*), a widely read newspaper famous for its speedy news coverage (figure 7.4). The newspapers' dazzling contents and images provided much for a visitor's eye to take in: on one corner of the wall the newspaper proclaimed that the state had made the decision to push high-tech industry ahead, on another it complained

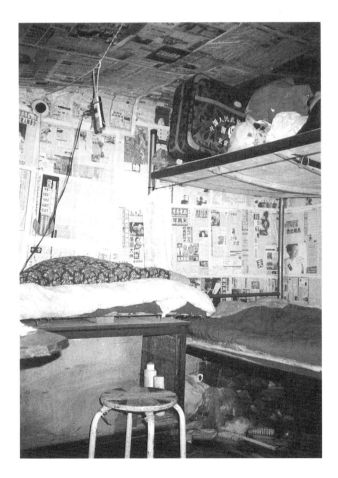

Figure 7.4. A corner of Wang's room (photo taken in 2000).

about the falseness of modern advertising, and on yet another it reported that two of former American President George H.W. Bush's sons were governors of two big American states. The monthly rent for the room was 430 RMB yuan (USD$50).

The life of Aunt Wang and her family was revealed to me bit by bit through dozens of conversations. I learned that Wang was initially brought to Beijing by her cousin 5 years ago to work as a housemaid. As she gradually achieved a stable income, she brought her husband, her son, and later her nephew, to the city. Among the family, Wang's income remained the highest, determining her high status in the family. Wang was openly proud that at present it was her husband who cooked meals and did laundry. When I asked why she did not take advantage of the unit public canteen which was only 3 minutes' walk from her home, Wang replied that home-cooked meals were much cheaper. Although she had lived in Beijing for 5 years, she had never visited any tourist attractions such as the Imperial Palace or the Great Wall. Wang's thriftiness had saved her enough money to build a brick-concrete house in her hometown. When I joked that it seemed a waste because Wang's whole family was absent from the new house most of the year, Wang responded, 'It was built for my grandsons. They don't have Beijing *hukou* and cannot go to school here. They have to stay in my hometown'.[11] Wang explained that although the reforms had reduced the importance of the decades old resident permit (*hukou*) system, the children of rural migrants still did not have access to schools in the city, unless they could afford expensive non-resident tuition fees.

While Wang was uneasy when talking about the future, she was fairly satisfied with her present life. Unlike live-in housemaids, Wang worked by the hour (*xiaoshi gong*) for 22 households (table 7.1). By working seven days a week at a wage of 5 RMB yuan (USD$0.60) per hour, she had a higher income and enjoyed greater freedom than live-in housemaids. As Wang was a hard worker, her clients continuously recommended her to other households; she gradually built up her own network of contacts in a few neighbourhoods. Although she did not have a telephone, her clients were able to contact her anytime through her son's mobile pager, and she could return calls by using the public phone. Knowing that Wang worked for households scattered in five units/neighbourhoods at different locations, I asked her if she could draw me a map identifying the sites of her daily routine.[12] Wang told me that because she was illiterate, she had never used a map in her life, nor even considered drawing one herself. She managed to travel to different places in the city by remembering the numbers of apartment buildings as well as the characteristics of the places. When Wang had to take buses to go long distances, she had more things to remember: the number of the first bus she would take, the number of stops between the transfers, the numbers of the subsequent buses, and the name of her destination. During the journey, Wang confessed, she

Table 7.1. Wang's weekly schedule.

	Morning	Afternoon	Evening
Monday	8.00–10.00am Household 1, apartment building of the bank	2.00–5.00pm Odd Week. Household 3, Building 33, SRI	5.30–7.30pm Household 5, Building 13, SRI
	11.00am–12.00 noon Household 2, Building 13, SRI	Even Week. Household 4, Building 33, SRI	
Tuesday	9.00am–12.00 noon Household 6, Zhaojunmiao District	2.00–5.00pm Household 7, Zizhu Garden	5.30–7.30pm Household 8, apartment building of the bank
Wednesday	9.00am–12.00 noon Household 9, Building 13, SRI	2.00–5.00pm Household 10, Building 31, SRI	5.30–7.30pm Household 11, Building 33, SRI
Thursday	9.00am–12.00 noon Households 12 and 13, apartment building of the bank	2.00–5.00pm Household 14, Zizhu Garden	5.30–7.30pm Household 15, apartment building of the bank
Friday	8.30–9.30am Household 16, the university	2.00–5.00pm Household 17, Zhaojunmiao District	5.30–7.30pm Household 18, Building 33, SRI
Saturday	8.30–11.30am Household 19, Zizhu Garden	2.00–5.00pm Household 20, Zizhu Garden	
Sunday	8.30–11.30am Household 21, Building 33, SRI	2.00–5.00pm Household 22, apartment building of the bank	

Source: Interview with Wang by the author, Beijing, 12 June 2000.

was so concentrated on counting the number of stops that she paid little attention to the urban landscape.[13]

Spatial Disruptions

Wang enjoyed the sense of security the seemingly chaotic compound gave her. 'I have never seen a single robbery, nor have I ever been robbed', she told me, 'Beijing is very safe, and our courtyard is always in good order'.[14] The city dwellers, however, generally perceived rural migrants and their 'congregating zones' as the source of urban disorder. The Chinese city under Mao provided urban residents a safe and stable living environment. As the country moved towards a market economy, the previous order wore away; crime and prostitution increased (Solinger, 1999). Although these 'urban ills' were closely related to changes brought about by the process of 'marketization', they were frequently attributed, in public discourse, to peasant migrants (Zhang, 2001, chapter 1). The latter, with their rural origins, spatial mobility and lower economic status, were considered money-driven and maliciously jealous of urban affluence (Solinger, 1999).

Although the institutional barriers that prohibited rural-to-urban migration were eroding in the reform era, new cultural and social boundaries were invented. Most urban residents were astute about the differences between themselves and migrants. The latter, according to several city dwellers with whom I talked, could be identified by their accent, gestures, darker complexion, formless clothes, worn-out belongings, and above all, their dispositions. Once their Otherness was identified, migrants were often discriminated against. Several migrants told me that city folk intentionally pointed the wrong way when consulted for directions. The unit gate attendant was particularly good at evaluating the status of outsiders: whether they were housemaids, newcomers to the city, or peasant-workers (*mingong*). Certainly, unlike in the past, the gate attendant no longer stopped just anyone whom he could not recognize for formal identification, as 'outsiders' were now an inseparable part of everyday life in the unit compound.

The unprecedented arrival of massive numbers of peasants in the city posed new challenges to urban order and drained already scarce urban resources. This made urban space itself, rather than anything else, the new scarcity in reform China. In 1995 the Ministry of Public Security enacted a policy which required all migrants to register with local authorities and obtain a 'temporary resident permit' (*wailai renkou zanzhu zheng*). Since then and up until 2003, the police have reserved the right to stop anyone looking like a migrant on the streets for an identification check. Indeed, officers were often particularly shrewd in assessing who was a migrant, and who was not. This, according to Wang, was because city dwellers and migrants had different bodily features: 'Beijing people have pale faces, they are bigger and their outfits are better than ours'.[15] Migrants without a temporary resident permit might be taken to the police substation (*paichusuo*) for further questioning and a fine would be imposed. If the migrant did not have enough money to pay the fine, he or she might be sent to suburban Beijing or somewhere in Heibei Province to perform physical labour.[16] Although Wang had a resident permit, she still feared being sent away. Her anxiety originated from a story widely circulated among rural migrants at the time:

One day a guy was stopped on the street by an officer for an identification check. The person handed his temporary resident card to the officer, but the latter tore it up, threw it away, and then asked, 'Do you have another one?' When the person answered no, the officer said to him, 'Then I have to send you to the police substation'.[17]

While rural migrants felt that they were sometimes the victims of unfair treatment by the authorities, they were perceived by the state and city dwellers as the source of disorder. During my stay in the SRI, a household was burgled: a thief broke into an apartment and stole possessions from one family. The most shocking part of the story was that the thief even stole the clothes the family took off the night before. While several versions of the story circulated, I noted that the thief was referred to as the 'peasant worker'. I inquired if the police had arrested anyone, but the answer was no. When I asked a storyteller how he knew that the criminal was a peasant worker, he spoke firmly: 'Only a peasant worker could be so poor that he would steal used clothes!'[18] Through this daily telling and retelling of the story, facts were mixed with imagination, constructing a firm boundary between 'Us' and 'Them'.

Once created, boundaries were carefully maintained through trivial everyday practices. The SRI public bathhouse, for instance, used to be reserved for the exclusive use of its employees and their families. Since the early 1990s, with the increasing shortage of social services in the city, the state encouraged work units to allow the general public to take advantage of their community resources. The SRI bathhouse was then opened up, and unit residents were forced to share the space with outsiders, many of whom were migrants. Facing the transition, some, believing that the bathhouse had become 'chaotic' and 'dirty', immediately stopped using it and started to shower at home. Those who continued to use the bathhouse complained that it had become crowded, inconvenient and unsafe. Some decided to visit the bathhouse only in the afternoon, when outsiders were few. Although no change was visible, some believed that cabinets and couches were 'polluted' by outsiders. To avoid being contaminated, they brought newspapers from home, spread them out before they sat down on the couch in the boudoir, and carefully placed all their personal items within the area of the newspaper. Through this subtle gesture, a line was drawn between themselves and their surroundings.

Soon after the unit bathhouse was opened to the public, a robbery took place. A woman's belongings were stolen while she was showering. She had to ask colleagues to call her family to bring her clothes. After the event, more residents preferred locking their personal possessions in the cabinets. But often there were insufficient cabinets to go round. One interviewee was angry because, she believed, many of those using the cabinets were outsiders. 'And they imitate us, bringing locks to lock the cabinets too!' she said.[19] To keep her belongings safe, she sought alternatives. Her favourite strategy was wearing worn-out homely clothes to the bathhouse. 'It was safe', she commented. 'No one would steal tattered clothes'.[20] With other like-minded members of her local community doing the same, an ironic reversal occurred: some rural migrants appeared more fashionable than the locals. After some time, as people from both sides began wearing similar clothes, it became difficult to identify who was the migrant and who was the local. When people undressed themselves for a shower, they became virtually indistinguishable: after all, there are not too many clues on a naked body.

Liquid Urban Space?

For years, the work unit had remained a largely self-contained entity, whose domain was closed to outside influences (Lü and Perry, 1997a). After the reforms, the free movement of people, capital and information across the borders of the work unit greatly increased. Yet as we have seen, the robust expansion of the mobile space created different consequences for different people. While those who adapted successfully to the new economic system drew on diverse offerings outside the unit compound, those who were less successful, mostly old and female members, still centred their lives on the work unit. The dual effect, though generated by quite different processes, echoed the observation Manuel Castells makes on the rising network society: on one side there are mobile elites, and on the other are the excluded whose lives and experiences are rooted in a fixed place and in their history (1996, pp. 415–416).

To be sure, many elements of social differentiation were 'no longer built around defined territorial limits' (Kaufmann, 2002, p. 101). The increased mobility of people, the advances in telecommunications and the expansion of the private sector brought new ways of escaping the previous social and spatial constraints, even for those who were located at the periphery of urban space. The life of the housemaid Wang is a case in point. The market opened up new opportunities for rural migrants to live and work in the city. Wang's routine as a housemaid involved 22 households, and sometimes she needed to go to five different locations within a single day. Through her movements, Wang not only created new paths between previously separated compartments, but also built up her own lifestyle outside the boundaries of the well-defined environment of the work unit. With newly acquired economic capital, Wang's dominant position was accepted at home, while her husband's power was reduced.[21] When Wang proudly stated that it was her husband who did most housework, part of her identity had changed. She was no longer the rural woman whose life was bounded by the family; instead, she was a free labourer connected to a larger network, through personal relations with her clients, her son's electronic pager and the public phone.

Nonetheless, the institutional legacies left from the former socialist system continued to limit rural migrants' capacity to move vertically and horizontally in the larger social space. Without a permanent resident permit, they were denied the access to perquisites such as free compulsory education for their children. The lack of economic and cultural capital thrust most rural migrants to the bottom of a ladder with little hope of climbing up. Their experience with the city was one of remarkable hardship. When Wang shuttled between her clients' homes by memorizing numbers, the city collapsed in front of her illiterate eyes into a series of nodes marked by numbers. With little economic capital, she was alienated from much of urban space where numerous alternative lifestyles had been created by the market. In one sense, Wang's urban experience was like the newspapers she pasted on the walls of her rental room: although many other worlds were juxtaposed there, for Wang, it was nothing more than a collage of fragmented and unrelated images, images without depth, which one could never enter.

The emergence of migrant enclaves produced new landscapes of scarcity in the city. The mobility of rural migrants and their substandard living condition created both real and imagined threats to the city dwellers. The differences between urban and rural disposition were employed to ensure the maintenance of urban order. Nonetheless, as this chapter shows, the increasing fluidity of urban space had allowed the everyday trajectories of urban and rural residents to intersect. As the two parties ran parallel to each other in close spatial proximity, disruptions and connections occurred in unpredictable ways. The formerly closed, unit-based welfare system, for instance, was opened up for outsiders' use in the reform era. This transition brought much uncertainty to unit residents as seen in the example of the bathhouse. As peasants now shared the space once reserved for the sole consumption of unit residents, the latter's trusted patterns of privilege disappeared. With anxiety, city dwellers invented new boundaries to differentiate Us and Them. The bathhouse became a site where identities were constructed, expressed and negotiated. Eventually, with the rise of a new homogeneous space, the turmoil of the changed urban realm was displaced, guaranteeing the appearance of a conceivable social order.

As Andrew Sayer points out, 'social processes do not occur on *tabula rasa* but "take place" within an inherited space' (2000, p. 115). This study shows that legacies from the previous system still play an important role in shaping intermediate solutions and conflicting realities in everyday practices. In the dancers' search for a place to train, for example, the gestures of actors pointed in different directions, each rooted in the interplay between the past and present. Dance on a daily basis as a way of amusement was made possible by the relaxed control of everyday life in the reform era, but the form in which it was organized – group activities – was nonetheless influenced by collectivism of the previous era. While residents created spaces of pleasure out of the rigid spatial grid of the work unit through leisure activities, their newly carved niches were threatened by the rising commercial interests. The work unit no longer had a monopoly of the organization of everyday life, but it continued to be responsible for welfare expenses. As 'soft budget constraints' became tightened in a mixed economy, the work unit was forced to take a new role in mobilizing its existing resources to generate additional revenues for its operation. Under such circumstances, emphasis on the use value of the former welfare space was reduced, while its exchange value was promoted. While dancers sought places of pleasure, for the canteen managers, the realization of profits was essential. The trade union adhered to its conventional role in the management of everyday life, but its endeavours failed in the new milieu where the needs of the market were dominant. These episodes remind us that in a fast changing society, tradition, as Nezar AlSayyad puts it, is 'what we make and sustain everyday and everywhere through the occasionally contemptuous act of living' (2004, p. 26). It is through these interrelated daily practices that an urban transition progressed slowly but steadily.

In his book *Liquid Modernity* (2000) Zygmunt Bauman characterizes the liquid society as one in which:

The prime technique of power is now escape, slippage, elision and avoidance, the effective rejection of any territorial confinement with its cumbersome corollaries of order-building, order-maintenance and the responsibility for the consequences of it all as well as of the necessity to bear their costs. (Bauman, 2000, p. 11)

Bauman speaks of advanced capitalist society in the era of consumerism, globalization and ephemerality. The fluidification of Chinese urban space has just started, in a different context and with different consequences. As such, it is necessarily fraught with confrontations: the confrontation between old and new, socialist and capitalist, the use and exchange value of space, and the privileged Us and the underprivileged Them. The Chinese city has indeed been a frontier which makes possible the spatial proximity and synchronic temporality of myriad heterogeneous practices. As these practices intersect, combine and ramify, layers of boundaries are dismantled, paths between distinct compartments multiply, and life unfolds as a strange conjuncture of different presents. It is this diversity that creates an everyday which is uncertain, yet full of potentials.

Notes

1. The main part of my fieldwork was conducted in 2000, supported by Social Science Research Council International Field Research Fellowship, 1999–2000. Follow-up research was undertaken in 2001, 2004 and 2005. In order to protect interviewees from official harassment, the names of both the work unit and individuals have been changed.
2. For recent discussion on social fluidity, see, for example, Bauman, 2000; Urry, 2000; Kaufmann, 2002. In classical sociology, a fluid society is one which allows individuals to 'move vertically in socio-professional space' (Kaufmann, 2002, p. 4). With the development of communication and transport systems, the social fluidity question has become more far-reaching in recent years. According to Vincent Kaufmann (*Ibid.*), the current fluidity debate concerns issues incuding vertical and horizontal movement in social space, transport and communication systems as manipulators of time and space,

and diverse barriers and margins for individual operation. Zygmunt Bauman (2000, p. 11) characterizes the state of the weakening of social structure, the rejection of territorial restrictions, and the dimunition of the mutual engagement 'between the supervisors and the supervised, capital and labour' and so on as 'liquid modernity'.

3. While my study has been informed by existing scholarship, I have decided not to delve into the theoretical discussion on everyday life in this chapter. For the discussion on the everyday in social and cultural studies, see Lefèbvre, 1984, 1997; Bourdieu, 1977, 1990; Certeau, 1984; Ortner, 1994; Highmore, 2002. For the relationship between everyday life and the built environment, see Thrift, 1996; McLeod, 1997; Crawford, 1999; Upton, 2002. For the application of the notion of everyday practice to the study of Chinese society, see, for instance, Farquhar, 1994; Liu, 2000.

4. Interview by the author, 17 May 2000.

5. Bourdieu's concept of *habitus* refers to a set of internalized dispositions that reflect the social conditions within which they were acquired (Bourdieu, 1977, 1990). These dispositions do not determine one's actions but provide the feel of the game which guides one's everyday practices. They are ingrained in such a way that they are not readily amenable to conscious reflection and modification (Thompson, 1991, pp. 12–13).

6. Interview by the author, 6 June 2000.

7. Interview by the author, 18 May 2000.

8. The building was divided into two parts before being redeveloped into the 'Entertainment Palace': one part was the social hall, and the other was a restaurant.

9. Interview by the author, 6 June 2000.

10. Interview by the author, 17 June 2001.

11. Interview by the author, 11 January 2000.

12. The approach to the spatial experiences of different social groups adopted here was inspired by Lynch, 1960; Upton, 1985.

13. Interview by the author, 18 January 2000.

14. Interview by the author, 18 January 2000.

15. Interview by the author, 12 June 2000.

16. The sending-away system was abolished in 2003.

17. Interview by the author, 12 June 2000.

18. Interview by the author, 3 June 2001.

19. Interview by the author, 7 June 2000.

20. Interview by the author, 7 June 2000.

21. Bourdieu (1986) categorizes the main components of social resources which define power and the capacities of the actors in the field into economic, cultural and social capital. Economic capital not only consists of capital in the Marxian sense, but also of other economic possessions. Cultural capital has three forms of existence: first, it exists as incorporated in the *habitus*; second, it is manifested in cultural articles such as dress and bodily decoration; third, it is institutionalized via cultural and educational institutions (Bourdieu, 1977). Social capital is a resource that is connected with group membership and social networks and based on mutual recognition.

Chapter Eight

Epilogue

Spatial reconfigurations are common in societies in transition. By giving frame and form to the material world, architecture defines the structure of human flows, creates a visual representation of power, and provides the physical site where everyday life occurs. Thus, the reordering of space is really a reordering of social relations. The Chinese attempt to reshape the built environment shared with modernist projects elsewhere a vision of social transformation through spatial reorganization by employing modern knowledge and techniques (Gregory, 1994; Scott, 1998). What is different is the unique outcome created as modernity unfolded within the specific national and social contexts (Gaonkar, 1999; Eisenstadt, 2002). Eventually every society produces its own space (Lefèbvre, 1991a).

In the preceding chapters, I have examined a number of critical aspects of how Chinese society constructed itself through the making and remaking of its urban form. I show that despite the nation's identification with 'the modern', the historical condition of scarcity limited the possibility that the desire for modernity could ever, in actuality, be fulfilled. Although planners attempted to apply modern planning techniques to the socialist city, their attempts were often effectively ignored. The realization of planning ideals such as the microdistrict schema was continuously postponed. The complex and often conflicting relationship between scarcity and the socialist system created specific spatial strategies, which eventually gave rise to the unique form of the work unit.

The unit-based Maoist city appeared modern, orderly, and devoid of tokens of extreme poverty. In contrast, in the countryside, most savings were drawn off to feed industrial growth. As such, the occasional efforts to improve the rural built environment – such as those during the people's commune movement – were inevitably defeated due to the scarcity of resources. In the end, despite the socialist aspirations to eliminate urban-rural inequities, the locomotive of urban development roared along on its own track, leaving a 'poor and blank' rural world extending endlessly on both sides. This history of the contemporary Chinese built environment, therefore, has been a narration of China's mixed experiences with socialist and Third World modernity.

The book demonstrates that, despite successive transformations, what endows the Chinese built environment with consistency is the significant role it plays in the construction, reproduction and transformation of the social order. Far from a neutral background, the space of the work unit had important socio-political implications for contemporary Chinese society. In Chapters 3 and 4, I show that the work unit offered a safety net through which industrial labour was reproduced at relatively low cost, facilitated the socialist mode of domination of everyday life, and provided a spatial basis for community building and social bonding. In Chapter 7, I look into the post-reform work unit as a site where, on one hand, interrelated heterogeneous practices fragmented the previous spatial grid, while continually restructuring a new social space, on the other. They did so, nonetheless, under the sustaining constraint of the work unit space.

Since 1978 radical changes have been brought to the Chinese city by the economic reforms and the nation's active participation in global economy (Ma and Wu, 2005a; Hsing, 1998). Earlier the Chinese city was organized around industrial production, but in the reform era it has been connected to the needs of the market, attracting domestic and international businesses, events, tourists and institutions in order to grow and prosper. The city has become increasingly differentiated, with distinct functional zones such as finance, commerce, residential and industrial districts (Gaubatz, 1995, 2005). This transition is accompanied by the development of the freeway system, improvement in the communications infrastructure, an increase in numbers of private cars, and the rise of new urban spaces such as CBDs and high-tech parks.

In this light, the Chinese city has become similar to cities in advanced capitalist societies. In other aspects, however, Chinese society continues to generate urban spaces that differ greatly from those of other societies (Ma and Wu, 2005b, pp. 10–12). The post-reform residential developments in major Chinese cities, for example, have been dominated by large-scale, high-rise and high-density projects due to the scarcity of urban land. The microdistrict schema, the decades-old socialist planning paradigm, was reinforced through planning codes as the dominant model for these large-scale real estate developments. As such, China's urban residential landscape is unfolding according to its inherited blueprint rather than becoming Western.

In fact, the high-density residential development pattern in China bears a great resemblance to some other East Asian cities such as Singapore and Hong Kong. It would, however, be erroneous to judge the resemblance merely as a result of cultural similarity, while ignoring the pressing problems of population pressure and the scarcity of land and other resources shared by these cities. To be sure, post-reform China displays plentiful signs of affluence. While in the past, urban residents struggled for basic necessities, many of them now join a perpetual quest for newest luxuries. Shopping malls have mushroomed rapidly throughout China, along with other new spaces of consumerism, such as karaoke bars and golf courses. With a total floor space of 6 million square feet, Beijing's Golden

Figure 8.1. Beijing's Golden Resources, the world's largest shopping mall by 2005, boasts over 1,000 shops, 230 escalators and 10,000 free parking spaces. One end of the building houses the Lufthansa Centre (photo taken in 2005).

Figure 8.2. The rapid growth of small businesses and the proliferation of single-family terrace houses have greatly changed the streetscape of Kanshi, a small town in Fujian (photo taken in 2005).

Resources Shopping Mall easily surpasses the largest mall in the United States – Minnesota's 4.2 million square feet Mall of America (figure 8.1), while the South China Mall in Guangdong features theme parks and a giant replica of Paris's Arc de Triomphe (Karnak, 2005). Even small rural towns now see a wide choice of modern products greeting customers on local streets (figure 8.2).

A new discourse of scarcity, however, arose at a time when material abundance has created a world of boundless desire. In 2004, the Chinese state launched a national campaign of building 'a conservation-minded society' (*jieyuexing shehui*) (Ma, 2004). The official statement conceptualized China as a country with scarce resources and established energy-efficient development as a crucial national goal (*Ibid.*). The campaign called for a better public awareness of the importance of conservation and the exploration of sustainable ways of production (*Renmin ribao*, 2005). With a new emphasis on the development of environmentally friendly buildings, the tendency to construct free-standing housing in urban suburbs was discouraged as being wasteful of land, while the high-density real estate development pattern was reinforced (Song, 2005).

The story of modernity, scarcity and space continues to unfold in China. In this book I have shown the workings of scarcity on social and spatial imaginations, and its impacts on human agency and the built environment. And perhaps more importantly, I have demonstrated the possibilities of producing other spaces and other knowledges by drawing upon indigenous experiences in the struggle against scarcity. It is my hope that the findings of this study will help to inform the design of better futures, not only for China, but also for other parts of the world. As we step into the twenty-first century, the battles over the control of resources show no sign of diminishing, and over one billion of the world's population still live below the povery line. Scarcity seems to be forever haunting modern society.

It is imperative to take steps to develop new imaginations about scarcity, so that solutions can be found to resolve conflict without resorting to vicious inequalities or violent actions.

Glossary

baojia 保甲
baowei ke 保卫科
bi 壁
changzhang jijin 厂长基金
cheng 城
da 大
dajiefang 大街坊
dang'an 档案
danwei 单位
dazayuanr 大杂院儿
dazibao 大字报
di cengci 低层次
difang danwei 地方单位
fan langfei 反浪费
fangguan ke 房管科
fanghuang 房荒
fuqiang 富强
gao xiaofei 高消费
gong 公
gonghui 工会
guangbo ticao 广播体操
hukou 户口
huiguan 会馆
jiceng danwei 基层单位
jiedao banshichu 街道办事处
jieyuexing shehui 节约型社会
jumin dian 居民点
jumin weiyuanhui 居民委员会
laonian disike 老年迪斯科
lilong 里弄
lingxing jianzhu 零星建筑
liutong 六统

loushang louxia,
diandeng dianhua 楼上楼下，电灯电话
mingong 民工
mu 亩
mulan quan 木兰拳
paichusuo 派出所
qiang 墙
qigong 气功
qilou 骑楼
qiufu 求富
shangpin fang 商品房
shehui shang 社会上
shenghuo jian 生活间
shenghuo qu 生活区
shequ jianshe 社区建设
siheyuan 四合院
taiji 太极
tiao nanbu 跳男步
wailai renkou zanzhu zheng 外来人口
暂住证
weizhang jianzhu 违章建筑
wuye guanli gongsi 物业管理公司
xiaoqu 小区
xiaoshi gong 小时工
yamen 衙门
yangge 秧歌
yongjiu peidu 永久陪都
yuan 垣
zhongyang danwei 中央单位
zhufang gongjijin 住房公积金
ziqiang 自强
zongwu ke 总务科

Illustration Credits and Sources

The author and publisher would like to thank all those who have granted permission to reproduce illustrations. We have made every effort to contact and acknowledge copyright holders, but if any errors have been made we would be happy to correct them at a later printing.

Cover: © Duanfang Lu.

Chapter 1
1.1. © Duanfang Lu.

Chapter 2
2.1. *Source*: Dong (1999), figure 5.2.2, p. 259.
2.2. *Source*: Juzhuqu xiangxi guihua keti yanjiuzu (1985), figure 1.13, p. 26.
2.3. *Source*: Wang and Chen (1964), figure 3, p. 9.
2.4. *Source*: Juzhuqu xiangxi guihua keti yanjiuzu (1985), figure 2.2, p. 55.
2.5. *Source*: Chengshi jianshe zongju guihua sheji ju (1956), figure 28.
2.6. *Source*: Li (1956), figure 2, p. 20.
2.7. *Source*: Nongyebu changbu guihuazu (1956), figure 3, p. 70.
2.8. *Source*: Zhao (1956), figure 4.
2.9. *Source*: Beijing gongye jianzhu shejiyuan (1963), figure 10, p. 32.
2.10. *Source*: Pei, Liu and Shen (1958), figure 'Hongqing gongshe Zaojiatun jumindian'.
2.11. *Source*: Wang (1962), figure 6, p. 9.
2.12. *Source*: Wang and Xu (1962), figure 1, p. 6.
2.13. *Source*: Beijing gongye jianzhu shejiyuan (1963), figures 1, 2 and 3, p. 34.
2.14. *Source*: Juzhuqu xiangxi guihua keti yanjiuzu (1985), figure 2.4, p. 56.
2.15. *Source*: Jiangsusheng chengshi jiansheting changzhou guihua gongzuozu (1959), figure 3, p. 38.

2.16. *Source*: Zhao (1963), figure 3, p. 2.

2.17. *Source*: Zhao (1963), figure 6, p. 2.

2.18–2.20. © Duanfang Lu.

Chapter 3

3.1. © Duanfang Lu

3.2. *Source*: Hunansheng chengshi jiansheju (1958), figure 1, p. 15.

3.3. *Source*: Shanghai gongye jianzhu shejiyuan meishan liantiechang shenghuoqu shejizu (1973), figure 1, p. 21.

3.4–3.5. © Duanfang Lu.

3.6. *Source*: Shanghai gongye jianzhu shejiyuan meishan liantiechang shenghuoqu shejizu (1973), figure 3, p. 21.

3.7–3.8. © Duanfang Lu.

3.9. *Source*: Lu (1964), figure 2, p. 17.

3.10 © Duanfang Lu.

3.11 © Tan Ying.

3.12–3.14 © Duanfang Lu.

3.15. *Source*: Gong and Li (1963), figure 8, p. 5.

3.16. *Source*: Yao and Wang (1962), figure 10, p. 24.

3.17. © Tan Ying.

3.18–3.19. © Duanfang Lu.

3.20. *Source*: Shanghai minyong jianzhu shejiyuan (1962), figure 41.

3.21. *Source*: Wang and Li (1961).

3.22–3.25. © Duanfang Lu.

Chapter 4

4.1. *Source*: Ao (1959).

4.2. *Source*: Qian and Ren (1959), p.14.

4.3. *Source*: Zheng (1960).

Chapter 5

5.1. *Source*: Wang (1961).

5.2. *Source*: Zhang and Tao (1961).

5.3. *Source*: Pei, Liu and Shen (1958), figures 5 and 6, p. 11.

5.4. *Source*: Wang, Wu and Deng (1958).

5.5. *Source*: Ru (1960).

5.6. *Source*: Wang and Cheng (1959), figure 1, p.10.

5.7. *Source*: Wang and Cheng (1959), figure 3, p. 12.

5.8. *Source*: Huanan gongxueyuan jianzhuxi (1958), figure 1, p. 11.

5.9. *Source*: Wang, Wu and Wan (1958), figure 6, p. 22.

5.10. *Source*: Tianjin daxue jianzhuxi (1958), figure 4, p. 16.

5.11. *Source*: Tianjin daxue jianzhuxi (1958), figure 6, p. 17.

5.12. *Source*: Wang (1958), figure 58, p. 26.

5.13. *Source*: Figure 13, in Huanan gongxueyuan jianzhuxi (1959), figure 13, p. 4.

5.14. *Source*: Wang, *et al.* (1958), figure 3, p. 15.

5.15. *Source*: Huanan gongxueyuan jianzhuxi (1958), figure 4, p. 12.

5.16. *Source*: Wu and Li (1959), p. 15.

5.17. *Source*: Wang (1962), figure 1, p. 10.

5.18. *Source*: Liu (1963), figure 1, p. 10.

Chapter 6

6.1. *Source*: Farmer (1976), p. 126.

6.2. © Song Huancheng.

6.3. *Source*: Liang (1986), figure 2, p. 64.

6.4–6.5. © Duanfang Lu.

Chapter 7

7.1–7.4. © Duanfang Lu.

Chapter 8

8.1–8.2. © Duanfang Lu.

Bibliography

Allen, J.B. (1966) *The Company Town in the American West*. Norman, OK: University of Oklahoma Press.

AlSayyad, N. (ed.) (1992) *Forms of Dominance: On the Architecture and Urbanism of the Colonial Enterprise*. Aldershot: Avebury.

AlSayyad, N. (2001) Hybrid culture/hybrid urbanism: Pandora's Box of the 'third place', in AlSayyad, N. (ed.) *Hybrid Urbanism: On the Identity Discourse and the Built Environment*. Westport: Praeger, pp. 1–17.

AlSayyad, N. (2004) The end of tradition, or the tradition of endings? in AlSayyad, N. (ed.) *End of Tradition?* London: Routledge, pp. 1–28.

Åman, A. (1992) *Architecture and Ideology in Eastern Europe during the Stalin Era: An Aspect of Cold War History*. Cambridge, MA: MIT Press.

Ao, S. *et al.* (1959) Xiwai dajie [Xiwai Street] (photomontage). *Renmin huabao* [People's Pictorial], No. 19, p. 18.

Arrighi, G. (2002) The rise of East Asia and the withering away of the interstate system, in Bartolovich, C. and Lazarus, N. (eds.) *Marxism, Modernity and Postcolonial Studies*. Cambridge: Cambridge University Press, pp. 21–42.

Augur, T.B. (1935) Some minimum standards in site planning for low-cost housing, in *Proceedings, Joint National Conference on Housing, Washington*. Chicago, IL: National Association of Housing Officials.

Bian, Y. *et al.* (1997) Work units and housing reform in two Chinese cities, in Lü, X. and Perry, E.J. (eds.) *Danwei: The Changing Chinese Workplace in Historical and Comparative Perspective*. Armonk, NY: M.E. Sharpe, pp. 223–250.

Ball, M. (1986) The built environment and the urban question. *Environment and Planning D: Society and Space*, **4**, pp. 447–464.

Banerjee, T. and Baer, W.C. (1984) *Beyond the Neighborhood Unit: Residential Environments and Public Policy*. New York: Plenum Press.

Barlow, T.E. (1997) Colonialism's career in postwar China studies, in Barlow, T.E.

(ed.) *Formations of Colonial Modernity in East Asia*. Durham, NC: Duke University Press, pp. 373–412.

Bartolovich, C. (2002) Introduction: Marxism, modernity, and postcolonial studies, in Bartolovich, C. and Lazarus, N. (eds.) *Marxism, Modernity and Postcolonial Studies*. Cambridge: Cambridge University Press, pp. 1–20.

Bater, J.H. (1980) *The Soviet City*. London: Edward Arnold.

Bauman, Z. (1976) *Socialism: The Active Utopia*. New York: Holmes & Meier Publishers.

Bauman, Z. (2000) *Liquid Modernity*. Cambridge: Polity Press.

BDG (1953) Beijingshi dang'an guan [Beijing Municipal Archives] Shiwei guanyu gaijian yu kuojian beijingshi guihua cao'an de yaodian [The municipality's summary on planning proposal for redeveloping and expanding the city of Beijing]. Category 131, Catalogue 1, Volume 10.

BDG (1954*a*) Guanyu jiaqiang Beijingshi fangwu jianzhu de tongyi lingdao de yijian (cao'an) [Proposal on strengthening the unitary leadership on housing construction in Beijing (draft)]. Category 131, Catalogue 1, Volume 11.

BDG (1954*b*) Jianzhu shiwu guanliju dangzu guanyu muqian ji 1955 nian jianzhu yongdi de chubu yijian [The preliminary proposal on construction land at present and in 1955 by the party group of Construction Affairs Management Bureau]. Category 131, Catalogue 1, Volume 12.

BDG (1955) Beijingshi 1955 nian jianzhu yongdi jihua cao'an [Draft plan of construction land use in Beijing in 1955], Category 131, Catalogue 1, Volume 225.

BDG (1956*a*) Beijingshi chengshi jianshe gongzuo zhong cunzai de jige wenti [Several problems in urban construction in Beijing]. Category 131, Catalogue 1, Volume 244.

BDG (1956*b*) Guanyu xunsu jiuzheng mujian jianzhu hunluan xianxiang de qingshi baogao [Proposal on the rapid rectification of the current chaotic construction situation]. Category 131, Catalogue 1, Volume 32.

BDG (1956*c*) Guowuyuan guanyu jiuzheng yu fangzhi guojia jianshe zhengyong tudi zhong langfei xianqiang de tongzhi [The State Council's notification on the rectification and prevention of wasting land in state requisition]. Category 131, Catalogue 1, Volume 286.

BDG (1956*d*) Guanyu jianzhu weizhang shigong qingkuang jiancha baogao [A survey of the state of illegal construction]. Category 131, Catalogue 1, Volume 32.

BDG (1956*e*) Guanyu chengqiang chaichu wenti de qingshi [Proposal on the issue of demolishing city walls]. Category 131, Catalogue 1, Volume 271.

BDG (1956*f*) Beijingshi chengshi guihua guanliju guanyu muqian gongzuo jiben qingkuang he wenti de baogao (chugao) [Beijing Planning Bureau's report on current work progress and problems (draft)]. Category 131, Catalogue 1, Volume 246.

BDG (1956g) 1956 nian di'er jidu weizhang gongzuo jihua ji 1955 nian weizhang gongzuo zongjie [Work plan for controlling illegal construction in the second season of 1956 and summary of work on illegal construction in 1955]. Category 131, Catalogue 1, Volume 285.

BDG (1956h) Guanyu zhengdun gongzuo zuofeng yu chufa weizhang jianzhu shanhou gongzuo de jihua [Work plan on the rectification of work style and handling the punishment of illegal construction]. Category 131, Catalogue 1, Volume 32.

BDG (1956i) Guihuaju guanyu chengfa weizhang jianzhu de jiancha [The planning bureau's self-criticism on punishing illegal construction]. Category 131, Catalogue 1, Volume 246.

BDG (1956j) Guanyu tuihuan 1954 nian weizhang fakuang de gongzuo qingkuang [Work progress on returning the fines on illegal construction in 1954]. Category 131, Catalogue 1, Volume 32.

BDG (1957a) Guanyu 1956 nian jianzhu shang hunluan qingkuang de baogao [Report on the chaotic construction situation in 1956]. Category 131, Catalogue 1, Volume 49.

BDG (1957b) Guihuaju waiqiang chengqiang xianzhuang de huibao [The planning bureau's report on the current state of outer city walls]. Category 131, Catalogue 1, Volume 271.

BDG (1957c) Guanyu yange kongzhi lingxin jianzhu de baogao [Report on strengthening control over small structures]. Category 131, Catalogue 1, Volume 309.

BDG (1957d) Guanyu yange kongzhi lingxing jianzhu de qingshi [Proposal on strengthening control over small structures]. Category 131, Catalogue 1, Volume 49.

BDG (1957e) 1956 nian weizhang jianfang danwei [Work units that built illegal projects in 1956]. BDG, Category 131, Catalogue 1, Volume 285.

BDG (1957f) Dianlibu shuili fadian jianshe zongju fangchan kezhang Wang Zhaitian tanhua jilu (zhaiyao) [Excerpts from the talk memo of Wang Zhaitian, Housing Manager of the General Bureau of Hydraulic Power Construction, the Ministry of Electric Power], Beijing Municipal Archives, Category 131, Catalogue 1, Volume 285.

BDG (1957g) Gexiang jianshe bixi jieyue de shiyong tudi [Use land economically in construction]. Category 131, Catalogue 1, Volume 31.

BDG (1957h) Guanyu guanli chaichu chengqiang wenti [On the management of demolishing city walls]. Category 131, Catalogue 1, Volume 271.

BDG (1957i) Guanyu guanli chaichu chengqiang wenti de qingshi [Proposal on the management of demolishing city walls]. Category 131, Catalogue 1, Volume 271.

BDG (1957*j*) Beijingshi caizhengju guanyu niding caiyong chengqiang zhuan shoufei de jixiang guiding [Beijing Finance Bureau's proposal on the rules of charging for city wall bricks]. Category 131, Catalogue 1, Volume 271.

BDG (1957*k*) Beijingshi renmin weiyuanhui guanyu zhanhuan chaichu chengqiang he shouji youguan chengqiang ziliao de tongzhi [Notification on postponing the demolishment of city walls and collecting related materials from Beijing People's Committee]. Category 131, Catalogue 1, Volume 271.

BDG (1957*l*) Guihuaju guanyu weixian bufen chengqiang chaichu de yijian [The planning bureau's proposal on demolishing the dangerous parts of city walls]. Category 131, Catalogue 1, Volume 271.

BDG (1958) Guanyu youxie danwei hushi chengshi jianshe jilü shijian fangwu de baogao [Report on the situation that some work units ignored urban construction rules and built without approval]. Category 131, Catalogue 1, Volume 71.

BDG (1959*a*) Guanyu chengshi guihua jige wenti de huibao tigang [Summary on several problems in urban planning]. Category 131, Catalogue 1, Volume 68.

BDG (1959*b*) Guihuaju guanyu weixian bufen chengqiang chaichu de yijian [The planning bureau's opinion on the demolishment of some dangerous city walls]. Category 131, Catalogue 1, Volume 271.

BDG (1959*c*) Chengqiang chaichu qingkuang de huibao [Report on the state of the demolishment of city walls]. Category 131, Catalogue 1, Volume 271.

BDG (1959*d*) Zhuanfa guanyu jiancha chengqiang weixian qingkuang he chuli yijian de baokao [Report on the dangerous state of city walls and related treatments]. Category 131, Catalogue 1, Volume 271.

BDG (1959*e*) Guanyu chengqiang chaichu de fang'an [Proposal for demolishing city walls]. Category 131, Catalogue 1, Volume 271.

BDG (1960*a*) Zongti guihua zhixing qingkuang de baogao [The progress of the implementation of master plan]. Category 131, Catalogue 1, Volume 101.

BDG (1960*b*) Guanyu shenpi lingshixing lingxing jianzhu wenti de qingshi [Proposal on the issue regarding approving small and temporary construction]. Category 131, Catalogue 1, Volume 307.

BDG (1960*c*) Guanyu shenpi lingshixing lingxing jianzhu wenti de pishi [Response to the proposal on the issue regarding approving small and temporary construction]. Category 131, Catalogue 1, Volume 307.

BDG (1960*d*) Guanyu gaijian jiucheng ruogang wenti de qingshi [Proposal on several issues related to urban redevelopment]. Category 131, Catalogue 1, Volume 101.

BDG (1961*a*) Guanyu 1960 nain yilai weizhang jianzhu qingkuang de baogao [Report on the state of illegal construction since 1960]. Category 131, Catalogue 1, Volume 422.

BDG (1961*b*) Guanyu 1958 nian yilai quanshi jiben jianshe yongdi shiyong qingkuang de jiancha baogao [Report on land use for basic construction in the city since 1958]. Category 131, Catalogue 1, Volume 116.

BDG (1963a) Guanyu benshi chengshi jianshe gongzuo dangqian cunzai de zhuyao wenti he jiejue yijian de baogao [Report on major problems in current urban construction and their solutions]. Category 131, Catalogue 1, Volume 128.

BDG (1963b) Guanyu chuli weizhang jianzhu de qingshi baogao [Proposal on handling illegal construction]. BDG, Category 131, Catalogue 1, Volume 462.

BDG (1964a) 1963 nian weizhang jianzhu qingkuang jianbao [Brief report on the state of illegal construction in 1963]. Category 131, Catalogue 1, Volume 493.

BDG (1964b) Guanyu jianshe danwei xiujian weiqiang wenti gei chengjianwei de qingshi baogao [Report to the Committee of Urban Construction on wall construction by work units]. Category 131, Catalogue 1, Volume 491.

BDG (1964c) Nongye chubanshe yinshuachang xiu zhuan weiqiang qingshi (1,000 gongchi) [Request for building brick walls by the Printing House of Agriculture Press (1,000 metres)]. Category 131, Catalogue 1, Volume 491.

BDG (1964d) Shenbao huairou, baihe biandianzhan xiujian weiqiang shi [Request for building walls for Huairou and Baihe substations]. Category 131, Catalogue 1, Volume 491.

BDG (1964e) Miyun shuili fadianchang wei baoqing shencha xiujian shenghuoqu weiqiang you [Reasons for building walls for the living quarter of Miyun Hydraulic Power Plant]. Category 131, Catalogue 1, Volume 491.

BDG (1964f) Qing pizhun jian nan zhuzhaiqu ji bei yanjiuqu peidianshi weiqiang shi [Request for building walls for the south living quarter and the power distributor room of the north research quarter]. Category 131, Catalogue 1, Volume 491.

BDG (1964g) Guanyu shenqing zhuanbao pizhun jianzhu weiqiang de han [A letter on the request for the approval of wall construction]. Category 131, Catalogue 1, Volume 491.

BDG (1965) Guanyu 1964 nian zhongxiaoxue jian weiqiang qingkuang de baogao [Report on wall construction by primary and middle schools in 1964]. Category 131, Catalogue 1, Volume 491.

Becker, J. (1996) Hungry Ghosts: Mao's Secret Famine. New York: Free Press.

Beijing gongye jianzhu shejiyuan (1963) Jianzhu sheji ziliao huibian xuanye [Selected pages from the collected material of architectural design]. Jianzhu xuebao [Architectural Journal], No. 12, p. 32.

Beijing wanbao [Beijing Evening News] (2001) Qiyue yiri qi Beijing danwei neibu shesi xiang shequ kaifang [The facilities of Beijing work units should be open to the community from 1 July on]. 13 June, p. B1.

Beijingshi jianzhu shejiyuan (1962) Miyun xinjian nongcun zhuzhai diaocha [A survey of new rural houses in Miyun]. Jianzhu xuebao [Architectural Journal], No. 10, pp. 3–6.

Beijingshi tongjiju (1999) *Beijing wushi nian* [Beijing's 50 years]. Beijing: Zhongguo tongji chubanshe.

Benjamin, W. (1973) *Charles Baudelaire: A Lyric Poet in the Era of High Capitalism.* London: NLB.

Benjamin, W. (1928, 1977) *The Origin of German Tragic Drama.* London: Verso.

Berman, M. (1982) *All that is Solid Melts into Air: The Experience of Modernity.* New York: Simon and Schuster.

Bhabha, H.K. (1994) *The Location of Culture.* London: Routledge.

Bian, Y. *et al.* (1997) Work units and housing reform in two Chinese cities, in Lü, X. and Perry, E.J. (eds.) *Danwei: The Changing Chinese Workplace in Historical and Comparative Perspective.* Armonk, NY: M.E. Sharpe, pp. 223–250.

Birtles, T.G. (1994) *Origins of the Neighbourhood Unit as a Twentieth Century Urban Residential Planning Ideal: A Tribute to Clarence Perry.* Belconnen: University of Canberra.

Bjorklund, E.M. (1986) The danwei: social-spatial characteristics of work units in China's urban society. *Economic Geography,* **62**(1), pp. 19–29.

Blakely, E. and Snyder, M.G. (1999) *Fortress USA: Gated Communities in the United States.* Washington DC: Brookings Institution Press.

Blecher, M.J. and White, G. (1979) *Micropolitics in Contemporary China: A Technical Unit during and after the Cultural Revolution.* Armonk, NY: M.E. Sharpe.

Bloch, E. (1986) *The Principle of Hope.* Oxford: Basil Blackwell.

Bourdieu, P. (1977) *Outline of a Theory of Practice.* Cambridge: Cambridge University Press.

Bourdieu, P. (1986) The forms of capital, in Richardson, J. (ed.) *Handbook of Theory and Research for the Sociology of Education.* New York: Greenwood Press, pp. 241–258.

Bourdieu, P. (1990) *The Logic of Practice.* Cambridge: Polity.

Boyd, A. (1962) *Chinese Architecture and Town Planning: 1500 BC–AD 1911.* Chicago, IL: University of Chicago Press.

Boyer, M.C. (1983) *Dreaming the Rational City: The Myth of American City Planning.* Cambridge, MA: MIT Press.

Bray, D. (2005) *Social Space and Governance in Urban China.* Stanford: Stanford University Press.

Broudehoux, A. (2004) *The Making and Selling of Post-Mao Beijing.* London: Routledge.

Brown, E.C. (1966) *Soviet Trade Unions and Labor Relations.* Cambridge: Harvard University Press.

Brownell, S. (1995) *Training the Body for China: Sports in the Moral Order of the People's Republic.* Chicago, IL: University of Chicago Press.

Brumfield, W.C. (1993) *A History of Russian Architecture.* Cambridge: Cambridge University Press.

Bucci, F. (1993) *Albert Kahn: Architect of Ford*. New York: Princeton Architectural Press.

Buck, D.D. (2000) Railway city and national capital: two faces of the modern, in Esherick, J.W. (ed.) *Remaking the Chinese City: Modernity and National Identity, 1900–1950*. Honolulu: University of Hawaii Press, pp. 65–89.

Buck-Morss, S. (2000) *Dreamworld and Catastrophe: The Passing of Mass Utopia in East and West*. Cambridge, MA: MIT Press.

Burgess, E.W. (1925) Can neighbourhood work have a scientific basis? in Park, R.E. and Burgess, E.W. (eds.) *The City*. Chicago, IL: University of Chicago.

Burke, G. (1971) *Towns in the Making*. London: Edward Arnold.

Butterfield, F. (1979) Getting a hotel room in China: you're nothing without a unit. *New York Times*, 31 October, p. C17.

Buzlyakov, N. (1973) *Welfare: The Basic Task*. Moscow: Progress Publishers.

Caldeira, T.P.R. (2000) *City of Walls: Crime, Segregation, and Citizenship in São Paulo*. Berkeley, CA: University of California Press.

Carson, M. (1990) *Settlement Folk: Social Thought and the American Settlement Movement, 1885–1930*. Chicago, IL: University of Chicago Press.

Cartier, C. (2005) City-space: scale relations and China's spatial administrative hierarchy, in Ma, L.J.C. and Wu, F. (eds.) *Restructuring the Chinese City: Changing Society, Economy and Space*. Abingdon: Routledge, pp. 21–38.

Castells, M. (1977) *The Urban Question: A Marxist Approach*. London: Arnold.

Castells, M. (1978) *City, Class, and Power*. London: Macmillan.

Castells, M. (1996) *The Rise of the Network Society*. Oxford: Blackwell.

Castells, M. (1998) *End of Millennium*. Oxford: Blackwell.

Castells, M. (2004) *The Power of Identity*. Oxford: Blackwell.

Castillo, G. (2003) Stalinist modern: constructivism and the Soviet company town, in Cracraft, J. and Rowland, D. (eds.) *Architectures of Russian identity: 1500 to the Present*. Ithaca, NY: Cornell University Press, pp. 135–149.

Certeau, M. de (1984) *The Practice of Everyday Life*. Berkeley, CA: University of California Press.

Chai, Y. (1996) Yi danwei wei jichu de zhongguo chengshi neibu shenghuo kongjian jiegou – lanzhou shi de shizheng yanjiu [The structure of work-unit-based living space in urban China – an empirical study of Lanzhou]. *Dili yanjiu* [Geographical Research], **15**(1), pp. 30–38.

Chakrabarty, D. (1997) The time of History and the times of Gods, in Lowe, L. and Lloyd, D. (eds.) *The Politics of Culture in the Shadow of Capital*. Durham, NC: Duke University Press, pp. 35–60.

Chakrabarty, D. (2000) *Provincializing Europe: Postcolonial Thought and Historical Difference*. Princeton, NJ: Princeton University Press.

Chan, C.L.W. (1993) *The Myth of Neighborhood Mutual Help: The Contemporary*

Chinese Community-Based Welfare System in Guangzhou. Hong Kong: Hong Kong University Press.

Chan, K.W. (1994) *Cities with Invisible Walls: Reinterpreting Urbanization in Post-1949 China*. Hong Kong: Oxford University Press.

Chang, S. (1977) The morphology of walled capitals, in Skinner, G.W. (ed.) *The City in Late Imperial China*. Stanford, CA: Stanford University Press, pp. 75–100.

Chao, K. (1968) *The Construction Industry in Communist China*. Chicago, IL: Aldine Publishing Company.

Chen, J. (1970) *Mao Papers: Anthology and Bibliography*. New York: Oxford University Press.

Chen, X. (1993) Urban economic reform and public housing investment in China. *Urban Affairs Quarterly*, **29**, pp. 117–145.

Chen, Z. (2005) Wushi nian hou lun shifei [An appraisal after fifty years], in Wang, R. (ed.) *Liang chen fang'an yu beijing* [The Laing-Chen Proposal and Beijing]. Shenyang: Liaoning jiaoyu chubanshe, pp. 113–124.

Cheng, T. and Selden, M. (1994) The origins and social consequences of China's *hukou* system. *The China Quarterly*, **139**, pp. 644–668.

Cheng, X. (1963) Jianpuzhai jianzhu [Cambodian architecture]. *Jianzhu xuebao* [Architectural Journal], No. 7, pp. 22–26.

Chengshi jianshe zongju guihua sheji ju (1956) Quanguo biaozhun sheji pingxuan huiyi jianxun [News in brief: the national conference of standardized design selection]. *Jianzhu xuebao* [Architectural Journal], No. 1, pp. 30–31.

Chi, W. (1967) The ideological source of the people's communes in communist China. *Pacific Coast Philology*, **2**, pp. 62–78.

Chicago Plan Commission (1946) *Preliminary Comprehensive City Plan of Chicago*. Chicago.

Clifford, J. (1989) Notes on travel and theory. *Inscriptions*, **5**, pp. 177–186.

Clifford, J. (1997) *Routes: Travel and Translation in the Late Twentieth Century*. Cambridge, MA: Harvard University Press.

Cody, J.W. (1996) American planning in Republican China. *Planning Perspectives*, **11**, pp. 339–377.

Cody, J.W. (1999) Columbia circle – an obscured Shanghai suburb, 1928–1932. *Dialogue*, **23**, pp. 130–135.

Cody, J.W. (2001) *Building in China: Henry K. Murphy's 'Adaptive Architecture', 1914–1935*. Hong Kong: The Chinese University Press.

Cody, J.W. (2003) *Exporting American Architecture, 1870–2000*. London: Routledge.

Collini, S. *et al.* (eds.) (1983) *That Noble Science of Politics: A Study in Nineteenth-Century Intellectual History*. Cambridge: Cambridge University Press.

Committee of Concerned Asian Scholars (1972) *China: Inside the People's Republic*. New York: Bantam Books.

Cooley, C.H. (1909) *Social Organization: A Study of the Larger Mind*. New York: Charles Scribner's Sons.

Crawford, M. (1995) *Building the Workingman's Paradise: The Design of American Company Towns*. London: Verso.

Crawford, M. (1999) Introduction, in Chase, J. *et al.* (eds.) *Everyday Urbanism*. New York: Monacelli Press, pp. 8–15.

Crysler, C.G. (2003) *Writing Spaces: Discourses of Architecture, Urbanism, and the Built Environment, 1960–2000*. New York: Routledge.

Dahir, J. (1947) *The Neighborhood Unit Plan: Its Spread and Acceptance*. New York: Russell Sage Foundation.

Dangdai zhongguo congshu bianjibu (1989) *Dangdai zhongguo de Beijing* [Beijing of Contemporary China]. Beijing: Dangdai zhongguo chubanshe.

Davis, D.S. *et al.* (eds.) (1995) *Urban Spaces in Contemporary China: The Potential for Autonomy and Community in Post-Mao China*. New York: Woodrow Wilson Center Press.

Davis, D.S. (ed.) (2000) *The Consumer Revolution in Urban China*. Berkeley, CA: University of California Press.

Dili zhishi [Geographical Knowledge] (1959) Beijing shida jinxing renmin gongshe guihua de gaikuang [Brief account: Beijing Normal University is carrying on commune planning]. No. 2.

Dirlik, A. (1994) *After the Revolution: Walking to Global Capitalism*. Hanover, NH: Wesleyan University Press.

Dirlik, A. (1997) *The Postcolonial Aura: Third World Criticism in the Age of Global Capitalism*. Boulder, CO: Westview Press.

Dirlik, A. (2000) *Postmodernity's Histories: The Past as Legacy and Project*. Lanham, MD: Rowman & Littlefield.

Dirlik, A. (2002) Modernity as history: post-revolution China: globalization and the question of modernity. *Social History*, **27**(1), pp. 16–39.

Dittmer, L. and Kim, S.S. (1993) In search of a theory of national identity, in Dittmer, L. and Kim, S.S. (eds.) *China's Quest for National Identity*. Ithaca, NY: Cornell University Press, pp. 1–31.

Dittmer, L. and Lü, X. (1996) Personal politics in the Chinese danwei under reform. *Asian Survey*, **3**, pp. 46–67.

Dixon, J. (1981) *The Chinese Welfare System, 1949–1979*. New York: Praeger.

Dong, J. (1999) *Zhongguo chengshi jianshe shi* [Chinese urban construction history]. Beijing: Zhongguo jianzhu gongye chubanshe.

Dong, Z. (1963) Yindunixiya jianzhu jieshao [An introduction to Indonesian architecture]. *Jianzhu xuebao* [Architectural Journal], No. 5, pp. 22–27.

Duara, P. (1995) *Rescuing History from the Nation: Questioning narratives of Modern China*. Chicago, IL: University of Chicago Press.

Dutton, M.R. (1992) *Policing and Punishment in China: From Patriarchy to the People*. Cambridge: Cambridge University Press.

Dutton, M. (1998) *Streetlife China*. Cambridge: Cambridge University Press.

Economist (2002) The antique that Mao destroyed, **365**(8296), p. 42.

Eisenstadt, S.N. (2002) Multiple modernities, in Eisenstadt, S.N. (ed.) *Multiple Modernities*. New Brunswick, NJ: Transaction Publishers.

Escobar, A. (1995) *Encountering Development: The Making and Unmaking of the Third World*. Princeton, NJ: Princeton University Press

Esherick, J.W. (2000*a*) Modernity and nation in the Chinese city, in Esherick, J.W. (ed.) *Remaking the Chinese City: Modernity and National Identity, 1900–1950*. Honolulu: University of Hawaii Press, pp. 1–18.

Esherick, J.W. (ed.) (2000*b*) *Remaking the Chinese City: Modernity and National Identity,1900–1950*. Honolulu: University of Hawaii Press.

Fairclough, N. (1989) *Language and Power*. London: Longman.

Fairclough, N. (1995) *Critical Discourse Analysis: The Critical Study of Language*. London: Longman.

Fanon, F. (1968) *The Wretched of the Earth*. New York: Grove Press.

Farmer, E. (1976) *Early Ming Government: The Evolution of Dual Capitals*. Cambridge, MA: Harvard University Press.

Farquhar, J. (1994) *Knowing Practice: The Clinical Encounter of Chinese Medicine*. Boulder, CO: Westview Press.

Federal Housing Administration (1941) *Successful Subdivisions: Planned as Neighborhoods for Profitable Investment and Appeal to Home Owners*. Land Planning Bulletin No. 1. Washington DC: FHA.

Fludernik, M. (1998) The constitution of hybridity: postcolonial interventions, in Fludernik, M. (ed.) *Hybridity and Postcolonialism: Twentieth-Century Indian Literature*. Tubingen: Stauffenburg Verlag, pp. 19–54.

Foucault, M. (1972) *The Archaeology of Knowledge*. London: Tavistock.

Francis, C. (1996) Reproduction of *danwei* institutional features in the context of China's market economy: the case of Haidian District's high-tech sector. *China Quarterly*, **147**, pp. 839–859.

Frank, A.G. (1998) *Reorient: Global Economy in the Asian Age*. Berkeley, CA: University of California Press.

French, R.A. (1995) *Plans, Pragmatism and People: The Legacy of Soviet Planning for Today's Cities*. Pittsburgh, PA: University of Pittsburgh Press.

French, R.A. and Hamilton, F.E.I. (1979) Is there a socialist city? in French, R.A. and Hamilton, F.E.I. (eds.) *The Socialist City: Spatial Structure and Urban Policy*. Chichester: Wiley, pp. 1–22.

Freud, S. (1939, 1967) *Moses and Monotheism*. New York: Vintage Books.

Friedmann, J. (2005) *China's Urban Transition*. Minneapolis, MN: University of Minnesota Press.

Fu, S. *et al.* (1958) Beijingshi xizhaosi juzhu xiaoqu guihua fang'an jieshao [An introduction to the planning proposal for the Xizhaosi microdistrict in Beijing]. *Jianzhu xuebao* [Architectural Journal], No. 1, pp. 10–16.

Fukuyama, F. (1992) *The End of History and the Last Man*. New York: Free Press.

Gaonkar, D.P. (1999) On alternative modernities. *Public Culture*, **11**(1), pp. 1–18.

Garner, J.S. (1992) *The Company Town: Architecture and Society in the Early Industrial Age*. New York: Oxford University Press.

Gaubatz, P. (1995) Urban transformation in post-Mao China: impacts of the reform era on China's urban form, in Davis, D.S. *et al.* (eds.) *Urban Spaces in Contemporary China: The Potential for Autonomy and Community in Post-Mao China*. New York: Woodrow Wilson Center Press, pp. 28–60.

Gaubatz, P. (1996) *Beyond the Great Wall: Urban Form and Transformation on the Chinese Frontiers*. Stanford, CA: Stanford University Press.

Gaubatz, P. (2005) Globalization and the development of new central business districts in Beijing, Shanghai and Guangzhou, in Ma, L.J.C. and Wu, F. (eds.) *Restructuring the Chinese City: Changing Society, Economy and Space*. Abingdon: Routledge, pp. 98–121.

Gaulton, R. (1981) Political mobilization in Shanghai, in Howe, C. (ed.) *Shanghai: Revolution and Development in an Asian Metropolis*. Cambridge: Cambridge University Press.

Gong, D. and Li, Z. (1963) Zhongxiaoxing gongchang changqianqu sheji [The design of the forecourt of small- and medium-type factories]. *Jianzhu xuebao* [Architectural Journal], No. 5, pp. 4–7.

Gong, T. and Chen, F. (1994) Institutional reorganization and its impact on decentralization, in Jia, H. and Tin, Z. (eds.), *Changing Central-Local Relations in China: Reform and State Capacity*. Boulder, CO: Westview Press, pp. 67–88.

Gordon, N.J. (1946) China and the neighborhood unit. *The American City*, **61**, pp. 112–113.

Goss, A. (1961) Neighbourhood units in British New Towns. *Town Planning Review*, **32**(1), pp. 66–82.

Gottdiener, M. (1985) *The Social Production of Urban Space*. Austin, TX: University of Texas Press.

Gregory, D. (1994) *Geographical Imaginations*. Oxford: Blackwell.

Gries, P. H. (2004) *China's New Nationalism: Pride, Politics, and Diplomacy*. Berkeley, CA: University of California Press.

Guo, Q. (2004) Changchun: unfinished capital planning of Manzhouguo, 1932–42. *Urban History*, **31**(1), pp. 100–117.

Guojia tongjiju shehui tongjisi (ed.) (1994) *Zhongguo shehui tongji ziliao* [Statistical Material on Chinese Society]. Beijing: Zhongguo tongji chubanshe.

Gupta, A. (1998) *Postcolonial Developments: Agriculture in the Making of Modern India*. Durham, NC: Duke University Press.

Hall, S. (1996) When was the 'post-colonial'? thinking at the limit, in Chambers, I. and Curtis, L. (eds.) *The Post-Colonial Question: Common Skies, Divided Horizons*. London: Routledge, pp. 242–260.

Hall, P. (2002) *Cities of Tomorrow: An Intellectual History of Urban Planning and Design in the Twentieth Century*, 3rd ed. Oxford: Blackwell.

Hansot, E. (1974) *Perfection and Progress: Two Modes of Utopian Thought*. Cambridge, MA: MIT Press.

Harris, L.C. and Worden, R.L. (1986) Introduction: China's Third World role, in Harris, L.C. and Worden, R.L. (eds.) *China and the Third World: Champion or Challenger?* Dover, VT: Auburn House Publishing Company, pp. 1–13.

Harvey, D. (1985) *The Urbanization of Capital: Studies in the History and Theory of Capitalist Urbanization*. Baltimore, MD: Johns Hopkins University Press.

Harvey, D. (1989) *The Condition of Postmodernity: An Enquiry into the Origins of Cultural Change*. Oxford: Basil Blackwell.

He, L. (1948) *Guojia zhuyi gailun* [An Outline of Nationalism]. Shanghai: Zhongguo renwen yanjiusuo.

Hein, C. (2003) Rebuilding Japanese cities after 1945, in Hein, C., Diefendorf, J.M. and Ishida, Y. (eds.) *Rebuilding Urban Japan after 1945*. Basingstoke: Palgrave Macmillan, pp. 1–16.

Henderson, G.E. and Cohen, M.S. (1984) *The Chinese Hospital: A Socialist Work Unit*. New Haven, CT: Yale University Press.

Heng, C.K. (1999) *Cities of Aristocrats and Bureaucrats: The Development of Medieval Chinese Cityscapes*. Singapore: Singapore University Press.

Hermassi, E. (1980) *The Third World Reassessed*. Berkeley, CA: University of California Press.

Highmore, B. (2002) *Everyday Life and Cultural Theory: An Introduction*. London: Routledge.

Hitchcock, H. and Johnson, P. (1932) *The International Style*. New York: W.W. Norton.

Hobsbawm, E.J. (1990) *Nations and Nationalism since 1780: Programme, Myth, Reality*. Cambridge: Cambridge University Press.

Holston, J. (1989) *The Modernist City: An Anthropological Critique of Brasilia*. Chicago, IL: University of Chicago Press.

Homer-Dixon, T.F. (1991) On the threshold: environmental changes as causes of acute conflict. *International Security*, Fall.

Homer-Dixon, T.F. (1999) *Environment, Scarcity, and Violence*. Princeton, NJ: Princeton University Press.

Howard, E. (1898) *To-Morrow: A Peaceful Path to Real Reform*. London: Swann Sonnenschein.

Howell, J. (ed.) (2004) *Governance in China*. Lanham, MD: Rowman & Littlefield.

Hsing, Y. (1998) *Making Capitalism in China: The Taiwan Connection*. New York: Oxford University Press.

Hsu, I.C.Y. (2000) *The Rise of Modern China*. New York: Oxford University Press.

Hu, X.H. and Kaplan, D. (2001) The emergence of affluence in Beijing: residential social stratification in China's capital city. *Urban Geography*, **22**, pp. 54–77.

Hua, N. (1956) Bu ying zai chengqiang shang jianzhu dianche dao [We should not build streetcar trail on city walls]. *Chengshi jianshe* [Urban Construction], November.

Huadong gongye jianzhu shejiyuan (1955) Dongbei mochang juzhuqu xiangxi guihua sheji de neirong jieshao [An introduction to the detailed planning of the residential district of a factory in northeast China]. *Jianzhu xuebao* [Architectural Journal], No. 2, pp. 24–39.

Huanan gongxueyuan jianzhuxi (1958) Henansheng suipingxian weixing renmin gongshe diyi jiceng guihua sheji [Planning proposal for the basic unit of Satellite Commune, Suiping County, Henan Province], *Jianzhu xuebao* [Architectural Journal], No. 11, pp. 9–13.

Huanan gongxueyuan jianzhuxi (1959) Guangdongsheng panyu renmin gongshe shaxu jumindian xinjian geti jianzhu sheji jieshao [An introduction to the design of new buildings in Shaxu Residential Cluster, Panyu People's Commune, Guangdong]. *Jianzhu xuebao* [Architectural Journal], No. 2, pp. 3–7.

Huang, Y. (2005) From work-unit compounds to gated communities: housing inequality and residential segregation in transitional Beijing, in Ma, L.J.C. and Wu, F. (eds.) *Restructuring the Chinese City: Changing Society, Economy and Space*. Abingdon: Routledge, pp. 192–221.

Hunansheng chengshi jiansheju (1958) Hunan lianhe riyongpin gongchang sheji [The design of the Lianhe Articles of Everyday Use Chemical Plant, Hunan]. *Jianzhu xuebao* [Architectural Journal], No. 9, pp. 15–17.

Huntington, S.P. (1996) *The Clash of Civilizations and the Remaking of World Order*. New York: Simon and Schuster.

Jiangsusheng chengshi jiansheting changzhou guihua gongzuozu (1959) Changzhoushi puqianzhen xiaoqu guihua jieshao [An introduction to the planning of Puqianzhen Microdistrict, Changzhou]. *Jianzhu xuebao* [Architectural Journal], No. 11, pp. 37–38.

Jianzhu xuebao (1955) nos 1 and 2.

Jihua jingji [Planned Economy] (1958) Guanyu jianli renmin gongshe de jihua he tongji gongzuo de yijian [Suggestions regarding the establishment of planning and statistics work in people's communes]. No. 11, pp. 10–11.

Jihua yu tongji [Planning and Statistics] (1960) Zhejiangsheng renmin gongshe tongji yuan xunlianban kaixue [A training class for statistics workers in people's communes opened in Zhejiang Province], No. 2, p. 9.

Johnson, D.L. (2002) Origins of the neighbourhood unit. *Planning Perspectives*, **17**, pp. 227–245.

Jørgensen, M.W. and Phillips, L. (2002) *Discourse Analysis: As Theory and Method.* London: Sage.

Juan, E.S. (1998) *Beyond Postcolonial Theory.* New York: St. Martin's Press.

Juzhuqu xiangxi guihua keti yanjiuzu (1985) *Juzhuqu guihua sheji* [The Planning of Residential Districts]. Beijing: Zhongguo jianzhu gongye chubanshe.

Kalia, R. (1999) *Chandigarh: The Making of an Indian City.* New Delhi: Oxford University Press.

Kang, J. (1998) *Huihuang de huanmie: Renmin gongshe qishi lu* [Brilliant Failure: Lessons from the People's Commune]. Beijing: Zhongguo shehui chubanshe.

Kang, Y. (1900, 1994) *Da Tong Shu.* Shenyang: Liaoning renmin chubanshe.

Kaplan, R. (1994) The coming anarchy. *Atlantic Monthly*, February, pp. 44–76.

Kaplan, R. (2000) *The Coming Anarchy: Shattering the Dreams of the Post Cold War.* New York: Random House.

Karnak, R. (2005) Beijing's mega mall. *The China Business Review* (online), www.chinabusinessreview.com/public/0511/last_page.

Kaufmann, E.C. (1936) Neighbourhood units as new elements of town planning. *Journal of the Royal Institute of British Architects*, **44**, pp. 165–175.

Kaufmann, V. (2002) *Re-thinking Mobility: Contemporary Sociology.* Aldershot: Ashgate.

King, A.D. (1990) *Urbanism, Colonialism and the World-Economy: Cultural and Spatial Foundations of the World Urban System.* London: Routledge.

King, A.D. (2004) *Spaces of Global Cultures: Architecture, Urbanism, Identity.* London: Routledge.

King, A. and Kusno, A. (2000) On Be(ij)ing in the world: 'postmodernism', 'globalization' and the making of transnational space in China, in Dirlik, A. and Zhang, X. (eds.) *Postmodernism and China*. Durham, NC: Duke University Press.

Knorád, G. and Szelényi, I. (1979) *The Intellectuals on the Road to Class Power: A Sciological Study of the Role of the Intelligentsia in Socialism.* New York: Harcourt.

Kornai, J. (1979) *The Dilemmas of a Socialist Economy: The Hungarian Experience.* Dublin: The Economic and Social Research Institute.

Kornai, J. (1980) *Economics of Shortage.* Amsterdam: North-Holland Publishing.

Kornai, J. (1992) *Socialist Economy.* Princeton: Princeton University Press.

Kusno, A. (2000) *Behind the Postcolonial: Architecture, Urban Space, and Political Cultures in Indonesia.* London: Routledge.

Kwok, R.Y.W. (1973) Urban-rural planning and housing development in the People's Republic of China. Ph.D. dissertation, Columbia University.

Kwok, R.Y.W. (1981) Trends of urban planning and development in China, in Ma, L.J.C. and Hanten, E.W. (eds.) *Urban Development in Modern China*. Boulder, CO: Westview Press, pp. 147–193.

Lai, D. (2005) Searching for a modern Chinese monument: The design of the Sun Yat-sen Mausoleum in Nanjing. *Journal of the Society of Architectural Historians*, **64**(1), pp. 22–55.

Langer, P. (1984) Sociology – four images of organized diversity: bazaar, jungle, organism, and machine, in Rodwin, L. and Hollister, R.M. (eds.) *Cities of the Mind: Images and Themes of the City in the Social Sciences*. New York: Plenum Press.

Le Corbusier (1957) *La Charte d'Athènes* [The Athens Charter]. Paris: Editions de Minuit.

Lee, H.Y. (1991) *From Revolutionary Cadres to Party Technocrats in Socialist China*. Berkeley, CA: University of California Press.

Lee, L.O. (2001) Shanghai modern: reflections on urban culture in China in the 1930s, in Gaonkar, D.P. (ed.) *Alternative Modernities*. Durham, NC: Duke University Press, pp. 86–122.

Lee, T.T. (1989) *Trade Unions in China, 1949 to the Present: The Organization and Leadership of the All China Federation of Trade Unions*. Singapore: Singapore University Press.

Lefèbvre, H. (1984) *Everyday Life in the Modern World*. New Brunswick, NJ: Transaction Books.

Lefèbvre, H. (1991a) *The Production of Space*. Oxford: Basil Blackwell.

Lefèbvre, H. (1991b) *Critique of Everyday Life*, vol. 1. New York: Verso.

Lefèbvre, H. (1997) The everyday and everydayness, in Harris, S. and Berke, D. (eds.) *Architecture of the Everyday*. New York: Princeton Architectural Press, pp. 32–37.

Leng, M. (1992) Beijing shimin 'yijia liangzhi' [Beijing residents practicing 'one family, two systems']. *Renmin ribao*, haiwai ban [*People's Daily*, overseas edition], 6 August.

Lethbridge, H.J. (1963) *The Peasant and the Communes*. Hong Kong: Dragonfly Books.

Levitas, R. (1990) *The Concept of Utopia*. London: Philip Allan.

Li, B. (1993) Danwei culture as urban culture in modern China: the case of Beijing from 1949 to 1979, in Guldin, G. and Southall, A. (eds.) *Urban Anthropology in China*. Leiden: E.J. Brill, pp. 345–354.

Li, B. (1997) Riben zai zhongguo de zhanlingdi de chengshi guihua lishi yanjiu [The historical research of the city planning of the Japanese occupied areas in China]. Ph.D. dissertation, Tongji University.

Li, H. (1956) Baiwanzhuang zhuzhaiqu he guomian yi chang shenghuo qu diaocha [A survey of Baiwanzhuang Residential District and the living quarter of

Guomian No. 1 Plant]. *Jianzhu xuebao* [Architectural Journal], No. 6, pp. 19–28.

Li, H., Wang, F. and Li, L. (1996) *Work Unit – The Basic Structure of Chinese Society Data Material for the Research of Chinese Danwei Phenomena.* Beijing: Beijing chubanshe.

Li, J. and Li, X. (1963) Caiyong huokang cainuan de loufang zhuzhai [Multi-storey apartment buildings with hearth heating]. *Jianzhu xuebao* [Architectural Journal], No. 1, p. 23.

Li, L. and Li, H. (2000) *Zhongguo de danwei zuzhi – ziyuan, quanli yu jiaohuan* [China's Work Unit Organization – Resources, Power and Exchange]. Hanzhou: Zhejiang renmin chubanshe.

Li, M. *et al.* (1996) Danwei: zhiduhua zhuzhi de neibu jizhi [Danwei: the inner mechanism of the institutionalized organization]. *Zhongguo shehui kexue jikan* [Chinese Social Science Quarterly], **16**.

Liang, S. (1986) Guanyu Beijing chengqiang cunfei wenti de taolun [Discussion on the issue of the conservation-or-demolition of Beijing city walls], in *Liang Sicheng wenji* [Collected Works of Liang Sicheng], Vol. 4. Beijing: Jianzhu gongye chubanshe.

Liaoningsheng jiansheting (1958) Renmin gongshe jumindian gonggong jianzhu ding'er de tantao [An inquiry into the quota of public facilities in the residential cluster of the people's commune]. *Jianzhu xuebao* [Architectural Journal], No. 12, pp. 36–37.

Lin, R. (1948) Jiejue fanghuang yu di jin qili [Solving the problem of housing scarcity and making full use of land]. *Jianshe pinglun* [Construction Review], **1**(8), pp. 3–4.

Linge, G.J.R. (1975) *Canberra: Site and City.* Canberra: Australian National University Press.

Liu, L. H. (1995) *Translingual Practice: Literature, National Culture, and Translated Modernity – China, 1900–1937.* Stanford, CA: Stanford University Press.

Liu, S. and Wu, Q. (1986) *China's Socialist Economy: An Outline History, 1949–1984.* Beijing: Beijing Review.

Liu, X. (2000) *In One's Own Shadow: An Ethnographic Account of the Condition of Post-Reform Rural China.* Berkeley, CA: University of California Press.

Liu, Y. (1963) Guba jianzhu gaikuan [A survey of Cuban architecture]. *Jianzhu xuebao* [Architectural Journal], No. 9, pp. 20–27.

Logan, J. (2002) *The New Chinese City: Globalization and Market Reform.* Oxford: Blackwell.

Lu, A. (2000) *China and the Global Economy since 1840.* New York: St. Martin's Press.

Lu, D. (2000) The changing landscape of hybridity: a reading of ethnic identity and urban form in late-twentieth-century Vancouver. *Traditional Dwellings and Settlements Review*, **11**(2), pp. 19–28.

Lu, D. (2004) Placing modernism, in Edquist, H. and Frichot, H. (eds.) *Limits: Proceedings of the 21st Annual Conference of the Society of Architectural Historians Australia & New Zealand*. Melbourne: RMIT, pp. 276–282.

Lu, D. (2005) Forgotten routes: other modernisms and the rise of regionalist architecture in China. Paper presented at the Society of Architectural Historians Annual Conference, April 2005 (Vancouver, Canada).

Lu, F. (1964) Changqianqu de guihua sheji [The planning of the factory frontyard]. *Jianzhu xuebao* [Architectural Journal], No. 5, pp. 17–19.

Lu, F. (1989) Danwei: yizhong teshu de shehui zuzhi xingshi [The work unit: a special form of social organization]. *Zhongguo shehui kexue* [Chinese Social Science]. No. 1.

Lü, J., Rowe, P.G. and Zhang, J. (2001) *Modern Urban Housing in China, 1840–2000*. Munich: Prestel.

Lü, X. (1997) Minor public economy: the revolutionary origins of the *danwei*, in Lü, X. and Perry, E.J. (eds.) *Danwei: The Changing Chinese Workplace in Historical and Comparative Perspective*. Armonk, NY: M.E. Sharpe, pp. 21–41.

Lü, X. and Perry, E.J. (eds.) (1997a) *Danwei: The Changing Chinese Workplace in Historical and Comparative Perspective*. Armonk, NY: M.E. Sharpe.

Lü, X. and Perry, E.J. (1997b) Introduction: the changing Chinese workplace in historical and comparative perspective, in Lü, X. and Perry, E.J. (eds.) *Danwei: The Changing Chinese Workplace in Historical and Comparative Perspective*. Armonk, NY: M.E. Sharpe, pp. 3–20.

Luard, D.E.T. (1960) The urban commune. *China Quarterly*, No. 3, pp. 74–79.

Ma, K. (2004) Jiakuai jianshe ziyuan jieyuexing shehui [Accelerate the construction of a conservation-minded society]. *Renmin ribao* [People's Daily], 26 May, B6.

Ma, L.J.C. (1981) Introduction: the city in modern China, in Ma, L.J.C. and Hanten, E.W. (eds.) *Urban Development in Modern China*. Boulder, CO: Westview Press, pp. 1–18.

Ma, L.J.C. and Hanten, E.W. (eds.) (1981) *Urban Development in Modern China*. Boulder, CO: Westview Press.

Ma, L.J.C. and Wu, F. (2005a) *Restructuring the Chinese City: Changing Society, Economy and Space*. Abingdon: Routledge.

Ma, L.J.C. and Wu, F. (2005b) 'Introduction', in Ma, L.J.C. and Wu, F. (eds.) *Restructuring the Chinese City: Changing Society, Economy and Space*. Abingdon: Routledge, pp. 1–20.

Ma, W. (ed.) (1982) *A Bibliography of Chinese-Language Materials on the People's Communes*. Ann Arbor, MI: Center for Chinese Studies, University of Michigan.

MacFarquhar, F. (1983) *The Origins of the Cultural Revolution*. Oxford: Oxford University Press.

MacNay, L. (2000) *Gender and Agency*. Cambridge: Polity.

MacPherson, K.L. (1990) Designing China's urban future: the greater Shanghai plan, 1927–37. *Planning Perspectives*, **5**, pp. 39–62.

MacPherson, K.L. (1998) Erzhan hou shanghai de chengshi guihua: 1945–1949 nian [Post-World War II Planning in Shanghai, 1945–49], in Wang, X. and Huang, K. (eds.), *Chengshi shehui de pianjian* [The Evolution of Urban Societies]. Beijing: Zhongguo shehui kexue chubanshe, pp. 322–337.

MacQueen, R. (1977) Housing and people. *Progress in Planning*, 8(2), pp. 133–142.

Maddison, A. (1991) *Dynamic Forces in Capitalist Development: A Long-Run Comparative View*. Oxford: Oxford University Press.

Magagna, V.V. (1989) Consumers of privilege: a political analysis of class, consumption and socialism. *Polity*, **21**(4), pp. 711–729.

Majid, A. (2000) *Unveiling Traditions: Postcolonial Islam in a Polycentric World*. Durham, NC: Duke University Press.

Malthus, T.R. (1798, 1960) *On Population*. New York: Modern Library,

Marianne, J. and Phillips, L. (2002) *Discourse Analysis as Theory and Method*. London: Sage.

Mao, Z. (1971) Introducing a co-operative (April 15, 1958), in *Selected Readings from the Works of Mao Tsetung*. Beijing: Foreign Languages Press, p. 500.

Marx, K. (1973) *Grundrisse*. Harmondsworth: Penguin.

Marx, K. (1867, 1976) *Capital*. Harmondsworth: Penguin.

Marx, K. and Engels, F. (1973) *Selected Works in Three Volumes*, vol. 3. Moscow: Progress Publishers.

Marx, L. (1994) The idea of technology and postmodern pessimism, in Smith, M.R. and Marx, L. (eds.) *Does Technology Drive History? The Dilemma of Technological Determinism*. Cambridge, MA: MIT Press, pp. 237–257.

McLoed, M. (1997) Henri Lefèbvre's critique of the everyday: an introduction, in Harris, S. and Berke, D. (eds.) *Architecture of the Everyday*. New York: Princeton Architectural Press, pp. 9–29.

Meisner, N. (1982) *Marxism, Maoism, and Utopianism*. Madison: University of Wisconsin Press.

Miliutin, N.A. (1974) *Sotsgorod: The Problem of Building Socialist Cities*. Cambridge, MA: MIT Press.

Min, Y. (1993) *Housing Layout and Space Use: A Study of Swedish and Chinese Neighbourhood Units*. Göteborg: Chalmers University of Technology.

Ministry of Health (1944) *Design of Dwellings* (The Dudley Report). London: HMSO.

Ministry of Housing (1944) *The Housing Manual*. London: HMSO.

Morrison, K. (1995) *Marx, Durkheim, Weber: Formations of Modern Social Thought*. London: Sage.

Moseley, G.E. (1974) Residential area planning in Canberra. *New Zealand Surveyor*, **27**, pp. 474–494.

Mote, F.W. (1977) The transformation of Nanking, 1350–1400, in Skinner, G.W. (ed.) *The City in Late Imperial China.* Stanford, CA: Stanford University Press, pp. 101–154.

Mumford, L. (1951) Introduction, in Stein, C.S. (ed.) *Toward New Towns for America.* Cambridge, MA: MIT Press.

Mumford, L. (1961) *The City in History: Its Origins, Its Transformations, and Its Prospects.* New York: Harcourt, Brace and World.

Mumford, L. (1973) Utopia, the city and the machine, in Manuel, F.E. (ed.) *Utopias and Utopian Thought.* London: Souvenir Press.

Nalbantoglu, G.B. and Wong, C.T. (eds.) (1997) *Postcolonial Space(s).* New York: Princeton Architectural Press.

National Capital Development Commission (1965) *The Future Canberra: A Long Range Plan for Land Use and Civic Design.* Sydney: Angus Robertson.

Naughton, B. (1988) The Third Front: defense industrialization in the Chinese interior. *China Quarterly,* **115**, pp. 351–386.

Naughton, B. (1996) *Growing Out of the Plan: Chinese Economic Reform, 1978–1993.* Cambridge: Cambridge University Press.

Naughton, B. (1997) Danwei: the economic foundations of a unique institution, in Lü, X and Perry, E.J. (eds.) *Danwei: The Changing Chinese Workplace in Historical and Comparative Perspective.* New York: M.E. Sharpe, pp. 169–194.

Nee, V. (1996) The emergence of a market society: changing mechanisms of stratification in China. *American Journal of Sociology,* **101**, pp. 908–949.

Nongyebu changbu guihuazu (1956) Guoying nongchang changbu guihua sheji litu jieshao [An introduction to the standard planning drawings for state farms]. *Jianzhu xuebao* [Architectural Journal], No. 3, pp. 68–77.

Oksenberg, M. (ed.) (1973) *China's Developmental Experience.* New York: Praeger.

Ophuls, W. and Boyan, A.S. (1992) *Ecology and the Politics of Scarcity Revisited: The Unraveling of the American Dream.* New York: W.H. Freeman.

Ortner, S.B. (1994) Theory in anthropology since the sixties, in Dirks, N.B., Eley, G. and Ortner, S.B. (eds.) Culture/Power/History. Princeton, NJ: Princeton University Press, pp. 372–411.

Packenham, R.A. (1973) *Liberal America and the Third World: Political Development Ideas in Foreign Aid and Social Science.* Princeton, NJ: Princeton University Press.

Pahl, R. (1971) Collective consumption and the state in capitalist and state socialist societies, in Scase, R. (ed.) *Industrial Society: Class, Cleavage and Control.* London: Allen and Unwin, pp. 153–171.

Pannell, C.W. (1977) Past and present city structure in China. *Town and Planning Review,* **48**(2), pp. 149–156.

Pannell, C.W. (1990) China's urban geography. *Progress in Human Geography,* **14**(2), pp. 214–236.

Pannell, C.W. and Ma, L.J.C. (1983) *China: The Geography of Development and Modernization*. New York: John Wiley.

Parish, M. and Parish, W.L. (1986) *Urban Life in Contemporary China*. Chicago, IL: University of Chicago Press.

Park, R. (1928) Human migration and the marginal man. *The American Journal of Sociology*, **6**, pp. 881–893.

Park, R. (1952) *Human Communities: The City and Human Ecology*. Glencoe, IL: The Free Press.

Patricios, N.N. (2002) The neighborhood concept: a retrospective of physical design and social interaction. *Journal of Architectural and Planning Research*, **19**(1), pp. 70–90.

Pei, X., Liu, J. and Shen, L. (1958) Renmin gongshe de guihua wenti [Problems in commune planning]. *Jianzhu xuebao* [Architectural Journal], No. 9, pp. 9–14.

Peng, Y. (1948) Xin dushi linli jihua qianshuo [An elementary introduction to new urban neighbourhood planning]. *Jianshe pinglun* [Construction Review], **1**(7), pp. 18–22.

Peluso, N.L. and Watts, M. (2001) Violent environments, in Peluso, N.L. and Watts, M. (eds.) *Violent Environments*. Ithaca, NY: Cornell University Press, pp. 3–38.

Perlman, J. (1976) *The Myth of Marginality*. Berkeley, CA: University of California Press.

Perry, C.A. (1911) *The Wider Use of School Plant*. New York: Russell Sage Foundation.

Perry, C.A. (1924) The relation of neighborhood forces to the larger community: planning a city neighborhood from the social point of view. *Proceedings of the National Conference of Social Work (51st Annual Session)*.

Perry, C.A. (1926) *The Urban Community*. Chicago, IL: University of Chicago Press.

Perry, C.A. (1929) *Regional Survey of New York and Its Environs, Volume VII: Neighborhood and Community Planning*. New York: Committee on Regional Plan of New York and Its Environs.

Perry, E.J. (1997) From native place to workplace: labor origins and outcomes of China's *danwei* system, in Lü, X. and Perry, E.J. (eds.) *Danwei: The Changing Chinese Workplace in Historical and Comparative Perspective*. Armonk, NY: M.E. Sharpe, pp. 42–59.

Pile, S. and Thrift, N. (1995) Mapping the subject, in Pile, S. and Thrift, N. (eds.) *Mapping the Subject: Geographies of Cultural Transformations*. London: Routledge.

Poe, E.A. (1986) The man of the crowd, in Galloway, D. (ed.) *The Fall of the House of Usher and Other Writings*. Harmondsworth: Penguin, pp. 179–188.

Pravda, A. and Ruble, B. (eds.) (1986) *Trade Unions in Communist States*. Boston, MA: Allen and Unwin.

Pye, L.W. (1968) *The Spirit of Chinese Politics: A Psychocultural Study of the Authority Crisis in Political Development*. Cambridge, MA: MIT Press.

Sartre, J. (1960, 1976) *Critique of Dialectical Reason*. London: NLB.

Saunders, P. (1986) *Social Theory and the Urban Question*. New York: Holms & Merier.

Sawers, L. (1978) Cities and countryside in the Soviet Union and China, in Tabb, W.K. and Sawers, L. (eds.) *Marxism and the Metropolis: New Perspectives in Urban Political Economy*. New York: Oxford University Press, pp. 338–364.

Sayer, A. (2000) *Realism and Social Science*. London: Sage.

Schurmann, F. (1968) *Ideology and Organization in Communist China*. Berkeley, CA: University of California Press.

Scott, J.C. (1998) *Seeing Like a State: How Certain Schemes to Improve the Human Condition Have Failed*. New Haven, CT: Yale University Press.

Seligman, E.R.A. (ed.) (1934) *Encyclopaedia of the Social Sciences, vol. 4*. London: Macmillan.

Shaked, S. (1970) Physical planning in Israel, in *Israel Builds 1970: Interdisciplinary Planning*. Jerusalem: Ministry of Housing.

Shanghai gongye jianzhu shejiyuan meishan liantiechang shenghuoqu shejizu (1973) Meishan liantiechang shenghuoqu guihua sheji [The planning of the living quarter of Meishan Ironworks]. *Jianzhu xuebao* [Architectural Journal], No. 1, pp. 20–24.

Shanghai minyong jianzhu shejiyuan (1962) Shanghai diqu 1962 nian zhuzhai fang'an zhi liu [The sixth housing proposal, Shanghai, 1962]. *Jianzhu xuebao* [Architectural Journal], No. 6.

Shils, E. (1981) *Tradition*. Chicago, IL: University of Chicago Press.

Shue, V. (1988) *The Reach of the State: Sketches of the Chinese Body Politics*. Stanford, CA: Stanford University Press.

Shue, V. (1994) State power and social organization in China, in Migdal, J.S., Kohli, A. and Shue, V. (eds.) *State Power and Social Forces: Domination and Transformation in the Third World*. Cambridge: Cambridge University Press, pp. 65–88.

Shui, Y. (1962) Guowai zhuzhaiqu he xiaoqu de xingzhi yu guimo [The nature and scale of foreign residential districts and microdistricts]. *Jianzhu xuebao* [Architectural Journal], No. 11, pp. 21–2

Sil, R. (1997) The Russian 'village in the city' and the Stalinist system of enterprise management: the origins of worker alienation in Soviet state socialism, in Lü, X. and Perry, E.J. (eds.) *Danwei: The Changing Chinese Workplace in Historical and Comparative Perspective*. Armonk, NY: M.E. Sharpe, pp. 114–141.

Simmel, G. (1964) The metropolis and mental life, in Wolff, K. (ed.) *The Sociology of Georg Simmel*. New York: Free Press, pp. 409–424.

Simpson, R.D., Toman, M.A. and Ayres, R.U. (2005) *Scarcity and Growth Revisited: Natural Resources and the Environment in the New Millennium*. Washington DC: Resources for the Future.

Sirén, O. (1924) *The Walls and Gates of Peking*. London: John Lane.

Sit, V.F.S. (1995) *Beijing: The Nature and Planning of a Chinese Capital City*. Chichester: Wiley.

Skinner, G.W. (1977a) *The City in Late Imperial China*. Stanford, CA: Stanford University Press.

Skinner, G.W. (1977b) Introduction: urban and rural in Chinese society, in Skinner, G.W. (ed.) *The City in Late Imperial China*. Stanford, CA: Stanford University Press, pp. 253–274.

Smith, A.D. (1998) *Nationalism and Modernism: A Critical Survey of Recent Theories of Nations and Nationalism*. London: Routledge.

Smith, N. (1996) *The New Urban Frontier: Gentrification and the Revanchist City*. London: Routledge.

Solinger, D.J. (1997) The impact of the floating population on the *danwei*: shifts in the pattern of labor mobility control and entitlement provision, in Lü, X. and Perry, E.J. (eds.) *Danwei: The Changing Chinese Workplace in Historical and Comparative Perspective*. Armonk, NY: M.E. Sharpe, pp. 195–222.

Solinger, D.J. (1999) *Contesting Citizenship in Urban China: Peasant Migrants, the State, and the Logic of the Market*. Berkeley, CA: University of California Press.

Solinger, D.J. (2002) Labor market reform and the plight of the laid-off proletariat. *China Quarterly*, **170**, pp. 304–326.

Song, C. (2005) Guannian, jishu, zhengce: guanyu fazhan 'jieneng shengdi xing' zhuzhai de sikao [Concepts, techniques and policies: reflections on the development of 'energy-and-land-efficient' housing]. *Jianzhu xuebao* [Architectural Journal], No. 4, pp. 5–7.

Song, L. (2002) *Zongluxian, dayuejin, renmin gongshehua yundong shimo* [The Whole Story of the General Guideline, the Great Leap Forward, and the People's Commune Movement]. Kunming: Yunnan renmin chubanshe.

Spence, J.D. (1969) *To Change China: Western Advisors in China, 1620–1960*. Boston, MA: Little Brown.

Spence, J.D. (1990) *The Search for Modern China*. New York: W.W. Norton.

Staleton, K. (2000) *Civilizing Chengdu: Chinese Urban Reform, 1895–1937*. Cambridge, MA: Harvard University Press.

Strand, D. (2000) New Chinese cities, in Esherick, J.W. (ed.) *Remaking the Chinese City: Modernity and National Identity, 1900–1950*. Honolulu: University of Hawaii Press, pp. 211–224.

Straus, K.M. (1997a) *Factory and Community in Stalin's Russia: The Making of an Industrial Working Class*. Pittsburgh, PA: University of Pittsburgh Press.

Straus, K.M. (1997b) The Soviet factory as community organizer, in Lü, X. and Perry, E.J. (eds.) *Danwei: The Changing Chinese Workplace in Historical and Comparative Perspective*. Armonk, NY: M.E. Sharpe, pp. 142–168.

Su, K. (1985) *Modern China: A Topical History*. Beijing: New World Press.

Sun, Y. (1963) Guangxi tongzu malan jianzhu jianjie [A brief description of the 'Malan' architecture of Tong Nationality, Guangxi]. *Jianzhu xuebao* [Architectural Journal], No. 1, pp. 9–11.

Szelenyi, I. (1993) East European socialist cities: how different are they? in Guldin, G. and Southall, A. (eds.) *Urban Anthropology in China*. Leiden: E.J. Brill, pp. 41–64.

Szelenyi, I. (1996) Cities under socialism – and after, in Andrusz, G., Harloe, M. and Szelenyi, I. (eds.) *Cities after Socialism: Urban and Regional Change and Conflict in Post-socialist Societies*. Oxford: Blackwell, pp. 286–317.

Taneff, L. (1958) Chengshi zhuzhaiqu de guihua he jianzhu [The planning and construction of urban residential districts]. *Jianzhu xuebao* [Architectural Journal], No. 1, pp. 23–31.

Tang, W.F. and Parish, W.L. (2000) *Chinese Urban Life under Reform*. Cambridge: Cambridge University Press.

Tang, X. (1996) *Global Space and the Nationalist Discourse of Modernity: The Historical Thinking of Liang Qichao*. Stanford, CA: Stanford University Press.

Tao, Q. (1981) *Soushen houji*. Beijing: Zhonghua shuju.

Tewei'ersikeyi, P.M. (1956) Zhuzhai-jiefang-xiaoqu [Housing, neighbourhood, and microdistrict]. *Chengshi jianshe yicong* [Translated Articles in Urban Construction], **14**(7), pp. 1–6.

Thompson, B. (1991) Editor's introduction, in Bourdieu, P., *Language and Symbolic Power*. Cambridge: Polity, pp. 1–3.

Thompson, E.P. (1955, 1976) *William Morris: Romantic to Revolutionary*. London: Merlin Press.

Thrift, N. (1996) *Spatial Formations*. London: Sage Publications.

Tianjin daxue jianzhuxi (1958) Tianjin shi xiaozhan renmin gongshe de chubu guihua sheji [The preliminary planning of Xiaozhan People's Commune, Tianjin]. *Jianzhu xuebao* [Architectural Journal], No. 10, pp. 14–18.

Tongji gongzuo [Statistical Work] (1958) Jianli renmin gongshe tongji wang de dongyuan ling [Mobilizing calls for establishing a statistics network in the people's communes]. No. 19, p. 22.

Tongji University *et al.* (1981) *Chengshi guihua yuanli* [The Principles of Urban Planning], Beijing: Zhongguo jianzhu gongye chubanshe.

Trolander, J.A. (1987) *Professionalism and Social Change: From the Settlement House Movement to Neighborhood Centers, 1886 to the Present*. New York: Columbia University Press.

Tsin, T. (1999) *Nation, Governance, and Modernity in China: Canton, 1900–1927*. Stanford, CA: Stanford University Press.

Tucher, D.V. (1999) Building our Manchukuo: Japanese city planning, architecture, and nation-building in occupied northeast China, 1931–1945. Ph.D. dissertation, The University of Iowa.

Uchida, Y. (1939*a*) Daido toshi keikakuan ni tsuite, 1 [On Datong urban planning proposal, 1]. *Kenchiku zasshi*, **53**(657), pp. 1281–1295.

Uchida, Y. (1939*b*) Daido toshi keikakuan ni tsuite, 2 [On Datong urban planning proposal, 2]. *Kenchiku zasshi*, **53**(658), pp. 1355–1360.

Unger, J. (ed.) (1996) *Chinese Nationalism*, Armonk: M.E. Sharp.

Upton, D. (1985) White and black landscapes in eighteenth-century Virginia. *Place*, **2**(2), pp. 357–369.

Upton, D. (1991) Architectural history or landscape history? *Journal of Architectural Education*, **44**(4), pp. 195–199.

Upton, D. (2002) Architecture in everyday life. *New Literary History*, 33(4), pp. 707–723.

Urry, J. (2000) *Sociology beyond Societies: Mobilities for the Twenty First Century*. London: Routledge.

Van Ness, P. (1993) China as a Third World state: foreign policy and official national identity, in Dittmer, L. and Kim, S.S. (eds.) *China's Quest for National Identity*. Ithaca: Cornell University Press, pp. 194–214.

Verdery, K. (1991) Theorizing socialism: a prologue to the 'transition'. *American Ethnologist*, **18**, pp. 419–439.

Walder, A.G. (1986) *Communist Neo-Traditionalism: Work and Authority in Chinese Industry*. Berkeley, CA: University of California Press.

Walder, A.G. (1989) Factory and manager in an era of reform. *China Quarterly*, **118**, pp. 242–264.

Wallerstein, I. (1979) *The Capitalist World-Economy: Essays*. Cambridge: Cambridge University Press.

Wallerstein, I. (1999) *The End of the World as We Know It: Social Science for the Twenty-First Century*. Minneapolis: University of Minnesota Press.

Wang, C. (1999) Greater Shanghai plan: a nationalist utopia. *Dialogue*, **23**, pp. 62–67.

Wang, D. (1947) Shiqu congjian yu jiejue fanghuang [Urban redevelopment and housing scarcity]. *Jianshe pinglun* [Construction Review], **1**(2), pp. 5–6.

Wang, D. (1956) Shanghai caoyang xincun zhuzhaiqu de guihua sheji [The planning of Shanghai Caoyang new village residential district]. *Jianzhu xuebao* [Architectural Journal], No. 2, pp. 1–15.

Wang, D. and Xu, C. (1962) Juzhu jianzhu guihua sheji zhong jige wenti de tantao [On several issues in residential planning]. *Jianzhu xuebao* [Architectural Journal], No. 2, pp. 6–13.

Wang, H. (1955) Women dui dongbei mochang juzhuqu guihua sheji gongzuo de jiancha [Our self-criticism on residential planning for a factory in northeast China]. *Jianzhu xuebao* [Architectural Journal], No. 2, pp. 20–40.

Wang, H. and Chen, Q. (1964) Shanghai juzhuqu guihua sheji zhong jige wenti de tantao [Inquiry into several issues in the planning of residential districts in Shanghai], *Jianzhu xuebao*, No. 2, pp. 8–14.

Wang, H., Wu, X. and Wan, G. (1958) Shanghaishi yige renmin gongshe xincun de guihua sheji fang'an [The planning proposal for a new village of the people's commune in Shanghai], *Jianzhu xuebao* [Architectural Journal], No. 10, pp. 19–23.

Wang, J. (1958) Shanghai jiaoqu Xianfeng nongyeshe nongcun guihua [The rural planning of Vanguard Cooperative Farm in Shanghai suburb]. *Jianzhu xuebao* [Architectural Journal], No. 10, pp. 24–28.

Wang, J. (1961) Lishang zhi jia [Family of courtesy] (photograph). *Renmin huabao* [People's Pictorial], No. 1, p. 21.

Wang, J. (2003) *Cheng ji* [The Tale of a City]. Beijing: Sanlian shudian.

Wang, J. and Li, L. (1961) Xiabanle [After work] (photograph). *Renmin huabao* [People's Pictorial], No. 12, p. 31.

Wang, J., Wu, N. and Deng, C. (1958) Yuanjing guihua [Long-term plan] (drawing). *Renmin huabao* [People's Pictorial], No. 10, p. 9.

Wang, S. (1962) Juzhu xiaoqu guihua sheji de tantao [An inquiry into the planning of residential microdistricts]. *Jianzhu xuebao* [Architectural Journal], No. 1, pp. 8–11.

Wang, S. (1995) The politics of private time: changing leisure patterns in urban China, in Davis, D.S. *et al.* (eds.) *Urban Spaces in Contemporary China: The Potential for Autonomy and Community in Post-Mao China*. New York: Woodrow Wilson Center Press, pp. 28–60.

Wang, S. and Cheng, J. (1959) Jumindian fenbu guihua de yanjiu [Research on the distribution of residential clusters]. *Jianzhu xuebao* [Architectural Journal], No. 1, pp. 10–14.

Wang, T. *et al.* (1958) Hebeisheng xushuixian suicheng renmin gongshe de guihua [The planning of Suicheng People's Commune, Xushui, Hebei]. *Jianzhu xuebao* [Architectural Journal], No. 11, pp. 14–18.

Wang, W. (2004) Shanghai jindai chengshi guihua shi gailun [An outline of the history of city planning in modern Shanghai]. Ph.D. dissertation, Tongji University.

Wang, Y. (1956) Guanyu juzhuqu guihua sheji xingshi de taolun [Discussion on the planning of the form of the residential district]. *Jianzhu xuebao* [Architectural Journal], No. 5, pp. 51–57.

Wang, Y. (1995) Public-sector housing in urban China, 1949–1988. *Housing Studies*, **10**(1), pp. 57–82.

Wang, Y.P. (1999) Commercial housing development in urban China. *Urban Studies*, **36**(9), pp. 1475–1494.

Wang, Y.P. and Murie, A. (1996) The process of commercialization of urban housing in China. *Urban Studies*, **33**(6), pp. 971–989.

Wang, Z. (1962) Zhejiang minju caifeng [A survey of Zhejiang vernacular dwellings]. *Jianzhu xuebao* [Architectural Journal], No. 7, pp. 10–18.

Wei, Y.H. and Ma, L.J.C. (1996) Changing patterns of spatial inequality in China, 1952–1999. *Third World Planning Review*, **18**, pp. 177–192.

Wei, Z. (1964) Jiana jianzhu [Ghanian architecture]. *Jianzhu xuebao* [Architectural Journal], No. 5, pp. 30–33.

Weiner, D.E.B. (1994) *Architecture and Social Reform in Late-Victorian London*. Manchester: Manchester University Press.

Weisskopf, T.E. (1980) The relevance of the Chinese experience for Third World economic development. *Theory and Society*, **4**, pp. 283–318

Wheatley, P. (1971) *The Pivot of the Four Quarters: A Preliminary Enquiry into the Origin and Character of the Ancient Chinese City*. Chicago, IL: Aldine.

Whyte, M.K. and Parish, W.L. (1984) *Urban Life in Contemporary China*. Chicago, IL: University of Chicago Press.

Wilson, J.L. (1986) The People's Republic of China, in Pravda, A. and Ruble, B. (eds.) *Trade Unions in Communist States*. Boston, MA: Allen and Unwin.

Wirth, L. (1938) Urbanism as a way of life. *American Journal of Sociology*, **44**, pp. 1–24.

Wright, A.F. (1977) The cosmology of the Chinese city, in Skinner, G.W. (ed.) *The City in Late Imperial China*. Stanford, CA: Stanford University Press, pp. 33–73.

Wolf, M. (1985) *Revolution Postponed: Women in Contemporary China*. Stanford, CA: Stanford University Press.

World Bank (1980) *World Development Report*. World Bank.

Wu, F. (1996) Changes in the structure of public housing provision in urban China. *Urban Studies*, **33**(9), pp. 1601–1627.

Wu, F. (1997) Urban restructuring in China's emerging market economy: towards a framework for analysis. *International Journal of Urban and Regional Research*, **21**, pp. 640–663.

Wu, F. (2002*a*) The transformation of urban space in Chinese transitional economy: with special reference to Shanghai, in Logan, J.R. (ed.) *The New Chinese City: Globalization and Market Reform*. Blackwell: Oxford, pp. 154–166.

Wu, F. (2002*b*) China's changing urban governance in the transition towards a more market-oriented economy. *Urban Studies*, **39**(7), pp. 1071–1093.

Wu, F. (2005) Rediscovering the 'gate' under market transition: from work-unit compounds to commodity housing enclaves. *Housing Studies*, **22**(2), pp. 235–254.

Wu, F. and Yeh, A.G.O. (1997) Changing spatial distribution and determinants of land development in China's transition to a market economy: the case of Guangzhou. *Urban Studies*, **34**, pp. 1851–1879.

Wu, H. (1997) The Hong Kong clock – public time-telling and political time/space. *Public Culture*, **9**(3), pp. 329–354.

Wu, H.J. (1964) 'Ping xifang shizuo jianzhu [A review of ten buildings in the West]. *Jianzhu xuebao* [Architectural Journal], No. 6, pp. 29–33.

Wu, H.X. (1994) Rural to urban migration in the People's Republic of China. *China Quarterly*, **139**, pp. 669–698.

Wu, J. (1993) The historical development of Chinese urban morphology. *Planning Perspectives*, **8**, pp. 20–52

Wu, L. (1959) Guanyu renmin gongshe guihua zhong de jige wenti de tantao [A discussion of several problems in the planning of the people's commune]. *Jianzhu xuebao* [Architectural Journal], No. 1, pp. 1–3.

Wu, L.Y. (1999) *Rehabilitating the Old City of Beijing: A Project in the Ju'er Hutong Neighborhood*. Vancouver: University of British Columbia Press.

Wu, S. (2003) *Xuechou dinglü: zhongguo lishi zhong de shengchun youxi* [The Rules of Recompense for Violence: The Game of Survival in Chinese History]. Beijing: Zhongguo gongren chubanshe.

Wu, X. and Li, S. (1959) Jianshe guihua [Construction planning] (photograph). *Renmin huabao* [People's Pictorial], No. 23, p. 15.

Xenos, N. (1989) *Scarcity and Modernity*. London: Routledge.

Xie, Z. and Zhu, H. (1956) Changfang shenghuojian sheji [The design of the life room of the factory workshop]. *Jianzhu xuebao* [Architectural Journal], No. 6, pp. 13–18.

Xu, Y. (2000) *The Chinese City in Space and Time: The Development of Urban Form in Suzhou*. Honolulu: University of Hawaii Press.

Xu, J. and Fang, R. (1958) Shanghai hudong zhuzhaiqu guihua sheji de yantao [A discussion on the planning of Hudong Residential District, Shanghai]. *Jianzhu xuebao* [Architectural Journal], No. 1, pp. 1–9.

Yang, J. (1987) *Xiandaihua yu zhongguo gongchan zhuyi* [Modernisation and Chinese Communism]. Hong Kong: Chinese University of Hong Kong Publishing House.

Yang, K. (1993) *Zhongguo gudai ducheng zhidu shi yanjiu* [A study of the history of the Capital City System in Ancient China]. Shanghai: Shanghai guji chubanshe.

Yang, M. (1989) Between state and society: the construction of corporateness in a Chinese socialist factory. *Australian Journal of Chinese Affairs*, **22**, pp. 31–60.

Yang, W. *et al.* (1958) *Dayuejin xuanchuanhua xuanji* [Selected Works of Great Leap Forward Propaganda Posters]. Shanghai: Shanghai renmin chubanshe.

Yang, X. and Zhou, Y. (1999) *Zhongguo danwei zhidu* [The Chinese Work Unit System]. Beijing: Zhongguo jingji chubanshe.

Yang, Z. *et al.* (1992) *Urban Land Use and Management in China*. Beijing: Jingji kexue chubanshe.

Yao, F. and Wang, S. (1962) Gaodeng xuexiao xuesheng shenghuoqu de sheji [The design of students' living quarter of colleges and universities]. *Jianzhu xuebao* [Architectural Journal], No. 9, pp. 23–25.

Yeh, A.G.O. and Wu, F. (1999) *The Transformation of the Urban Planning System in China from a Centrally-planned to Transitional Economy*. Oxford: Pergamon.

Yeh, W. (1997) The Republican origins of the *danwei*: the case of Shanghai's Bank of China, in Lü, X. and Perry, E.J. (eds.) *Danwei: The Changing Chinese Workplace in Historical and Comparative Perspective*. Armonk: M.E. Sharpe, pp. 42–59.

Yi, X. (1948) Zhuzhai de jiti sheji [Collective housing design]. *Jianshe pinglun* [Construction Review], **1**(4), pp. 6–10.

Yi, X. (1991) Danwei yishi de shehui xue fenxi [An sociological analysis of the danwei conscious]. *Shehui xue yanjiu* [Sociological Research], no. 7.

Yin, H. (1964) Guba nongcun zhuzhai [Rural housing in Cuba]. *Jianzhu xuebao* [Architectural Journal], No. 3, pp. 34–39.

Yin, H., Shen, X. and Zhao, Z., (2005) Industrial restructuring and urban spatial transformation in Xi'an, in Ma, L.J.C. and Wu, F. (eds.) *Restructuring the Chinese City: Changing Society, Economy and Space*. Abingdon: Routledge, pp. 155–174.

You, Z. (2000) *Neibu fenhua yu liudong – yijia guoyou qiye de ershi nian* [Internal Differentiation and Mobility – A State Enterprise's Twenty Years]. Beijing: Shehui kexue wenxian chubanshe.

Young, R.J.C. (1995) *Colonial Desire: Hybridity in Theory, Culture and Race*. London: Routledge.

Yu, D. (1989) *Yu Dafu xiaoshuo xuanpian* [Selected Works of Yu Dafu]. Hangzhou: Zhejiang wenji chubanshe.

Zhang, F. et al. (1963) Chaoxianzu zhuzhai de pingmian buzhi [The layout of Korean housing]. *Jianzhu xuebao* [Architectural Journal], No. 1, pp. 15–16.

Zhang, H. and Tao, T. (1961) Xuri dong sheng [The sun rising in the eastern sky] (drawing). *Renmin huabao* [People's Pictorial], No. 3, p. 22.

Zhang, J. (2001) *Beijing guihua jianshe wushi nian* [Beijing Planning and Construction in the Past Fifty Years]. Beijing: Zhongguo shudian.

Zhang, J. (2004) Neighborhood-level governance: the growing social foundation of a public sphere, in Howell, J. (ed.) *Governance in China*. Lanham, MD: Rowman & Littlefield, pp. 121–142.

Zhang, L. (2001) *Strangers in the City: Reconstructions of Space, Power, and Social networks within China's Floating Population*. Stanford, CA: Stanford University Press.

Zhang, X. (2003) *Mingqing Beijing chengyuan he chengmen* [*The Walls and Gates of Beijing during the Ming and Qing Dynasties*]. Shijiazhuang: Hebei jiaoyu chubanshe.

Zhang, Z., Zheng, R. and Dai, E. (1982) *Jiben jianshe jingjixue* [Economics of Basic Construction]. Beijing: Zhongguo caizheng jingji chubanshe.

Zhao, D. (1956) Lun yiyuan jianzhu [On hospital architecture]. *Jianzhu xuebao*

[Architectural Journal], No. 1, pp. 32–83.

Zhao, D. (1963) Beiyangcun shinyan xiaoqu guihua yu zhuzhai sheji [The planning and residential design of Beiyangcun experimental microdistrict]. *Jianzhu xuebao* [Architectural Journal], No. 3, pp. 1–6.

Zhao, D. *et al.* (1958) Beijingshi baizifang juzhu xiaoqu gaijian guihua fang'an [Proposal for redevelopment planning of the Baizifang microdistrict in Beijing]. *Jianzhu xuebao* [Architectural Journal], No. 1, pp. 17–22.

Zheng, G. (1960) Zaoshang shangban [Going to work in the morning] (photograph). *Renmin huabao* [People's Pictorial], No. 16, p. 4.

Zheng, Y. (2000) *Lengzhan yiye* [A Page in the Cold War]. Beijing: Zhongguo qingnian chubanshe.

Zhonggong zhongyang wenxian yanjiushi (ZZWY) (ed.) (1995) *Jianguo yilai zhongyao wenxian xuanbian, di shiyi ce* [Selected important documents since the founding of the People of Republic, vol. 11]. Beijing: Zhongyang wenxian chubanshe.

Zhongguo chengshi jianshe nianjian bianweihui (1989) *Zhongguo chengshi jianshe nianjian* [Yearbook of Urban Construction in China, 1986–87]. Beijing: Zhongguo jianzhu gongye chubanshe.

Zhongguo shehui kexue yuan and zhongyang dang'anguan (ZSKYZD) (eds.) (1989) *Zhonghua renmin gongheguo jingji dang'an ziliao xuanbian: jiben jianshe touzi he jianzhu ye juan, 1949–1952* [Selected Economic Archival Material of the People's Republic of China: Basic Construction Investment and Building Industry, 1949–1952]. Beijing: Zhongguo chengshi jingji shehui chubanshe.

Zhongguo shehui kexue yuan and zhongyang dang'an guan (ZSKYZD) (eds.) (1998) *Zhonghua renmin gongheguo jingji dang'an ziliao xuanbian: guding zichan touzi he jianzhu ye juan, 1953–1957* [Selected Economic Archival Material of the People's Republic of China: Investment in Fixed Assets and Building Industry, 1953–1957]. Beijing: Zhongguo wujia chubanshe.

Zhonghua renmin gongheguo jianshebu (2002) *Zhonghua renmin gongheguo guojia biaozhun chengshi juzhuqu guihua sheji guifan GB 50180–93 (xiugaiben)* [Planning standards for urban residential districts, People's Republic of China (revised edition)]. Beijing: Zhongguo jianzhu gongye chubanshe.

Zong, H. (1995) Miandui 'yulegong' [Facing the 'Entertainment Palace']. *SRI Newsletter*, 25 January, p. B1.

Zou, D. (2001) *Zhongguo xiandai jianzhu shi* [Modern Chinese Architectural History]. Tianjin: Tianjin kexue jishu chubanshe.

Index